D1433634

The Encyclopedia of
INDIAN COOKING

The Encyclopedia of
INDIAN COOKING

Khalid Aziz

TREASURE PRESS

Notes

☐ All recipes serve four unless otherwise stated.

☐ All spoon measures are level unless otherwise stated. Spoon measures can be bought in both imperial and metric sizes to give accurate measurements of small quantities.

☐ Egg sizes are specified only where exact quantities are vital to the recipe.

☐ Metric and imperial measurements have been calculated separately. Use one set of measurements only as they are not exact equivalents.

☐ Cooking times may vary depending on the individual oven. Always preheat the oven to the specified temperature.

☐ All flour is plain and all sugar granulated unless otherwise specified.

Author's dedication
To my daughter Fleur

First published in Great Britain in 1983 by
Park Lane Press

This edition published in 1985 by
Treasure Press
59 Grosvenor Street
London W1

This book was designed and produced by
George Rainbird Limited
40 Park Street, London W1Y 4DE

Text copyright © Khalid Aziz 1983

ISBN 1 85051 080 6

Printed in Hong Kong

Contents

Introduction

The way of life in the Indian subcontinent is rich and varied, encompassing the widest ranges of climates, religions, wealth, language and, above all, cooking styles to be found in any country. The climate means that in the temperate north, where in the foothills of the Himalayas there is an almost European climate, there is an abundance of good meat and dairy products such as milk and yogurt. Wheat is the predominant source of carbohydrate and the cooking of northern India abounds with recipes for a variety of breads, leavened and unleavened, griddle cooked and fried.

Move further south and as the temperatures rise towards the Equator, the wheat culture gives way to rice. In the central states of the subcontinent as many varieties of rice are grown as there are potatoes in the western world, and the food becomes hotter. Many people ask why in searing temperatures people insist on eating hot food. The answer lies in the fact that hot food makes you perspire and as you drink more water to replace the liquid lost through the skin the body is flushed of toxic waste products.

Overlaying the climatic considerations are those of religion. Indians are by and large highly religious. Predominant are the Hindus, who are, in the main, vegetarians. This vegetarianism has given rise to myriad intricate dishes as well as more simple treatments of everyday vegetables. One factor that controls the sort of food eaten is cost. Most Indians simply could not afford to eat meat except on very rare occasions such as the great feast days like Holi, when everyone runs wild in a carnival atmosphere and small boys cover each other in brightly coloured dye. Outside the festivals poorer Indians have learned to cook the hundred and one varieties of pulses, creating tasty and filling meals with the addition of just a few spices.

The other main religious group are the Muslims. Their faith precludes them from eating pork, but the dominance of the Mogul emperors led to Indian cooking rising to what many consider to be its culinary height with dishes of great richness. Many of these elaborate dishes are still cooked today, particularly in Pakistan, where there too they are brought out on holy days such as Eid-ul-Fitr, when dishes of milk-soaked vermicelli covered in finely beaten silver leaf are served to visitors.

As there is such a spread of food across the Indian subcontinent the chapters are divided up in such a way as to identify clear geographical areas and whether the recipes are for meat, fish or vegetables. All the recipes are designed for ease of cooking; some clearly are more complicated than others. None are difficult but the ones with smaller numbers of ingredients are best for beginners to try their hand at.

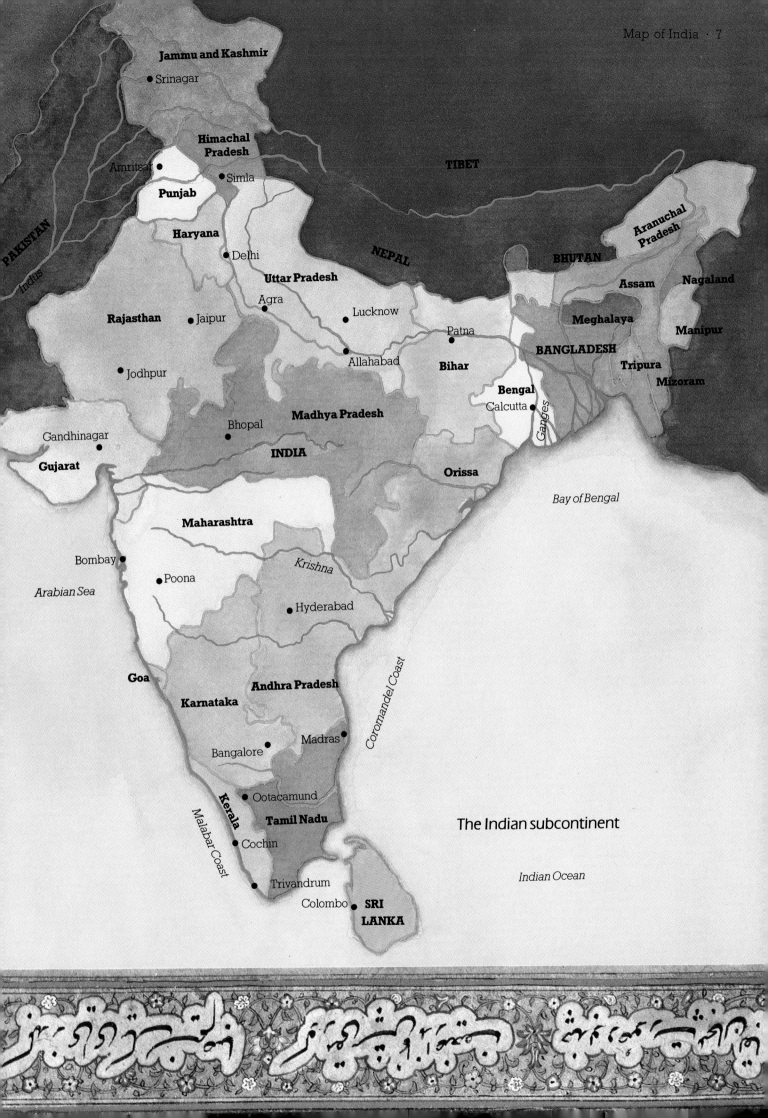

The Indian subcontinent

How to read an Indian menu

Many people quite understandably tend to stick to the one or two dishes that they know when they eat out in an Indian restaurant. There is a way of extending your knowledge of Indian food served in Indian restaurants without over-extending your pocket and committing the cardinal sin of over-ordering! For a start, resist any pressure to order more than one of any dish with the exception of rice and bread. Even with rice it is usually best to order half the amount, so for four people order two portions of rice. You can always order more later.

Order one main dish per person and one vegetable dish for every two people plus yogurt, dal or raeta. If you are having a vegetarian meal, order one and a half dishes per person. If you want to have a starter ask for kebabs, one main portion between two people, or perhaps a quarter Tandoori Chicken each. In most restaurants Tandoori Chicken servings are for half a chicken but invariably it arrives at the table in two quarters so you should have no qualms about sharing dishes.

When it comes to puddings ask when they were made. Some puddings such as Gulab Jamun and Jallebi keep reasonably well in syrup for up to a week; after that they tend to become stale and the syrup can go ropey. Other sweetmeats, such as Halwas, keep for weeks. The golden rule about ordering in an Indian restaurant is do not be afraid to ask about the meanings of words, cooking processes and the freshness of vegetables.

Menu planning

Planning an Indian meal is not difficult largely because there are no hard and fast rules about what to serve. Common sense is the best guide to compiling a list of dishes. There has to be a balance between protein and carbohydrate, richness and simplicity and of course between mildness and high spicing. On the subject of how spicy you should make the menu, do consider the preferences of your guests. Someone just being introduced to Indian cooking can get completely the wrong impression if the first Indian meal he ever eats has all the fire of a volcano in full spate! Do have on hand the 'fire extinguishers' such as raeta and natural yogurt.

When it comes to how much carbohydrate to serve it is always better to have more rather than less. One rule I try to stick to is not to mix the wheat culture of the north with the rice culture of the south, so I tend to serve either rice or bread. If you are just setting out on Indian cooking then rice is perhaps easier to cook.

In India itself the number of dishes served at a meal varies according to wealth and religion. Muslims and Sikhs, who tend to eat more meat dishes, will generally serve one or two dishes based on meat (including perhaps a kebab of some sort), supported by bread and two or three vegetable dishes. Hindus favour the vegetarian dishes and serve rather more of them at one sitting. Traditionally a Hindu meal is eaten from a thali. This can be a silver plate or in its simplest form a banana leaf. Each guest takes a small amount from each of the dishes laid out and places each sample of food around the edge of the thali. The centre of the thali is then used to mix the food rather as an artist mixes oils on a palette. Rice is predominately served with vegetarian meals. Here are some dishes that would go well together at an Indian dinner party for four to six people:

Vegetarian menu 1

Suji pakora (Semolina fritters) · 1
Karela (Spiced courgettes) · 2
Palak dal (Lentils with spinach) · 3
Gajjar bhajji (Carrots with cashew nuts) · 4
Aloo bhindi bhajji (Okra with potatoes) · 5
Tamatar ka salan (Tomato curry) · 6
Aloo paratha (Stuffed paratha) · 7
Chaat (Spicy fruit salad) · 8
Sharbat sandal (Sandalwood drink) · 9

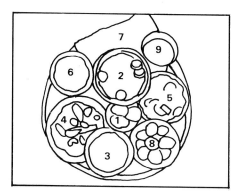

Vegetarian menu 2

Pakora (Fritters) · 1
Kela kofta (Curried banana balls) · 2
Shahi dal (Royal lentil curry) · 3
Dum ka subzi (Steamed French beans) · 4
Raeta (Yogurt cooler) · 5
Pillao (Spiced rice) · 6
Am (Mangoes) · 7
Nimboo pani (Lemonade) · 8

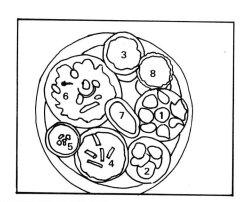

Non-vegetarian menu 1

Tandoori chicken · 1
Nargisi kofta (Indian Scotch egg) · 2
Baigan tamatar (Aubergines and tomatoes) · 3
Tarka dal (Lentils with a spicy topping) · 4
Bhindi bhajji (Okra curry) · 5
Saag aloo (Spinach and potato chutney) · 6
Dahi (Yogurt) · 7
Chapatti (Unleavened bread) · 8
Kulfi (Ice cream) · 9
Lussi (Yogurt drink) · 10

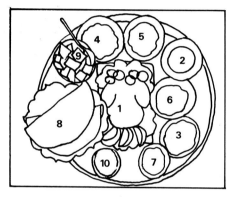

Non-vegetarian menu 2

Samosa (Stuffed pastry cases) · 1
Gosht dopiazah (Beef with onions) · 2
Jhinghe saag (Prawns with spinach) · 3
Goodhi bhajji (Marrow curry) · 4
Baigan bhagar (Aubergines with tamarind) · 5
Kesari chawal (Saffron rice) · 6
Raeta (Yogurt cooler) · 7
Chachumber (Indian salad) · 8
Gulab jamun (Sweet dumplings in syrup) · 9
Podina ka sharbat (Mint drink) · 10

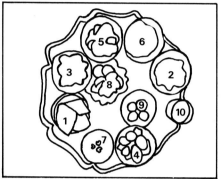

Glossary of Indian foods

Chick-pea Flour Ground chick peas are used to make a flour known as besan, which is also sold as gram flour. It is used to make bread, and also as a thickening agent for curry sauces.

Coconut Coconut is widely used in both sweet and savoury dishes, particularly those from the south of India. Choose coconuts that are still reasonably fresh. Test for this by first shaking the nut to ensure there is still a fair amount of liquid inside. Then examine the 'eyes' at one end of the nut. They should be intact and should just yield to pressure from the thumbs. Having selected your coconut, pierce two of the eyes with a screwdriver and pour out the liquid. Put this to one side. Wrap the nut in a tea towel and break it with a hammer.

Some people put the pieces of nut into a hot oven to help separate the flesh from the shell, but this has the disadvantage of making the flesh too dry. It is better to remove as much flesh as possible using a sharp knife. The flesh may now be sliced or grated depending on the recipe. Some dishes call for the preparation of coconut milk made by liquidising the grated flesh with the liquid and a little extra water. Such milk serves to thicken and flavour a dish. If fresh coconut is not available, then desiccated coconut may be used. 170–225 g/ 6–8 oz of desiccated coconut corresponds to one fresh coconut, although naturally rather more water has to be added when making coconut milk.

Colouring In India much of the food is brightly coloured. Any proprietary food colours may be used – the predominant colours are yellow (for rice dishes), red/orange (for tandoori food) and green (for sweets and ice cream). Remember that Indian colourings tend to be rather livid so do not be afraid to add more rather than less.

Dal This is the collective name given to the wide variety of pulses cooked in India. The best known in the West is Masoor Dal which is the pink split lentil. It is cooked in exactly the same way as Pease Pudding, that is by boiling the lentils until they form a smooth thick sauce. Other dals include: Urhd Dal which is either split when it is white in colour, or whole when it is black; Mung Dal which is green in colour; Chenna Dal which is the Indian equivalent to chick peas; and Kabli Chenna which is very much like a pea but darker and smaller.

Ghee This is the fat universally used in Indian cooking. Traditionally only pure ghee made from clarified cow's butter is used. It is made by gently heating the butter until it melts. Any floating solids are then skimmed off and the remaining clear liquid poured into a container to set, leaving behind any solids which may have settled out. With so many vegetarians in India who take their vegetarianism to the point where in addition to meat, animal products such as milk and butter are also shunned, ghee substitute made from vegetable oil has been developed. Although this is not as rich as animal fat ghee it makes very little difference to the flavour of the final dish. It also has the advantage of being less than half the price of animal fat ghee and it keeps better too. For this reason I tend to use ghee substitute most of the time. Ghee substitute is available in tins in all Asian stores. Once opened the ghee tin should be covered with cling film and stored in the refrigerator. Pure ghee (animal fat) should keep for about a week and vegetable ghee will keep for about a month. If ghee is not available, a good vegetable oil (but not olive oil!) can be used, although the flavour will not be the same. If using oil, you can remove some from the surface before serving.

Kewra water This is used to impart a flowery fragrance to a variety of dishes ranging from rice to ice cream. It is made from a particular type of cactus plant and is available at some Asian stores. Rose water may be used as a substitute.

Poppadums These are made from mixtures of various dals ground into a flour and formed into a very hard dough. This dough is often mixed with chillies and other spices to make spiced poppadums. It is rolled out into very thin rounds and allowed to dry. The rounds are deep-fried until they crisp up. Because of the very dry climate needed to make poppadums no one, it seems, bothers to make them in the West. It is much easier to buy them ready-made and fry them as necessary. The secret of frying poppadums is first to shake them free of any excess dust (too much dust and the oil will spoil very quickly) and then fry them two at a time, turning them over after about 15 seconds. In this way the poppadums will tend to curl against each other and remain flat.

Sesame seed oil This oil is used in small quantities, usually to fry spices before adding them to a dish. The oil has a very high smoking point and can therefore be used at much higher temperatures than other oils.

Silver leaf Finely beaten silver is used as a decoration on both sweet and savoury dishes. It was first used by the Moguls to decorate their already very elaborate dishes. At times gold leaf was used too. Silver leaf is known as varak and is available at some Asian stores. It can be quite safely eaten and some say it is an aid to digestion. Watch out for the effects when it hits your fillings! Aluminium foil should not be used as a substitute!

The spices

Spices have always been an integral part of the Indian culture. They are mentioned in the *Vedas* – the holy books of the Hindus which stretch back more than five thousand years. Not only are spices used in cooking but also as invaluable cures for every ailment known to man.

When it comes to cooking with spices the golden rules are freshness and dry, dark storage. It is difficult to be sure of the freshness of spices that have travelled thousands of miles by sea and air. Usually your nose is your best guide to freshness. Spices such as ginger and coriander should be quite pungent. Similarly fresh green chillies should almost threaten to leap up and bite you so strong should their smell be. Obviously drier spices such as cinnamon and turmeric will not have such a strong odour. With the aromatics such as cardamoms and cloves, the stronger smelling they are the better.

Resist the temptation to buy larger quantities of spices than you really need. In India cooks purchase their spices at least once a week to ensure freshness. As long as they are kept dry in airtight jars and away from sunlight, most spices will remain useable for at least a month.

Cardamoms (1) These are used in the same way as cloves. There are two types of cardamom; green cardamoms are about 1 cm/½ inch long and black cardamoms which can be up to 4 cm/1½ inches long. Both varieties may be added to a recipe either whole or the seeds removed from the skin and added alone.

Garam masala (8): From left to right: Cinnamon sticks, white cumin seeds, chilli powder, black peppercorns, cardamoms, coriander seeds and freshly ground nutmeg.

Chillies (2) These come in several forms. Green chillies are the mildest form. When they have ripened to red they are hotter. Red chillies are dried in the sun and are hotter still. Dried red chillies are ground to a powder to provide the hottest form of the spice.

Cinnamon (3) In India this is known as 'pea sugar'. It is used either in its original bark form or powdered to add aromatic flavouring.

Cloves (4) These are nearly always used whole in Indian food to provide aromatic flavouring.

Coriander (5) This comes either as seed, powder or leaves. Seed is used when more aroma is wanted in a dish. The powder gives more flavour and body to a curry sauce. Green, sprouted coriander leaves are used chopped in the same way as parsley for garnish and last-minute flavouring.

Cumin (6) This is used both as seed (more aromatic) and powder.

Fenugreek (7) This is used either in whole seed or in powder form, mainly to remove 'fishyness' from a dish. It is particularly useful with prawns.

Garam Masala (8) Literally translated this means 'hot spice'. It is made in a variety of ways but nearly always includes cloves, cardamoms, cumin and coriander. It is used to add a final flavouring towards the end of cooking.

Garlic (9) This is absolutely essential to cooking good curries. Many people do not realise they are eating garlic in a curry. Test for freshness by choosing only firm bulbs of garlic with the cloves tightly held together.

Ginger (10) This is another root spice, best used in root form with the outer bark-like skin removed and the flesh cut into thin strips. When ginger is dried it can be ground into a fine powder which is much hotter than the root itself, the hotness tending to mask the true ginger flavour.

Poppy seeds (11) These are used to add a nutty flavour to curries.

Saffron (12) This is used primarily for the rich yellow colour just a few saffron threads can give.

Sesame seeds (13) These are tiny small seeds, usually white in colour and rich in protein and oil.

Tamarind (14) This is the semi-dried fruit of the tamarind tree. The fruit is soaked in boiling water and after half an hour or so (depending on the strength of flavouring desired) the pulp is squeezed out and the liquid used to impart a bitter flavour to the dish. Tamarind is often used to cut down the oiliness in fish dishes.

Turmeric (15) This is the ground root of a plant grown predominantly in India. It imparts a bright yellow colour to any sauce and adds its own unique musty flavour.

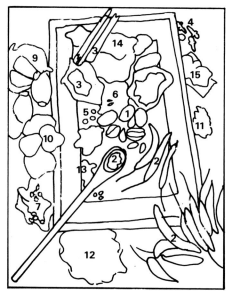

Chicken Murgh

Throughout the north of India much use is made of poultry. The reason for this is twofold, firstly because poultry is widely available and does very well indeed in the rather more temperate climates and secondly that there are quite a number of Muslims in the north and in particular of course in Pakistan. They will not eat pork on religious grounds, preferring lamb or goat meat. This tends to be expensive so poultry is very attractive.

When you buy chickens in India you usually buy them alive! You can of course get the chicken dealer to dress them for you, but the Indian way is not to laboriously pluck every feather away leaving the chicken covered with its skin. As most Indian dishes call for skinned chicken, the chicken is skinned with the feathers intact all in one go. However, for most of these recipes you will probably be using oven-ready frozen chickens as these are the easiest to come by in the West, and so it is necessary to skin them before cooking them. In addition, there are very few recipes that call for whole chickens, so you will need to learn how to joint them. It is of course possible to use chicken joints although these are more difficult to skin and the disadvantage is that you are never quite sure of the quality of the chicken you are buying when you buy chicken joints. So, in my view it is best to use good oven-ready chickens that are sold for roasting and learn the simple but noble art of skinning and jointing chicken!

How to skin a chicken

Most oven-ready chickens come with the wings fully attached plus the bottom joints of the leg. The feet are usually cut off. Cut off the first joint on the wing section and the bottom joint on the leg section. Do this for each joint. There is very little waste here as there is hardly any meat on these pieces.

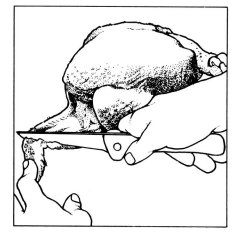

Next, sit the bird upright with the breast uppermost, and the cavity towards you. Pinch the skin above the breast and with a very sharp knife cut away from you, pulling the skin as you do.

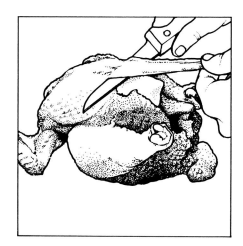

When you get to the neck end of the bird turn the chicken over and continue to cut this narrow strip of skin all the way across the underside of the bird to the parson's nose. Then cut off the parson's nose and discard.

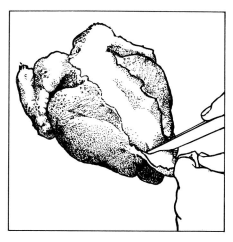

Now ease your fingers under the remaining skin on one side of the bird and using a kitchen towel or tea towel (this helps you grip the skin more easily), pull gently to remove the skin from the leg section and the wing section, plus the side of the bird. You may find that some skin is left on the wing section but this can be removed with a knife later. Repeat for the other side of the chicken. You have now skinned your chicken and it is ready for jointing.

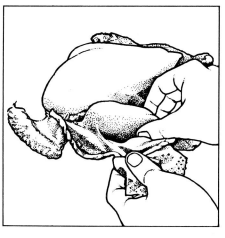

How to joint a chicken

Sit the bird upright with its breast uppermost, grasp the two legs and pull them back towards you.

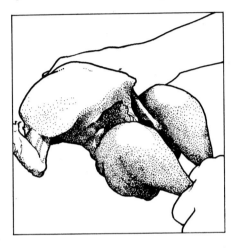

With a sharp knife cut down parallel to the breast bone so that the leg section tends to fall away.

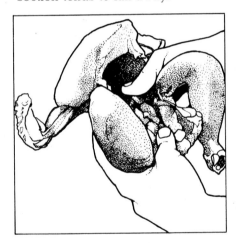

Bend the leg section backwards from the body section until you hear a sharp crack. This is the back bone breaking. With a sharp knife, just cut through any remaining flesh. You will now have two sections of chicken, one containing the chest cavity with the wings on and one consisting of the two leg sections.

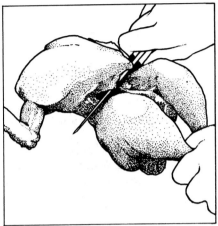

With a cleaver or heavy sharp knife, chop down either side of the leg section in the middle to remove the remaining back bone. You will now have two separate leg joints, cut these into two at the joints. In some cases one of the joints can be further divided into two, depending on the size of the chicken.

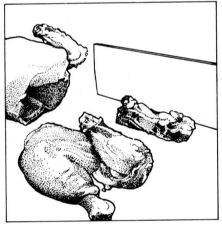

Now turn to the remaining breast part of the chicken. Hold the bird upright on its neck end, chop down either side of the back bone to remove the back bone centre section (about 2 cm/¾ inch wide).

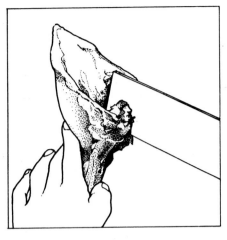

Place the chicken breast downwards on the chopping board so that the cavity is now uppermost. Spread the breast so that pressure is put on the breast bone and chop along the breast bone, one chop either with a heavy knife or cleaver (it really is best to have a small cleaver for this) and you will then have two breasts of chicken; again using the cleaver, chop these breasts into three pieces each.

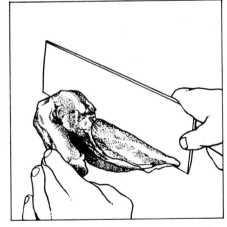

You have now skinned and successfully jointed your chicken and all that you have to do now is count your fingers!

Chapter One
Accompaniments

It is rather difficult to equate the style of serving Indian food with that of food in the West. As a rule everyone sits down to eat at once and virtually all the dishes appear at the same time. There is one exception to this. Often when people are invited to someone's house for a meal it is for a far longer time than in the West. In the West where you are invited for dinner at 8 o'clock, in India you may well be invited for about 5 o'clock. Very often you are first of all given tea to drink, accompanied by a number of snacks, some of them quite substantial. Naturally enough, quite a gap in time is left between the serving of tea and snacks and the serving of the meal proper.

The traditional Hindu method of eating is to use a thali. A thali is the name given to the dish on which each individual serves himself a small quantity of the food on offer. This can be a metal plate (if you are very rich it could be silver or even gold!), an ordinary porcelain plate or in the case of the very poor, simply a banana leaf. Small amounts of food are taken from each bowl and placed around the edge of the thali. The food is then mixed and eaten with the right hand.

In this chapter you will find recipes for a number of accompaniments, from the various Indian breads to the chutneys and some of the really spicy pickles.

Unleavened bread
Chapatti

꿎꿎꿎꿎꿎꿎꿎꿎꿎꿎꿎꿎꿎꿎꿎꿎

Chapattis are perhaps the easiest form of Indian bread and probably the one with which most people are familiar. Quite simply they are flat, unleavened pancakes made from wholemeal flour. The secret to good chapattis is to cook them and eat them within the space of half an hour. Any longer delay and they tend to become very tough. As you can imagine, this means that the person doing the cooking gets little time to sit down to enjoy the food with everyone else, but as long as the chapattis are put into a warm tea towel in a basket as soon as they are cooked and kept covered to prevent the moisture disappearing, they will keep reasonably well. In this way it is possible to cook a dozen chapattis half an hour in advance of the meal. This recipe makes approximately eight chapattis.

350 g/12 oz chapatti or wholemeal flour
1 teaspoon salt

Preparation time: 15 minutes plus 3 hours chilling
Cooking time: 30 minutes

Sift the flour and the salt together into a large bowl and gradually add a little water to obtain a hard dough. Knead the dough for 5 minutes until it becomes elastic. Return the ball of dough to the bowl, cover with foil or cling film and place in the refrigerator to chill for 2–3 hours.

To cook, break off a lump of dough and form it into a ball approximately 5 cm/2 inches in diameter. On a floured board, roll each ball into a disc measuring 15–23 cm/6–9 inches in diameter and about 0.25 cm/$\frac{1}{8}$ inch thick. Traditionally, chapattis are cooked on a convex iron plate known as a *tawa*, but if you do not have one of these, they can be cooked with a high degree of success in a dry frying pan.

Sprinkle a little flour into the frying pan, heat it and place the chapatti in it. Cook until it is dry on one side, turn it over and cook the other side. This should take about a minute. Once you have done this, remove the frying pan from the heat and using tongs place the cooked chapatti directly onto a low heat source. If this is gas you should leave it there for a couple of seconds and then flick it over onto the other side. It takes slightly longer on electric cookers. You will see that brown spots begin to form on either side and the chapatti should puff up almost into a sphere. Place the chapatti in a tea towel and wrap, keeping warm in a low oven before serving.

Deep-fried bread
Puri

꿎꿎꿎꿎꿎꿎꿎꿎꿎꿎꿎꿎꿎꿎꿎꿎

Puris are deep-fried chapattis and are traditionally eaten at breakfast time. It is the custom in many families to send out for puris rather than make them in the home and there are many stalls in the bazaars of the big cities specialising in puris and a special kind of Chenna chutney – made with whole chick peas. Puris and chutney make a very filling breakfast which sets you up for the day! This recipe makes approximately twelve.

350 g/12 oz chapatti flour
1 teaspoon salt
100 g/4 oz ghee
vegetable oil for deep frying

Preparation time: 3 hours 15 minutes
Cooking time: 10 minutes

Sift the chapatti flour and salt into a large bowl, rub in the ghee, and add enough water to form a hard dough. Cover the bowl with cling film or aluminium foil and put to one side for 2–3 hours or overnight.

Then, break off 4-cm/1$\frac{1}{2}$-inch pieces of dough and roll out into discs approximately 13 cm/5 inches in diameter. Roll the puris out at one time, keeping them separate either between greaseproof paper or by dusting with a little chapatti flour.

Heat the oil in a deep fryer or, failing that, a frying pan until a puri dropped into the oil immediately sizzles and rises to the surface. The puris should puff up and be cooked within 30–45 seconds. Using a slotted spoon, turn the puris from time to time to ensure that both sides are cooked evenly. Lift out from the deep fryer, drain off the excess oil and serve hot.

Leavened bread
Naan

꿎꿎꿎꿎꿎꿎꿎꿎꿎꿎꿎꿎꿎꿎꿎꿎

Traditionally, naan is the perfect accompaniment to Tandoori food, and it is usually prepared in the clay oven known as a tandoor. Just as in former times in Western countries every village had its own bakery, in the country areas of India and Pakistan every village has its own bread oven or tandoor. Often this is more than 3 metres/10 feet deep and set in the ground. The charcoal fire is lit 3 hours in advance of cooking and when all the smoke has disappeared and just a thin film of white ash is left on the charcoal, the tandoor is ready to cook the naan. The baker reaches

down into the tandoor with an uncooked naan placed on a cushion of canvas and horsehair and slaps it on the inside walls. Both sides cook simultaneously and once cooked, using a long-handled spatula and a hook, the naan-wallah scoops the naan off the wall and hoists it out of the tandoor in one deft operation. This is the traditional way to cook naan, but do not worry as it can be made quite satisfactorily in an ordinary, conventional oven. This recipe makes eight naan.

350g/12 oz flour
1 teaspoon salt
100 ml/4 fl oz natural yogurt
150 ml/¼ pint milk
2 teaspoons sugar
½ teaspoon bakers' yeast
1 tablespoon poppy seeds
50 g/2 oz ghee or butter

Preparation time: 25 minutes plus 5 hours proving
Cooking time: 20 minutes

Sift the flour together with the salt into a bowl and mix in the yogurt. Warm the milk slightly and stir in the sugar and the yeast. Add to the dough and continue to mix. Add a little water or flour as necessary, to get the dough to the correct hard consistency. Knead well for at least 15 minutes. Return to the bowl and cover with a damp tea towel. Put in a warm place to prove for 4–5 hours. The dough should rise to twice its original size.

To cook the naan, pull off lumps of dough approximately 5–8 cm/2–3 inches across and, using a combination of rolling and pulling, form into elongated shapes. Put the poppy seeds into a saucer, wet the hands with a little water, pick up a few poppy seeds on your wet hands and press them into the top of the naan.

Lay each naan out on a baking tray, brush with a little of the melted ghee or butter and bake in a pre-heated hot oven, 230°C/450°F/Gas Mark 8, for about 10 minutes until the naan puff up and turn golden brown. Serve immediately, keeping the naan warm in a cloth.

From left to right: Chapatti, Puri and Naan.

Shallow-fried bread
Paratha

A paratha is very similar to a chapatti except it contains ghee, which turns the chapatti mix into a kind of flaky pastry. Parathas are much thicker than chapattis and are lightly fried as opposed to dry cooked. Most people find them tastier although it has to be said they are very much heavier than chapattis. This recipe makes approximately six chapattis.

350 g/12 oz chapatti flour
1 teaspoon salt
170 ml/6 fl oz water
100 g/4 oz ghee or 120ml/4 fl oz
  cooking oil
ghee for frying

Preparation time: 15 minutes plus 3
  hours chilling
Cooking time: 30 minutes

Sift the chapatti flour and salt together in a large bowl, gradually add the water and knead into a hard, elastic dough. Cover the bowl with cling film or aluminium foil and leave to chill for 2–3 hours in a refrigerator.

Then, break off a lump of the dough and form into a ball about 9 cm/3½ inches in diameter, sprinkle a little chapatti flour onto your work surface and roll the dough out into a thin circle. The dough should be as thin as possible at this stage.

Heat the ghee in a small saucepan and as soon as it has melted, use a pastry brush to spread some of it on the dough. Now roll the dough from one end to form several layers.

Hold one end of the dough with your thumb and first finger and wind the other end round and round to form another ball of dough. Flatten the ball that you have now made, roll it out again and coat once again with ghee.

Roll it up once more and wind it round and round to form a ball. Then roll the whole circle out to about 20 cm/8 inches in diameter, about 0.5–1 cm/¼–½ inch thick. Repeat the process.

Heat a little ghee in a frying pan and fry the parathas for about 2–3 minutes on each side until crisp. Serve immediately.

Stuffed parathas
Aloo paratha

Stuffed Parathas are generally served on their own as they make a very filling snack. The stuffing can consist of virtually anything. Often it can be simply a mixture of minced meat and peas or a concoction of vegetables.

This particular recipe is a typical filling, consisting of potato, chopped coriander and parsley, plus, quite naturally enough, a few spices. Use the basic paratha dough method. This recipe makes approximately six parathas.

350 g/12 oz paratha dough mixture
500 g/1 lb potatoes
1 teaspoon salt
½ teaspoon black pepper
1 small onion
50 g/2 oz ghee or 120 ml/4 fl oz
  cooking oil
½ teaspoon ground ginger
½ teaspoon ground turmeric
1 teaspoon whole cumin seeds
1 teaspoon ground coriander
1 tablespoon chopped parsley
ghee for frying

Preparation time: 15 minutes plus 3
  hours chilling
Cooking time: 40 minutes

Make the dough in the paratha mixture and divide it up into pieces 9 cm/3½ inches in diameter. Roll out each piece three or four times, coating with melted ghee to make discs as for parathas.

Roll out the discs quite thinly and rather larger than you would normally do to make ordinary parathas, to 30–35 cm/12–14 inches across, and place them to one side.

Boil the potatoes in a little water until they are soft. Drain and mash them, adding the salt and the black pepper. Peel the onion and chop it very finely. Heat the ghee or cooking oil in a frying pan and fry the onion until soft. Add the remaining ingredients with the exception of the coriander and parsley. Mix the ingredients together in the frying pan over a gentle heat and cook for about 2 minutes.

Now add the mashed potato, stir it in well ensuring that the onion and spice mixture is well distributed throughout the potato. Sprinkle in the

Above left to right: Paratha and Chapatti malai; below left to right: Aloo paratha and Tamatar ka raeta.

coriander and parsley and stir in well. Put spoonfuls of the mixture on one side of each circle of paratha. Fold the parathas over and seal the edges to make a kind of patty. Heat a little ghee in a frying pan and fry the parathas gently for about 2–3 minutes on each side until brown on all sides. Serve immediately.

Tomato cooler
Tamatar ka raeta

ᘐᘐᘐᘐᘐᘐᘐᘐᘐᘐᘐᘐᘐᘐᘐᘐᘐ

Raeta is the general name given to a combination of yogurt and vegetables. It is made as a vegetable dish, serving as a 'fire extinguisher' to the hottest of the Indian dishes. Raeta can be made with virtually any vegetable, but the most popular ones are cucumber, potato or tomato. This recipe calls for 300 ml/½ pint of yogurt to two tomatoes, although the ratios of quantities are infinitely variable.

2 medium tomatoes
½ teaspoon salt
pinch of paprika
300 ml/½ pint natural yogurt
a little black pepper

Preparation time: 10 minutes

Wash the tomatoes and cut them into quarters and then crossways again, to form eight pieces from each tomato. Place the tomatoes in a bowl, sprinkle on the salt and the paprika and pour on the yogurt. Sprinkle a little ground black pepper over the top as a garnish and serve.

Chapatti with cream
Chapatti malai

ᘐᘐᘐᘐᘐᘐᘐᘐᘐᘐᘐᘐᘐᘐᘐᘐᘐ

This is a dish from my youth and is a very good way of using up old, tough chapattis that have been left over from an Indian meal.

Simply take the chapatti and spread it with jam and then with malai. Traditionally, Indian malai is the cream which floats to the top of ordinary milk when it is boiled; however, whipped double cream will do just as well.

Once the chapatti has been spread with jam and cream, roll it into a cylinder, chill for 2 hours and serve. It makes a great change from a jam butty!

Indian crisps
Poppadum

❧❧❧❧❧❧❧❧❧❧❧❧❧❧❧❧❧

Poppadums are perhaps among the most popular of the so-called Indian breads. They are usually served with a meal, as a starter to a meal or simply on their own as a snack.

They are extremely difficult to make in the West as the dough is made from lentils and chick peas ground together to form a very fine flour rolled out into ultra-thin wafers and left to dry. Without the very dry conditions that exist, particularly in the south of India, it is difficult indeed to make poppadums and no poppadums are made during the rainy season in India. This is because the poppadums absorb water from the atmosphere very quickly which renders them useless when it comes to cooking them.

So, it is best to buy poppadums ready made (they are widely available) and it goes without saying they should be kept in a dry place.

The normal savoury poppadum is, in its raw state, 10–13 cm/4–5 inches across, but there are also spicy poppadums, which are often in much bigger sizes, up to 30–35 cm/12–14 inches across.

Cooking time: 10 minutes

As poppadums swell up with cooking, it is best to fold them into four before frying them. Some suppliers of poppadums recommend grilling them but in my view this is an unsatisfactory method of cooking as they never become properly cooked through. The best method is to fry them in about 5 cm/2 inches of vegetable oil.

There are, though, techniques to remember when frying poppadums. The first is to remove any dust that may have rubbed off the poppadums during their journey from India. Do this by taking however many poppadums you wish to cook (work on the ratio of at least 2½ per person!) and holding the poppadums loosely in two hands on the edge and shaking them so that the dust falls out.

One chef I knew used to take the poppadums, two at a time, and bash them on the edge of a table to beat any excess dust from them. Whenever I tried this I ended up with too many broken poppadums, so I think the previous method is perhaps more satisfactory. Removing the dust serves to help preserve the oil as small amounts of dust will quickly blacken in the hot oil.

In a deep-sided frying pan heat the oil until it is the correct temperature. Test this by breaking off a small piece of poppadum and throwing it into the oil. It should sizzle immediately and begin to curl up. Until it does, do not start to fry your poppadums, otherwise they will go soggy.

Once this temperature has been reached you have to work quickly. The secret is to fry poppadums in twos. Put the poppadums two at a time into the oil and using a fish slice or slotted spoon spin them in the oil as they cook for 5–10 seconds, and then quickly flick them over until the other poppadum cooks.

The reason for frying them two at a time is to ensure that they do not curl up. If you fry poppadums singly, they curl up to look like brandy snaps. By frying them two at a time each poppadum is curling against the other and this keeps them relatively flat. After another few seconds, the other poppadum will be cooked; lift them out and give them a quick shake over the pan so that any excess oil drops back into the pan. Drain the poppadums on kitchen paper. Poppadums are best eaten freshly cooked although they will keep, but not for much longer than a day or so, depending on the atmospheric humidity.

Chick pea bread
Basni roti

❧❧❧❧❧❧❧❧❧❧❧❧❧❧❧❧❧

This is a very similar bread to a paratha – the difference being that the bread is made with chick-pea flour. This is variously known in India as gram flour or besan. The flour is very fine and tends to form into lumps easily. It is vital for this recipe that it is sifted well before mixing with the yogurt to form the dough.

170 g/6 oz chick-pea flour
2 teaspoons salt
1 teaspoon black pepper
150 ml/¼ pint natural yogurt
½ tablespoon chopped coriander
    leaves
50 g/2 oz butter
oil for frying

Preparation time: 1 hour 30
    minutes
Cooking time: 15 minutes

Sift the chick-pea flour, together with the salt and black pepper, into a large mixing bowl and gradually add the yogurt to form a dough. Depending on how liquid the yogurt is, you may have to add a little water or more flour to make a fairly hard dough. Fold in the chopped coriander leaves. Leave to stand for 1 hour. Then, break off pieces of the dough about 5 cm/2 inches in diameter and roll out into circles about 0.25 cm/⅛ inch thick.

Heat the butter and brush it over the rolled-out dough. Roll it up lengthways and repeat the process twice. Finally roll out into a circle about 0.5 cm/¼ inch thick and dry fry in a hot frying pan until golden brown on both sides. Serve hot.

From above: Poppadum, Dahi and Basni roti.

Yogurt
Dahi

✥✥✥✥✥✥✥✥✥✥✥✥✥✥✥

Yogurt-making at home has found fame relatively recently in the West and it has been accompanied by all manner of gadgets designed to make yogurt-making easy.

There are three things to be said about these gadgets: one, they are unnecessary; two, they are expensive and three, they do not usually make enough yogurt for the purpose of cooking. Yogurt-making without the use of gadgets is simplicity itself although you will need to do a little experimenting.

You need to find exactly the right place in your house where the yogurt bacteria, which turn ordinary milk into yogurt, can thrive and flourish. This may be an airing cupboard, although many people find their airing cupboards a little too warm, or it may simply be a warm shelf in the kitchen.

Either way, do experiment before buying expensive yogurt-making equipment. Once you have tried making just 600 ml/1 pint of yogurt and it has turned out successfully you are ready to make larger quantities.

Preparation time: 12 hours 30 minutes

The making of yogurt is simplicity itself. Bring the milk to the boil and boil for 3 or 4 minutes. Remove from the heat and cover the saucepan. Allow to cool to blood temperature, then beat in your 'starter' yogurt, which can be any plain shop-bought yogurt. Allow about 100 ml/4 fl oz to 1.2 litres/2 pints of milk. It is essential to allow the milk to cool to blood temperature otherwise the yogurt bacteria will be killed off. Beat the yogurt in well, cover the saucepan again and place in a warm position to maintain at blood heat. After 12 hours or so you will see that the milk has turned into yogurt. Taste it and you will find it is much better than any yogurt you can buy in a shop. You can then go on using your home-made yogurt to seed new batches of yogurt. However, after about 6 or 7 batches, it is best to start again with a new carton of shop-bought yogurt. For some reason, yogurt this old tends to have a rather fizzy taste to it.

Home-mixed curry powder
Garam masala

Literally translated, Garam masala means hot spice and that really is what it is. It is the combination of a number of spices and aromatics which form the basis of most dishes in an Indian kitchen. The idea is that the Garam masala is then added with other spices to change the flavour of the dish. Quite often Garam masala is added towards the end of cooking to give an extra spicy punch to the dish just before serving. There are almost as many recipes for Garam masala as there are cooks in India, but here now are two variations.

100 g/4 oz coriander seeds
5 bay leaves
100 g/4 oz white cumin seeds
25 g/1 oz cardamoms
25 g/1 oz cloves
1 × 5-cm/2-inch stick of cinnamon
50 g/2 oz chilli powder
50 g/2 oz black pepper
1 teaspoon freshly grated nutmeg

Preparation time: 30 minutes

Preheat the oven to 200°C/400°F/Gas Mark 6. Put the coriander seeds, bay leaves, cumin seeds, cardamoms and cloves together with the cinnamon stick onto a flat baking tin, and roast in the hot oven for 20 minutes. Then put the spices into a grinder and grind very finely. Combine them with the powdered ingredients, the chilli powder, black pepper and nutmeg, and store in an airtight jar. If the jar is kept well sealed and out of sunlight the spices will last for several months.

The second recipe uses the same ingredients except black pepper and chilli powder. This makes a far blander Garam masala, which consists purely of aromatics. The effect of this is to produce a far more fragrant dish when the Garam masala is added to the dish, usually 5 minutes from the end of cooking.

Above: Baigan ka achar; centre left: Piaz ka chatni; centre right: Am chatni; below: the spices for a Garam masala.

Sweet mango chutney
Am chatni

꿩꿩꿩꿩꿩꿩꿩꿩꿩꿩꿩꿩꿩꿩꿩

Mango Chutney is an abomination in as much as it often serves to mask the true flavour of many Indian dishes. Often in the West, particularly in England, a curry is served as some kind of nondescript stew plonked on top of a bed of boiled rice with a dollop of Mango Chutney on top. This quite clearly is not true Indian food, but nonetheless many people enjoy this form of cooking. This recipe uses honey instead of the traditional sugar and I think it produces a chutney that is more exotic and better tasting. Start the preparations the day before.

500 g/1 lb underripe mangoes
50 g/2 oz salt
1.2 litres/2 pints boiling water
1 × 10-cm/4-inch piece of fresh
   ginger
4 cloves garlic
2 teaspoons garam masala
4 teaspoons ground turmeric
4 teaspoons chilli powder
50 g/2 oz sultanas
500 g/1 lb honey
300 ml/½ pint vinegar

Preparation time: 15 minutes plus
   overnight soaking
Cooking time: 40 minutes

Choose only really firm mangoes which ought not to be too ripe. If they are overripe you will find the chutney turns into a kind of mush. The idea is that at the end you will finish up with a chutney that has discernible pieces of mango in it. Peel the mangoes and trim away the flesh in large pieces from the central stone. Cut these pieces into strips measuring approximately 5 × 2.5 cm/2 × 1 inch across. Place in a bowl, sprinkle with the salt and pour over the boiling water. Cover the bowl and soak overnight.

The next day, peel the ginger and garlic and chop very finely. Mix together with the remaining spices and the sultanas. Transfer this mixture to a large saucepan, pour a little of the liquid from the mangoes into the saucepan, bring to the boil and add the honey, vinegar, mangoes and remaining liquid.

Cook for 20–25 minutes until the mixture begins to thicken. If you are worried about the thickness of the mixture, increase the heat to boil off the excess moisture. When the mixture has thickened sufficiently, cool and transfer to preserving jars to store.

Aubergine pickle
Baigan ka achar

꿩꿩꿩꿩꿩꿩꿩꿩꿩꿩꿩꿩꿩꿩꿩

This is one of the rarer pickles not often seen. Certainly you will not have it served to you often in an Indian restaurant. However, if you have a good source of firm, hard aubergines, it is a good pickle to make yourself as it keeps very well for months.

500 g/1 lb aubergines
300 ml/½ pint sesame seed oil
4 cloves garlic
1 × 5-cm/2-inch piece of fresh
   ginger
1 teaspoon ground turmeric
6 dried red chillies
4 bay leaves
2 teaspoons mustard seeds
1 teaspoon cumin seeds
2 tablespoons salt
100 g/4 oz clear honey

Preparation time: 15 minutes
Cooking time: 20 minutes plus
   1 month storing

Remove the hard green leaves from the end of the aubergines and cut into 2.5-cm/1-inch pieces. The best way to do this is to cut the aubergines lengthways and then keeping the pieces together, cut lengthways in the other direction. Then cut across the aubergines at 2.5-cm/1-inch intervals to make the cubes.

Heat a little of the sesame seed oil in a frying pan and fry the aubergine pieces until they just begin to change colour. Remove from the frying pan and put into a bowl. Peel the garlic and ginger and slice and chop them very finely. Fry the garlic and ginger in a little more of the sesame seed oil and add the turmeric and chillies. Crumble the bay leaves into the frying pan (if they are not crisp put them in a moderate oven to crisp). Cook for 2–3 minutes, remove the frying pan from the heat and put to one side.

Heat the remaining sesame seed oil in a saucepan until it starts to smoke. Add the mustard and cumin seeds and cook for 3–4 minutes. Allow to cool.

Arrange the aubergine pieces in a bowl and sprinkle with the salt. Put the spice mixture from the frying pan in a bowl with the oil from the saucepan, stir well to ensure it is well dispersed, and then pour over the aubergines. Finally pour over the honey and turn the aubergines well.

Transfer the pickle to preserving jars. Cover and store for a month or so before serving. The pickle should keep for a year if properly sealed.

Onion chutney
Piaz ka chatni

꿩꿩꿩꿩꿩꿩꿩꿩꿩꿩꿩꿩꿩꿩꿩

This is a very simple chutney, which goes well with most Indian dishes. You can make it hotter by adding a few chopped green chillies!

2 large onions
1 clove garlic
1 × 8-cm/3-inch piece of fresh
   ginger
1 lemon
1 teaspoon salt
2 teaspoons chilli powder
1 teaspoon black pepper

Preparation time: 10 minutes plus 1
   hour chilling

Peel the onions and cut them into slices about 0.5 cm/¼ inch thick. Peel the garlic and chop it very finely. Remove the outer skin from the ginger and cut the flesh into thin strips. Mix the ginger, onions and garlic together. Sprinkle the juice of the lemon into the bowl and mix in the salt, chilli powder and black pepper. Chill for 1 hour and serve.

Tomato chutney
Tamatar chatni

If the chilli pickle is the dynamite of the chutney world, then Tomato Chutney must be one of the mildest and a most acceptable chutney for any palate. Use slightly underripe tomatoes for this recipe and remember that the chutney will not keep for very long, so you will have to serve it immediately. It is a good chutney to serve with a rather special dinner party.

225 g/½ lb tomatoes
1 small lemon
2 bay leaves
1 small onion
1 × 5-cm/2-inch piece of fresh
    ginger
½ teaspoon black pepper
½ teaspoon chilli powder
½ teaspoon ground turmeric

Preparation time: 20 minutes
Cooking time: 40 minutes plus
    2 hours chilling

Using a fork, hold the tomatoes over a gas flame until their skins split. Remove the skins and cut the tomatoes into thin strips using a sharp knife. (If you do not have a gas flame, then remove the skins by pouring boiling water over the tomatoes.) Squeeze the juice from the lemon over the tomatoes and then grate, with a very fine grater, half of the lemon peel into the tomato mixture. Be sure not to grate any of the pith into the tomatoes as this will make the chutney bitter.

Preheat the oven to 180°C/350°F/ Gas Mark 4. Put the bay leaves into the oven on a tray until they are crisp. This should take about 20–30 minutes. Then, peel the onion and ginger and chop very finely. Mix the ginger and onion together with the black pepper, chilli powder and turmeric and crumble in the roasted bay leaves. Add this mixture to the tomatoes and stir in well to ensure it is well dispersed throughout the dish. Chill for 2 hours in the refrigerator and serve.

From left to right: Tamatar chatni; Nimboo ka achar and Dhania ka chatni.

Lime pickle
Nimboo ka achar

Lime Pickle is one of the best pickles ever produced in Indian cooking. It has a hotness and sharpness which complements most of the southern Indian dishes. Traditionally in Indian restaurants the pickle tray is offered to diners and equally traditionally most diners usually opt for the sweet mango chutney that they have come to know and love. Mango chutney has a place, but not with most of the Indian food that one is served with because it is far too sweet and sickly and tends to mask the real flavours. Lime Pickle, on the other hand, is so much better, so do have a go at making your own. The recipe calls for limes but equally well you could use half the number of lemons.

15 limes
6 teaspoons salt
4 teaspoons black pepper
300 ml/½ pint sesame seed oil
1 tablespoon mustard seeds
2 teaspoons fenugreek seeds
½ teaspoon aniseed
6 green chillies
4 cloves garlic
100 g/4 oz fresh ginger

Preparation time: 40 minutes plus
    2 weeks storing

Cut the limes in half or into quarters if they are very large. (The best limes to use are the small ones that are only 2.5–5 cm/1–2 inches across and are almost spherical in shape.) Arrange the limes in a large pickling jar, placing them so that by and large the cut surfaces are uppermost. Sprinkle each layer with salt and black pepper.

Once you have put the limes in the jar, heat the sesame seed oil in a saucepan and when it is just on the verge of smoking, throw in the mustard seeds, fenugreek, aniseed and the green chillies, topped and tailed but not chopped. Cook for 30–60 seconds or so. Remove the saucepan from the heat and allow to cool. Remove the limes, salt and pepper from the pickling jar and place in a large bowl. Peel the garlic and ginger and chop finely. Mix the garlic and the ginger together with the limes and then transfer the limes and oil to the pickle jar, cover and

leave for 2 weeks to allow the spices and oil to penetrate the limes.

If you use lemons for this recipe then leave the jar to stand for at least a month as it takes longer for the lemon peel to break down than it does for the lime peel. The longer you leave this pickle the stronger it becomes. When you come to serve the pickle, if you want to do it in the real Indian way, always serve it from the jar and people then fish out the bits they want. Usually half a small lime is enough for 1 person.

Coriander chutney
Dhania ka chatni

The name chutney is given to any rather liquid sauce, served cold with a main dish. Unlike the chutneys in the West, Indian chutneys are not designed to be kept for any length of time; normally the Indians use very fresh ingredients and coriander chutney is one of the most refreshing tastes once you have got used to the rather brackish flavour of the coriander.

170 g/6 oz coriander leaves
1 small onion
2 lemons
2 tablespoons vinegar
1 tablespoon desiccated coconut
2 green chillies
2 teaspoons ground cumin
2 teaspoons salt
½ teaspoon black pepper
½ teaspoon chilli powder

Preparation time: 15 minutes

Wash the coriander leaves and chop them roughly. It does not matter if you include some of the stalks. 50 g/ 2 oz of coriander leaves should fill a 600-ml/1-pint container when pressed down gently. Peel the onion. Squeeze the juice of the lemons into a liquidiser and add the rest of the ingredients, together with the coriander. Liquidise until smooth. If necessary, add a little water to keep the chutney liquid.

Serve immediately or pour into a jar with a screw-top lid. It can be kept in a refrigerator for up to a week. Alternatively, put some to one side for immediate serving and freeze the remainder.

Chilli pickle
Mirch achar

This really is the hot one! I used to have an uncle who would never sit down to any meal unless he had, as an accompaniment, five fresh green chillies and a little dish of salt in which to dip them. He would then eat them raw. He was also a great devotee of chilli pickle.

This chilli pickle is only for those who can take the hottest of spices and even then my advice is to use it in moderation. However, if you want to try your hand at what is perhaps one of the most revered recipes in the Indian cuisine, then why not have a go.

500 g/1 lb green chillies
50 g/2 oz salt
25 g/1 oz black pepper
5 bay leaves
600 ml/1 pint sesame seed oil
50 g/2 oz aniseed
50 g/2 oz mustard seeds
2 tablespoons mustard powder

Preparation time: 1 hour 10 minutes
Cooking time: 40 minutes plus 1 month storing

Remove the stalks from the green chillies and with a sharp knife split each one lengthways. It is not necessary to slit the chilli into two, simply to split it open. Arrange the chillies in a bowl and sprinkle over the salt and black pepper. Put to one side for 1 hour.

Preheat the oven to 180°C/350°F/ Gas Mark 4. Put the bay leaves on a tray in the oven and warm through for about 30 minutes so that they become crisp.

Heat the sesame seed oil until it starts to smoke. Throw in the aniseed and mustard seeds and sprinkle in the mustard powder. Remove the bay leaves from the oven and crumble them into the oil. Reduce the heat and stir in well. Cook for about 1 minute, remove from the heat and allow to cool. Then pour onto the green chillies. Mix well, being careful not to break the green chillies up.

Transfer the mixture to a large, clear pickle jar, or two small ones. Cover and keep for 1 month. Remember, when serving the pickle, it will turn out to be dynamite!

Chick pea chutney
Chenna chatni

This is the traditional accompaniment with puris for breakfast, although it can be cooked on its own, and makes a very filling meal in itself. Start the preparations the day before.

225 g/½ lb chick peas
100 g/4 oz ghee or 120 ml/4 fl oz cooking oil
1 large onion
2 cloves garlic
1 teaspoon ground turmeric
1 teaspoon chilli powder
2 teaspoons fenugreek seeds
1 teaspoon ground cumin
1 teaspoon ground coriander
3 cardamoms
1 × 5-cm/2-inch stick of cinnamon
4 cloves
2 green chillies
½ lemon
1½ teaspoons salt
300 ml/½ pint beef stock
1 teaspoon cornflour
2 teaspoons garam masala

Preparation time: 10 minutes plus overnight soaking
Cooking time: 2 hours 30 minutes

Wash the chick peas well and soak them overnight in plenty of water. The next day, bring the water to the boil and simmer gently for 2 hours until the chick peas become tender. Drain them and put to one side.

Heat the ghee or cooking oil in a large saucepan. Peel and thinly slice the onion and fry in the ghee until soft. Now peel and finely chop the cloves of garlic and add to the saucepan.

Then add the turmeric, chilli powder, fenugreek seeds, cumin and coriander and stir well for 2–3 minutes on a very moderate heat.

Then add the cardamoms, cinnamon, cloves and chick peas. Continue to stir until you are sure the chick peas are well coated with the spice mixture.

Top and tail the green chillies and cut them into 0.5-cm/¼-inch pieces. Add to the saucepan and cook for a further minute. Now squeeze in the juice from the lemon and add the salt, together with the beef stock. Bring to the boil and continue to boil for 5 minutes.

Mix up the teaspoon of cornflour with a little cold water so that it forms a smooth paste and add to the saucepan. Cook for a further 5 minutes, and then sprinkle in the garam masala. As the sauce begins to thicken, check that the chick peas are fully softened. Cook for a further 10 minutes and serve.

Mint chutney
Podina ka chatni

ᘰᘰᘰᘰᘰᘰᘰᘰᘰᘰᘰᘰᘰᘰᘰᘰᘰ

This is a very good sauce to go with Tikka Kebabs or Tandoori Chicken. It is not quite so sweet as the mint sauce made in the West and the slight sourness of the yogurt gives the chutney its rather distinct flavour.

4 heaped tablespoons finely chopped fresh mint
1 small onion
1 teaspoon chilli powder
1 teaspoon black pepper
1 teaspoon salt
4 tablespoons natural yogurt
2 teaspoons honey
2 tablespoons vinegar

Preparation time: 10 minutes plus 1 hour chilling

Peel the onion and chop it finely. Combine it with the finely chopped mint. Sprinkle in the chilli powder, black pepper and salt and mix together with the yogurt. Dissolve the honey in the vinegar and stir into the yogurt mixture. Chill for 1 hour and then serve.

From left to right: Mirch achar, Chenna chatni and Podina ka chatni.

Nut sauce
Badam pista chatni

This sauce is best served with Seekh Kebabs. Its ingredients are quite expensive and so it is often served for special occasions. It is possible to buy pistachio nuts ready shelled and in some cases already chopped.

If you are unable to buy shelled pistachio nuts, then buy the sort which have been roasted in their shells and salted. Soak them for an hour or two in water to remove the salt and then remove the shells from the nuts.

50 g/2 oz pistachio nuts
50 g/2 oz almonds
½ teaspoon saffron threads
150 ml/¼ pint chicken stock
6 cardamoms
25 g/1 oz ghee or 30 ml/1 fl oz
   cooking oil
1 small onion
300 ml/½ pint cream
2 teaspoons salt
1 teaspoon black pepper

Preparation time: 40 minutes
Cooking time: 20 minutes

Put the saffron threads into a cup and pour on sufficient boiling water to three-quarters fill the cup. Leave to soak for 30 minutes, and then pour the threads together with the water in which they have been soaking into a liquidiser or food processor. Add the shelled pistachios and almonds and the chicken stock. Blend together for 1 minute.

Remove the seeds from the cardamoms, discard the husk, and grind the seeds. This can be done by putting the cardamoms between two sheets of greaseproof paper and pounding with a rolling pin. Alternatively, use a mortar and pestle. Add the ground cardamom seeds to the liquidiser and blend for a further 15 seconds.

Heat the ghee or cooking oil in a saucepan. Peel the onion and chop it finely. Cook the onion gently in the ghee until it begins to soften and then pour in the stock mixture. Bring to the boil and continue to stir while boiling away the stock until it is reduced by about half. Reduce the heat and gradually add the cream, salt and black pepper, stirring in well. When the sauce begins to thicken, remove from the heat and serve immediately.

This sauce may also be served cold, but do not over-chill it otherwise the ghee will congeal.

Dried fish
Bombay duck

The name makes Bombay Duck sound quite an elegant dish, but if you have ever tried them you will know that they are far from elegant.

However, many people do like this particular dish. A Bombay Duck is not in fact anything to do with a fowl. It is a fish. To be more precise it is the Bummaloe fish.

This fish is found swimming in many estuaries of the Indian sub-continent and it seems to be capable of withstanding quite sizeable amounts of pollution now typical in much of the industrial parts of the subcontinent. You could say it is the fish that boldly goes where no others can! For that reason, perhaps, it received its name, for it is believed that the name Bombay Duck is a corruption of Bombay Dock, an area not noted for its cleanliness, but well known for the Bummaloe fish, which seems to thrive among all the flotsam and jetsam that finds its way into the docks there.

There is no way of buying fresh Bummaloe fish in the Western world. Instead, in the West you will only find Bombay Ducks in packets, already dried and salted.

Cooking time: 10 minutes

All that remains is to cook them. This simply consists of grilling them gently until they are heated through. They are served as a starter and are also a very good accompaniment to beer, as their salt content tends to stimulate the thirst. One other thing, beware of the smell as you grill them.

Spiced apples
Seb sambal

A sambal is the name given to any combination of uncooked vegetables or in some cases seafood in a spicy dressing. This recipe uses sour apples rather than sweet ones; good green cooking apples are ideal.

225 g/½ lb apples
300 ml/½ pint boiling water
50–75 g/2–3 oz desiccated coconut
2 lemons
½ teaspoon ground ginger
½ teaspoon ground cumin
½ teaspoon ground turmeric
1 teaspoon chilli powder
1 medium onion
1 clove garlic
2 green chillies
50 g/2 oz ghee or 60 ml/2 fl oz
   cooking oil

Preparation time: 1 hour 30
   minutes
Cooking time: 15 minutes plus 1–2
   hours chilling

Make the coconut milk by combining the boiling water with the desiccated coconut. Allow this to steep for an hour or so and then liquidise in a blender. Squeeze in the juice from the lemons and add the ginger, cumin, turmeric and chilli powder. Blend for a further minute.

Peel the onion, garlic and chillies and chop finely. Fry them in the ghee or cooking oil until they begin to soften. Transfer this fried mixture to a liquidiser and blend with the other ingredients. Peel and core the apples. Cut into slices about 0.5–1 cm/¼–½ inch thick. Arrange in a small serving dish and pour the sauce. Chill for an hour or two and serve.

From left to right: Badam pista chatni, Bombay duck and Seb sambal.

Onion fritters
Piaz ka bhajji

This dish does not really exist in Indian cuisine in the Indian sub-continent, but it has shot to fame, courtesy of the numerous Indian restaurants in the West. It seems there is a definite taste for these strange-looking objects, without which I know many people would feel an Indian meal to be incomplete.

300 ml/½ pint natural yogurt
170 g/6 oz chick-pea flour
2 teaspoons chilli powder
½ teaspoon mustard powder
1 teaspoon salt
½ lemon
2 large onions
vegetable oil for deep frying

Preparation time: 2 hours 30 minutes
Cooking time: 15 minutes

Put the yogurt into a large bowl and sift in the chick-pea flour. You will find that quite often the flour forms very hard lumps and the back of a spoon is useful to break these lumps down as they go through the sieve. As you sift the flour into the yogurt, beat it with a fork to ensure it is well mixed in. Now stir in the chilli powder and mustard powder, together with the salt.

Transfer the mixture to a liquidiser or food processor. Squeeze in the juice from the lemon and then grate as much of the lemon peel as possible. Add to the yogurt mixture and liquidise for 1 minute until well combined, return to the bowl, cover with cling film and put into a refrigerator to stand for 2 hours.

Then peel the onions and cut crossways to form 4–6 large, thick wedges. These will break up, but not to worry as they will be just the right size to combine together with the batter. To cook the bhajjis, dip the onion slices in the batter, gather two or three together in a ball and deep fry in very hot cooking oil. To test whether the oil is the right temperature flick a little of the batter into it. If the batter sizzles immediately and floats to the surface, the oil is at the right temperature. When the bhajjis are golden brown on all sides, lift them out with a slotted spoon. Drain on kitchen paper and serve.

Mushroom fritters
Mushroom bhajji

As with Onion Bhajji, this recipe is a creation of the Indian restaurants in the Western world. Mushrooms are very difficult to come by in India and Pakistan, and I seldom cook them this way, coated in batter. However, I have to confess it is a very tasty recipe.

170 g/6 oz large button mushrooms
170 g/6 oz chick-pea flour
1 teaspoon salt
300 ml/½ pint natural thick yogurt
½ teaspoon black pepper
1 teaspoon chilli powder
½ lemon
1 medium onion
1 clove garlic
vegetable oil for deep frying

Preparation time: 2 hours 30 minutes
Cooking time: 15 minutes

Sieve the chick-pea flour together with the salt into the yogurt. Use a spoon to press through any stubborn lumps of chick-pea flour. Sprinkle in the black pepper and chilli powder and transfer the mixture to a liquidiser.

Squeeze in the juice from the lemon and grate in the peel. Peel the onion and cut it into small pieces and add to the liquidiser. Do the same with the clove of garlic.

Liquidise all the ingredients together for 1½ minutes until a smooth batter is obtained. Put the batter to rest for 2 hours in a refrigerator, covered with cling film or aluminium foil.

Then, prepare the mushrooms by cutting away any hard pieces. There are various schools of thought on how to prepare the mushrooms for this dish; one calls for the mushrooms to be cut up into thin strips but, personally, I prefer to coat whole mushrooms with the spiced batter and cook them individually in hot oil. In any event, plenty of batter has to be combined with the mushrooms to produce a good bhajji.

To cook the bhajjis, dip the mushrooms in the batter and deep fry in very hot cooking oil. Test that the oil is at the right temperature by flicking in a small piece of batter, which should immediately start to sizzle and rise to the surface of the oil. The oil is then at the correct temperature.

Cook the bhajjis until they are golden brown on all sides, remove with a slotted spoon and place on kitchen paper to drain. Serve hot.

From left to right: Mushroom bhajji, Piaz ka bhajji and Mulligatawny soup.

Spicy chicken soup
Mulligatawny soup

ᖰᖰᖰᖰᖰᖰᖰᖰᖰᖰᖰᖰᖰᖰᖰᖰᖰ

Soup as such does not exist in the traditional cooking of India but it was especially created to pander to the whims of the officers of the British Raj, who insisted on soup to start their evening meal. So, Mulligatawny was born. Translated from the Tamil it means 'Pepper Water' and that really is what it is. This recipe uses a good quality stock cube but real chicken stock can, of course, be used instead.

1 medium onion
1 clove garlic
4 green chillies
50 g/2 oz ghee or 60 ml/2 fl oz cooking oil
1 × 5-cm/2-inch piece of fresh ginger
1 teaspoon ground coriander
1½ teaspoons ground cumin
2 teaspoons black pepper
1 teaspoon ground turmeric
1 good quality chicken stock cube made up to 1.2 litres/2 pints with boiling water
1 teaspoon salt

Preparation time: 10 minutes
Cooking time: 30 minutes

Peel the onion and garlic and chop very finely. Top and tail the green chillies and chop them into 2.5-cm/1-inch pieces. Heat the ghee or cooking oil in a saucepan and fry the onion, garlic and chillies together for about 2 minutes until the onions begin to soften. Peel the ginger and cut it into thin strips. Fry for about 1 minute.

Now add the coriander, cumin, black pepper and the turmeric and stir for a further 3 minutes, cooking gently. Add the stock, bring to the boil and add the salt. Simmer for 10–20 minutes and serve.

Chapter Two
Meat dishes of southern India

The majority of food in southern India is vegetarian and vegetarianism has been one of the tenets of the Hindu religion for centuries. However, in the last twenty or thirty years habits have changed and a Western influence has crept in, albeit slowly. Increasingly, the more affluent classes of Hindus have been turning to meat dishes. By and large the women of India, though, do not receive the same education as the men, and are still very much vegetarian. However, a number of meat dishes have developed in southern India, mostly eaten by the Muslims and the Christians, found mainly in the region of Goa, a Portuguese colony until as recently as 1956. In particular there are the Vindaloo dishes which people in the West, brought up on Indian food served in Indian restaurants, quite often see as yet another hot and spicy dish. This is not strictly true, although it is correct to say that most of the southern Indian dishes are hot. Vindaloo cooking is a specific art in itself and depends not so much on hotness but on the use of vinegar in the cooking. The same techniques are applied to different meats – lamb, chicken and pork. There is still little domestic pork in India, most of it coming from the wild boar which inhabit the sugar-cane plantations. This tends to be a far spicier meat with a much stronger flavour.

Beef with coconut
Gosht molee

The name Molee is applied to a range of dishes generally found in southern India. The technique has spread to other places such as Ceylon and the Malay peninsula. Essentially a Molee is any dish which contains thick coconut milk. Originally these dishes were made purely from vegetables but nowadays they have been adapted to contain meat and poultry. Ideally, the coconut milk should be made from fresh coconuts although it can be made from desiccated coconut. For every fresh coconut substitute 170–225 g/6–8 oz of desiccated coconut.

500 g/1 lb beef
1 lemon
1 fresh coconut
100 g/4 oz ghee or 120 ml/4 fl oz
    cooking oil
1 large onion
2 cloves garlic
1 tablespoon ground coriander
1½ teaspoons ground turmeric
1 × 5-cm/2-inch stick of cinnamon
4 cloves
4 cardamoms
1 teaspoon black pepper
2 green chillies
2 teaspoons salt

Preparation time: 30 minutes
Cooking time: 1 hour 15 minutes

Trim away any fat from the beef and cut into 2.5-cm/1-inch pieces. Squeeze over the juice from the lemon and put to one side.

Make 2 holes in the end of the coconut and drain out any liquid into a bowl. Break open the nut and remove the meat from the inside of the shell. Grate this finely and mix together with the coconut liquid. Transfer this to a liquidiser and add 300 ml/½ pint water. Liquidise together for 5–7 minutes, pour through a double thickness of muslin and squeeze out the thick milk.

Turn the coconut pulp into a liquidiser and add another 300 ml/½ pint of water. Liquidise for a further 1½ minutes and squeeze the second milk through the muslin into a separate bowl. This is the thin milk.

If you use desiccated coconut instead of fresh coconut, then liquidise it with 450 ml/¾ pint of water and do not try to produce a second milk from it, but instead add half the remaining leftover pulp into the saucepan towards the end of the cooking process. Discard the other half.

Heat the ghee or cooking oil in a heavy saucepan. Peel and slice the onion and garlic thinly and fry gently for 2–3 minutes. Now add the coriander, turmeric, cinnamon, cloves, cardamoms and black pepper. Top and tail the green chillies and cut them lengthways. Add to the saucepan and cook for a further 2–3 minutes. Now add the beef and the thin coconut milk. Bring to the boil and simmer for 20 minutes. Pour in the thick coconut milk, add the salt, and continue to cook for another 30 minutes or so until the beef is tender.

From left to right: Gosht molee, Madoo thuckalee and Gosht madras.

Beef with tomatoes
Madoo thuckalee

This is a good recipe for a curry that is not too hot. The tomatoes add sweetness to the dish which is counteracted by the addition of natural yogurt.

500 g/1 lb braising beef
100 g/4 oz ghee or 120 ml/4 fl oz
    cooking oil
1 medium onion
2 cloves garlic
½ teaspoon ground cumin
1 teaspoon ground coriander
1 teaspoon ground turmeric
½ teaspoon ground ginger
1 teaspoon black pepper
1 teaspoon chilli powder
3 cloves
3 cardamoms
1 × 2.5-cm/1-inch stick of cinnamon
1 × 225-g/8-oz tin plum tomatoes
150 ml/¼ pint natural yogurt
1 tablespoon vinegar
1 teaspoon salt

Preparation time: 10 minutes
Cooking time: 2 hours

Trim away any excess fat from the beef and cut into 2.5-cm/1-inch cubes. Heat the ghee or cooking oil in a saucepan and fry the cubes of meat until they are sealed on all sides. Lift out with a slotted spoon and put to one side. Peel and thinly slice the onion and garlic and fry until they begin to soften.

Then, add the cumin, coriander, turmeric, ginger, black pepper and chilli powder and cook for a further 2 minutes. Add the cloves, cardamoms and cinnamon and cook for a further minute. Now add the beef, together with the tomatoes and any juice they have. Bring to the boil, stirring well so that the tomatoes break up, stir in the yogurt and vinegar and bring to the boil once again. Reduce the heat and cover the saucepan. Simmer for 1–1½ hours until the beef is tender. Add the salt towards the end of the cooking and serve.

Hot beef curry
Gosht madras

This hot curry comes from the city of Madras. A fairly dry mixture of spices used to produce a thick sauce.

500 g/1 lb braising beef
1 lemon
2 teaspoons salt
1 large onion
2 cloves garlic
2 dried red chillies
50 g/2 oz ghee or 60 ml/2 fl oz
    cooking oil
2 teaspoons ground coriander
1 teaspoon ground cumin
1 teaspoon ground turmeric
1 teaspoon ground ginger
2 teaspoons black pepper
100 g/4 oz tomato purée
300 ml/½ pint beef stock
2 teaspoons garam masala

Preparation time: 15 minutes
Cooking time: 1 hour 30 minutes

Cut the beef into 2.5-cm/1-inch cubes and squeeze over the lemon juice. Then sprinkle on the salt. Peel the onion and garlic, chop them very finely and mix together with the whole dried chillies, so that the chillies break up and are well dispersed in the chopped onion and garlic.

Heat the ghee or cooking oil in a heavy saucepan and fry the onion, garlic and chilli mixture for 2 minutes. Then add the coriander, cumin, turmeric, ground ginger and black pepper. Stir in well and cook for a further 2–3 minutes.

Add the beef, together with any remaining lemon juice, and turn the beef so that it is well coated with the spices. Cook for a further 5–10 minutes. Stir in the tomato purée and add the beef stock, bring to the boil and simmer gently, with the saucepan covered, for 30–40 minutes until the beef begins to become tender. Sprinkle in the garam masala and cook for a further 10 minutes. The gravy should by this stage be quite thick, if it is not, increase the heat, remove the lid from the saucepan and boil off any excess moisture until the gravy thickens.

Baked beef
Taskebab

This recipe is particularly used in the south for cooking tougher cuts of beef. It is almost exclusively a Christian dish for the Hindu majority abhor cooking their sacred animal, the cow. However, a very similar dish can be prepared using lamb instead of beef. You need to start preparations the day before.

500 g/1 lb stewing beef
2 lemons
2 teaspoons salt
2 large onions
120 ml/4 fl oz sesame seed oil
2 green chillies
2 cloves garlic
6 cloves
6 cardamoms
1 × 5-cm/2-inch stick of cinnamon
2 teaspoons black peppercorns
1 teaspoon ground ginger
2 teaspoons ground coriander
1 teaspoon ground cumin
2 teaspoons ground turmeric
2 teaspoons chilli powder

Preparation time: 15 minutes plus marinating overnight
Cooking time: 2 hours

Trim away any excess fat from the meat and cut into slices approximately 1 cm/½ inch thick. Squeeze the lemon juice over the meat and sprinkle with the salt. Leave overnight in the refrigerator to marinate.

The next day, peel one of the onions and cut it into thin slices. Heat the sesame seed oil and fry the onion until it is softened. Top and tail the green chillies, cut into 0.5-cm/¼-inch pieces and add to the saucepan. Fry until the chillies begin to brown. Peel and thinly slice the garlic, fry for a further 2 minutes. Then add the cloves, cardamoms, cinnamon and peppercorns and fry for a further 4 minutes.

Meanwhile, peel and chop the remaining onion finely. Arrange the onion in the bottom of an ovenproof casserole, put the marinade and beef on top and cover with the hot spice mixture. Sprinkle on the ginger, coriander, cumin, turmeric and chilli powder, cover the casserole and bake in a preheated moderate oven, 180°C/350°F/Gas Mark 4, for 1½ hours. From time to time turn the meat to ensure that it does not dry up. The dish should not be served until the beef is tender. If necessary increase the cooking time to take account of tougher cuts of beef.

Sweet and sour beef
Gosht chasnidargh

Sweet and sour cooking is usually associated with Chinese cooking. However, independently of China the Indian subcontinent, particularly in the south, has developed its own sweet and sour dishes, using honey for sweetness and lime juice for sourness. Sometimes a combination of vinegar is used with the lime juice to create the sourness, but either way it makes for an interesting dish. Common to most of the dishes is the use of rice flour to thicken the sauce.

500 g/1 lb braising beef
4 small limes or 2 lemons
1 tablespoon vinegar
2 tablespoons honey
4 cardamoms
4 cloves
2 teaspoons powdered rice
50 g/2 oz ghee or 60 ml/2 fl oz cooking oil
1 small onion
2 cloves garlic
1 × 5-cm/2-inch piece of fresh ginger
1 teaspoon ground cumin
2 teaspoons ground coriander
½ teaspoon saffron threads
2 teaspoons black pepper
1½ teaspoons salt
300 ml/1 pint beef stock
2 teaspoons garam masala
1 teaspoon kewra water

Preparation time: 15 minutes
Cooking time: 1 hour 30 minutes

Trim away any excess fat from the beef and cut into strips about 1 cm/½ inch thick. In a small saucepan squeeze the juice from the limes or lemons and add the vinegar and honey. Heat together with the cardamoms and cloves and boil for 2–3 minutes. Mix in the powdered rice and put the syrup to one side.

Heat the ghee or cooking oil in a heavy saucepan. Peel and thinly slice the onion and garlic and fry until they soften. Add the beef and continue to fry until it is sealed on all sides. Peel the ginger and cut into thin strips. Add to the pan. Add the cumin and coriander. Crush the saffron and add, together with the black pepper and salt. Pour in the beef stock and bring to the boil. Simmer gently for 40–45 minutes. Pour in the sweet and sour syrup and the garam masala, stir in well, and continue to cook for a further 10–15 minutes until the sauce begins to thicken. Check the tenderness of the beef, sprinkle in the kewra water and serve.

Sweet and sour pork
Shikar chasnidargh

ananananananananananan

This recipe is virtually identical to the Beef Chasnidargh but twice as much lime or lemon juice is used to counteract the fattiness of the pork.

500 g/1 lb pork
8 limes or 4 lemons
2 tablespoons clear honey
2 tablespoons vinegar
1 tablespoon powdered rice
50 g/2 oz ghee or 60 ml/2 fl oz cooking oil
1 small onion
3 cloves garlic
1 × 5-cm/2-inch piece fresh ginger
1 teaspoon fenugreek seeds
2 bay leaves
2 teaspoons poppy seeds
1 teaspoon mustard seeds
1 teaspoon black pepper
2 teaspoons chilli powder
600 ml/1 pint chicken stock
2 teaspoons salt

Preparation time: 15 minutes plus 3 hours marinating
Cooking time: 1 hour 30 minutes

Trim any excess fat from the pork and cut into 2.5-cm/1-inch cubes. Squeeze the juice of 4 of the limes or 2 of the lemons over the pork and leave to marinate for 2–3 hours.

Then mix together the honey, vinegar and juice from the remaining limes or lemons and add the powdered rice. Blend into a thick sauce.

Heat the ghee or cooking oil in a heavy saucepan. Remove the pork from the marinade and fry gently until the cubes are sealed on all sides. Keep to one side any juice left from the marinade. Remove the pork from the saucepan with a slotted spoon and put to one side.

Peel and thinly slice the onion and garlic and fry until they are soft. Peel the ginger and cut it into long, thin strips. Add the fenugreek seeds, bay leaves, poppy seeds, mustard seeds, black pepper and chilli powder and stir well for a further 2 minutes. Add the chicken stock and bring to the boil.

Once it is boiling, lower the pork in, together with the lime or lemon juice left over from the marinade. Simmer for 30 minutes and then add the sweet and sour syrup. Continue to cook until the sauce begins to thicken, check the tenderness of the pork and cook for a further 15 minutes until the pork is very tender. Add the salt and serve.

From left to right: Taskebab, Gosht chasnidargh and Shikar chasnidargh.

Pork chops with almonds
Punny valthumai

This is another dish specifically developed by the Christians of the south of India. It calls for a double cooking process. The first part is to seal the chops and the second part is designed to infuse the almond flavour. As with the Lamb with Almonds and Coconut recipe, milk is used to gently braise the pork.

4 pork chops
100 g/4 oz ghee or 120 ml/4 fl oz
  cooking oil
2 cloves of garlic
1 medium onion
3 teaspoons ground coriander
1½ teaspoons black pepper
2 teaspoons ground cumin
1 × 5-cm/2-inch stick of cinnamon
1 teaspoon ground turmeric
600 ml/1 pint milk
100 g/4 oz chopped almonds
½ teaspoon ground nutmeg
1½ teaspoons salt
150 ml/¼ pint double cream

Preparation time: 10 minutes
Cooking time: 1 hour 15 minutes

Wash the chops well and trim half the fat away from the chops. This is essential, as too much fat in this dish detracts from the flavour of the pork. Heat the ghee or cooking oil in a heavy saucepan. Peel the cloves of garlic and chop them very finely. Fry in the ghee or cooking oil until they just begin to turn brown. Then add the chops, continuing to fry until they are sealed on both sides. This should take about 1 minute for each side. Remove the chops from the saucepan and put to one side.

Peel and thinly slice the onion and cook in the ghee until it softens. Now add the coriander, black pepper, cumin, cinnamon and turmeric and cook for a further minute. Add the milk and bring to the boil. Once it is boiling, add the chopped almonds and continue to simmer for another 10–15 minutes. Now lower the pork chops into the saucepan and simmer for 25 minutes or so. Sprinkle in the nutmeg and salt and continue to cook for a further 15 minutes until the pork chops are cooked. Stir in the double cream and serve.

Pork in vinegar
Shikar ka vindaloo

The chances of obtaining wild boar in the West are perhaps fairly slim, nonetheless you can make do with the stronger flavoured cuts of pork, such as shoulder, to make this dish. The amount of fat on the pork is not too critical. In India the fattiness tends to be counteracted by adding extra vinegar. This is a fairly hot dish, so watch out.

900 g/2 lb pork, boned
100 g/4 oz ghee or 120 ml/4 fl oz
  cooking oil
2 green chillies
2 red chillies
4 cloves garlic
2 tablespoons ground coriander
1 tablespoon ground cumin
2 teaspoons black pepper
1 teaspoon ground turmeric
2 bay leaves
5 cloves
5 cardamoms
2 tablespoons vinegar
1 lemon
1 large onion
1 × 5-cm/2-inch piece fresh ginger
450 ml/¾ pint boiling water
1 tablespoon garam masala
2 teaspoons salt

Preparation time: 10 minutes
Cooking time: 1 hour 15 minutes

Trim away any excess fat from the pork. (This is a matter of judgement, if you leave all the fat on and think the pork too fatty, then add a little more vinegar towards the end of the cooking process.) Cut the pork into 2.5 - cm/1-inch cubes. Heat the ghee or cooking oil in a heavy saucepan and gently fry the pork until it is sealed on all sides. Lift it out with a slotted spoon and put to one side.

Now make the vindaloo paste. Roast the bay leaves and cloves on a baking tray in a preheated hot oven, 200°C/400°F/Gas Mark 6 for 15 minutes. Meanwhile, top and tail the green and red chillies and peel the garlic. Mince together the chillies and ·garlic and then grind these, together with the coriander, cumin, black pepper and turmeric. Remove the seeds from the cardamoms and grind together with the roasted cloves and bay leaves. Mix them into the garlic and spice paste and add the vinegar. Squeeze in the juice from the lemon. Mix this paste in with the pork cubes.

Reheat the remaining ghee or cooking oil in the heavy saucepan. Peel and slice the onion and fry it until it is just beginning to soften. Peel and slice thinly the ginger and fry for 2 minutes. Now add the pork, together with the paste, and fry for a further 5 minutes. Pour in the boiling water, bring to the boil and simmer for 40 minutes with the saucepan tightly covered. Then add the garam masala and the salt. Stir in well and simmer for a further 10–15 minutes until the pork is tender.

Braised lamb
Lamb korma

ଙ୍କ୍ଟ୍ଟ୍ଟ୍ଟ୍ଟ୍ଟ୍ଟ୍ଟ୍ଟ୍ଟ୍ଟ୍ଟ୍ଟ

A korma is the name applied to any dish where the meat is braised with a small amount of liquid. The following recipe is for a fairly rich lamb dish incorporating not only nuts and sultanas but also saffron and cream.

The best cuts of lamb should be used, preferably shoulder. You need to start preparations the day before.

Above left to right: Punny valthumai, Shikar ka vindaloo; below: Lamb korma.

750 g/1½ lb shoulder of lamb
1 lemon
1 teaspoon black pepper
½ teaspoon saffron threads
100 g/4 oz ghee or 120 ml/4 fl oz cooking oil
1 medium onion
3 cloves garlic
1 × 5-cm/2-inch piece of fresh ginger
1 teaspoon ground coriander
1 teaspoon ground cumin
1 teaspoon ground turmeric
1 × 2.5-cm/1-inch stick of cinnamon
4 cloves
4 cardamoms
300 ml/½ pint beef stock
1 tablespoon tomato purée
2 teaspoons salt
100 g/4 oz cashew nuts
100 g/4 oz sultanas
300 ml/½ pint double cream
1 tablespoon coriander leaves

Preparation time: 15 minutes plus marinating overnight
Cooking time: 1 hour 15 minutes

Trim away any excess fat from the lamb and cut into 2.5-cm/1-inch cubes. Put into a bowl and squeeze over the juice of the lemon, sprinkle over the black pepper and marinate overnight.

Next day, put the saffron threads into a cup and pour on boiling water to three-quarters fill the cup. Heat the ghee or cooking oil in a saucepan, peel and thinly slice the onion and garlic and fry for 3–4 minutes until they begin to soften. Peel and cut the ginger into thin strips and fry for 1 minute.

Now add the ground coriander, cumin, turmeric and cinnamon together with the cloves and cardamoms. Stir well and cook for a further 2–3 minutes.

Add the lamb, together with the lemon juice in which it has been marinating. Turn the lamb well so that it is cooked on all sides, then add the saffron water together with the saffron threads. Pour in the beef stock, bring to the boil and simmer for 30 minutes.

Now add the tomato purée, salt, cashew nuts and sultanas and cook for a further 5–10 minutes. Check to see that the sauce has begun to thicken. If it has not, increase the heat to boil off any excess moisture. Just before serving reduce the heat, add the cream and chopped coriander leaves, stir well and serve.

Lamb with almonds and coconut Althoo molee

Perhaps one of the most exotic of the southern Indian meat dishes, this is a combination of lamb braised in milk thickened with a coconut and almond mixture. It calls for fairly careful cooking so as not to cause the lamb to toughen through overcooking. Certainly it is a very different recipe from the average curry.

500 g/1 lb lamb
2 lemons
100 g/4 oz ghee or 120 ml/4 fl oz
    cooking oil
1 medium onion
4 cloves garlic
1 × 2.5-cm/1-inch piece of fresh
    ginger
2 teaspoons poppy seeds
2 teaspoons cumin seeds
2 teaspoons fenugreek seeds
4 cloves
4 cardamoms
1 teaspoon ground turmeric
1 teaspoon chilli powder
2 teaspoons black pepper
150 ml/¼ pint milk
1½ teaspoons salt
1 green chilli
½ fresh coconut
100 g/4 oz chopped almonds

Preparation time: 15 minutes plus
    3 hours marinating
Cooking time: 1 hour 15 minutes

Trim away any excess fat from the lamb and cut into 2.5-cm/1-inch pieces. Squeeze the juice of one of the lemons over the lamb and leave to marinate for 2–3 hours.

Put the poppy seeds, cumin seeds and fenugreek seeds on a baking tray in a preheated hot oven, 200°C/400°F/Gas Mark 6, for 20 minutes.

Heat the ghee or cooking oil in a heavy saucepan, strain the lamb cubes from the marinade (put this to one side) and fry until sealed on all sides. Peel the onion and garlic and cut into thin slices. Peel and slice the ginger and fry together until soft. This must be done very slowly.

Crush the baked spices with a rolling pin and add to the saucepan with the cloves and cardamoms. Increase the heat so the spices fry quite fiercely. Sprinkle in the turmeric, chilli powder and black pepper and add the milk, salt and the lamb pieces. Bring to the boil and simmer gently for 40–50 minutes.

Meanwhile top and tail the green chilli, cut into 0.5-cm/¼-inch pieces and add to the saucepan. Remove the meat from the coconut and grate it. Mix it together with the almonds.

After the lamb has simmered for 30 minutes, add the grated coconut and almonds to the saucepan. By this stage much of the milk should have boiled away. Continue to turn the meat gently over the heat to mix in the coconut and almond mixture. Squeeze in the juice from the remaining lemon together with any marinade left over. Cook for a further 5 minutes and serve.

Above left to right: Althoo molee and Pukkan; below: Masala kaleja.

Spiced liver
Masala kaleja

This is a particularly tasty dish which is very easy to prepare. Traditionally it is made with lambs' liver and to my mind this is the best liver to use. However, pigs' liver can be substituted; if so, leave it to soak overnight in the masala as opposed to just a couple of hours.

500 g/1 lb lambs' liver
2 lemons
2 teaspoons salt
2 green chillies
1 teaspoon ground ginger
1 teaspoon black pepper
1 tablespoon sesame seed oil

Preparation time: 30 minutes plus
  3 hours marinating
Cooking time: 15 minutes

Wash the liver well and cut it into thin strips, about 0.5–1 cm/$\frac{1}{4}$–$\frac{1}{2}$ inch wide. Squeeze the juice of the lemons over the liver and sprinkle on the salt. Top and tail the green chillies and chop them very finely. Mix them together with the ginger and black pepper.

Heat the sesame seed oil and add the chilli, ginger and black pepper mixture. Cook for 30 seconds, remove from the heat and pour over the lambs' liver. Allow to cool, cover with cling film, and marinate for 3 hours.

To cook the liver, transfer it together with the marinade to a frying pan and fry fairly quickly for about 15 minutes until the liver is tender. Serve immediately.

Kidney curry
Pukkan

Kidneys are not particularly popular in India but the Christians have developed various methods of cooking kidneys and liver.

500 g/1 lb lambs' kidneys
2 teaspoons salt
2 tablespoons vinegar
2 bay leaves
2 teaspoons sesame seeds
1 × 2.5-cm/1-inch stick of cinnamon
100 g/4 oz ghee or 120 ml/4 fl oz
  cooking oil
1 medium onion
1 clove garlic
$\frac{1}{2}$ teaspoon ground turmeric
1 teaspoon ground ginger
2 teaspoons chilli powder
600 ml/1 pint beef stock

Preparation time: 15 minutes plus
  3 hours marinating
Cooking time: 1 hour

Wash the kidneys well, cut them in half lengthways and sprinkle with the salt and vinegar. Leave them to marinate for 2–3 hours. Then put the bay leaves, sesame seeds and cinnamon into a preheated oven, 200°C/400°F/ Gas Mark 6 on a baking tray for 20 minutes.

Meanwhile, heat the ghee or cooking oil in a heavy saucepan. Peel and thinly slice the onion and fry gently until it begins to soften. Peel and thinly slice the garlic and add to the saucepan.

After 20 minutes remove the bay leaves, sesame seeds and cinnamon from the oven and pound, using a mortar and pestle. Add this mixture to the saucepan. Add the turmeric, ginger, chilli powder and the kidneys together with the marinade. Stir well to ensure that the kidneys are well coated with the spice mixture. Add the stock and bring to the boil. Simmer with the saucepan uncovered over a fairly high heat. The idea is to drive off most of the moisture while the kidneys are cooking. After 20 minutes, check to see that the kidneys are cooked and serve.

Hot chicken curry Murgh madras

This recipe is very similar to that of Beef Madras, the main difference is the slightly subtler spicing to take into account the more delicate flavour of chicken.

In many Indian restaurants this dish is cooked literally in the frying pan with precooked chicken, removed from the bone, and stir fried in spices to produce the Madras effect. This is not the authentic way of cooking the dish as there is a certain amount of special preparation.

1 × 1.5-kg/3–3½-lb chicken
1 lemon
2 teaspoons chilli powder
2 teaspoons black pepper
1 teaspoon salt
100 g/4 oz ghee or 120 ml/4 fl oz
    cooking oil
2 large onions
3 cloves garlic
1 × 5-cm/2-inch piece of fresh
    ginger
4 teaspoons ground cumin
2 teaspoons ground coriander
1½ teaspoons ground turmeric
1 green chilli
2 bay leaves
900 ml/1½ pints boiling water
2 teaspoons garam masala

Preparation time: 2 hours 20
    minutes
Cooking time: 1 hour 15 minutes

Skin the chicken and joint it into 10–12 pieces. Make two cuts in each piece and put the joints into a bowl. Squeeze the juice of the lemon over the joints. Mix together the chilli powder, black pepper and salt and sprinkle over the chicken pieces. Cover the bowl and put to one side for 2 hours.

Then heat the ghee or cooking oil in a heavy saucepan. Peel the onions, garlic and ginger, chop very finely and fry together for 3 minutes until they soften. Now add the cumin, coriander and turmeric, stir well in and cook for a further 2 minutes. Top and tail the green chilli and add to the saucepan, together with the chicken pieces and the juices in which they have been marinating.

Fry the joints until they have changed colour on the outside and add the bay leaves and boiling water. Bring to the boil and simmer for 35–40 minutes. Then sprinkle in the garam masala, turn well and continue to cook for a further 10 minutes until the chicken is tender and falls off the bone.

Chicken in vinegar Kholee vindaloo

This recipe is the basic Vindaloo method, involving the preparation of a curry paste using vinegar. It is a fairly hot dish.

1 × 1.5-kg/3–3½-lb chicken
100 g/4 oz ghee or 120 ml/4 fl oz
    cooking oil
2 red chillies
2 green chillies
4 cloves garlic
2 bay leaves
4 cloves
4 cardamoms
4 teaspoons ground coriander
1 tablespoon ground cumin
1½ teaspoons ground turmeric
1½ teaspoons fenugreek
2 tablespoons vinegar
1 lemon
1 medium onion
300 ml/½ pint boiling water
2 teaspoons black pepper
2 tablespoons garam masala
2 teaspoons salt

Preparation time: 15 minutes
Cooking time: 1 hour 45 minutes

Skin the chicken and cut it into ten joints. Heat the ghee or cooking oil in a heavy saucepan and fry the chicken joints gently until they are sealed on all sides. Top and tail the chillies. Peel the garlic and mince it, together with the red and green chillies. Put the bay leaves and cloves on a baking tray and place in a preheated hot oven, 200°C/400°F/Gas Mark 6. Remove the outer peel from the cardamom seeds. After 15 minutes remove the bay leaves and cloves from the oven and grind together with the cardamom seeds into a fine powder. Mix together with the coriander, cumin, turmeric, fenugreek, garlic and chilli mixture and add the vinegar. Put this mixture into a liquidiser and blend together into a thick paste. Add the juice from the lemon.

Spread the spice paste over the chicken joints. Reheat the remaining ghee or cooking oil in a heavy saucepan and fry the joints together with the paste for a further 2–3 minutes. Peel and finely chop the onion and add to the pan. Fry for a further 2 minutes and pour in the boiling water, black pepper and garam masala. Bring to the boil, add the salt and simmer for 45 minutes with the saucepan tightly covered.

Chicken with scrambled egg Kholee coongee

This recipe is ideal for using up chicken leftovers. It makes a very filling breakfast dish and is often served with Kitcheree.

225 g/8 oz chicken leftovers
2 large onions
1 × 5-cm/2-inch piece of fresh
    ginger
50 g/2 oz ghee or 60 ml/2 fl oz
    cooking oil
½ teaspoon ground cinnamon
1 teaspoon black pepper
½ teaspoon ground turmeric
½ teaspoon chilli powder
1 teaspoon salt
4 eggs
2 tablespoons milk

Preparation time: 10 minutes
Cooking time: 15 minutes

Peel the onions and ginger and chop them very finely. Heat the ghee or cooking oil in a large saucepan and fry the ginger and onion mixture until it just begins to brown. Cut the leftover chicken up into small pieces, add to the ginger and onion and continue to stir.

Sprinkle in the cinnamon, black pepper, turmeric, chilli powder and salt and stir for a further 2–3 minutes. Beat the eggs together and add the milk. Pour into the saucepan and continue to cook as you would for scrambled egg, mixing in well and scraping the eggs off the side of the saucepan. Serve hot with toast.

From left to right: Murgh madras, Kholee coongee and Kholee vindaloo.

Hot egg curry
Madras anday

Strictly speaking this is not a meat dish, but in the south of India eggs are eaten very much as meat would be elsewhere and Madras Egg Curry is so popular it is often served as a main course. This recipe calls for the addition of some fish but this is optional. If you have never tried Indian cooking before, then this is one of the simplest dishes to try.

6 eggs
50 g/2 oz ghee or 60 ml/2 fl oz cooking oil
1 large onion
1 clove garlic
1 teaspoon ground coriander
2 teaspoons ground cumin
1 teaspoon ground turmeric
½ teaspoon ground ginger
1 teaspoon chilli powder
1 teaspoon black pepper
100-g/4-oz piece of white fish (optional)
100 g/4 oz desiccated coconut
300 ml/½ pint warm water
2 tablespoons tomato purée
1 lemon
1 teaspoon salt

Preparation time: 10 minutes
Cooking time: 30 minutes

Hardboil the eggs, cool them, shell them and put to one side. Heat the ghee or cooking oil in a large saucepan, peel and slice the onion and garlic and fry them until they are soft. Now add the coriander, cumin, turmeric, ginger and chilli powder, together with the black pepper. Stir well and fry for another 2 minutes.

If you are using the fish, add it now, stirring it around so that it flakes into pieces as it cooks. Put the desiccated coconut into a liquidiser and add the warm water. Liquidise together for 2 minutes. While this is happening, add the tomato purée to the saucepan, stir well and pour in the coconut water mixture. Bring to the boil and squeeze in the juice from the lemon and add the salt. Cut the hardboiled eggs in halves lengthways and arrange in a shallow dish. Pour the curry mixture over the eggs, cover with aluminium foil and put in a preheated moderate oven, 180°C/350°F/Gas Mark 4, to bake for 10 minutes. Serve immediately.

Hare curry
Muyal

Hares are found throughout India although they tend not to be eaten except when shot on hunting trips, which are usually in pursuit of larger game. In India they are skinned and prepared as soon as they are caught. However, in the cooler climate of the West it is best to have the hare hung for 2–3 days, depending on the temperature, before cooking this dish.

1 hare, jointed
2 lemons
5 cloves garlic
2 tablespoons dry mustard
4 tablespoons vinegar
2 teaspoons black pepper
10 cardamoms
100 g/4 oz ghee or 120 ml/4 fl oz cooking oil
1 medium onion
1 teaspoon ground ginger
2 teaspoons chilli powder
6 bay leaves
4 green chillies
2 teaspoons salt
600 ml/1 pint chicken stock

Preparation time: 1 hour 30 minutes plus 3 hours marinating
Cooking time: 1 hour 30 minutes

Ask your butcher to joint the hare. Make two or three deep cuts in each joint with a sharp knife. Rub over with the juice from the lemons and leave to one side for an hour or so. Peel the cloves of garlic and mince them very finely. Mix together the dry mustard, garlic, vinegar and black pepper into a paste. Remove the seeds from the cardamoms, discarding the husks, and add to the paste. Pour this paste over the hare joints and leave for 2–3 hours in a cool place.

To cook the hare, heat the ghee or cooking oil in a heavy saucepan. Peel and thinly slice the onion, fry it until it begins to soften, then add the ginger, chilli powder and bay leaves. Stir for a further few minutes and add the pieces of hare, together with the garlic and mustard paste. Top and tail and chop the chillies and add them together with the salt. Turn for a further 2 minutes and add the chicken stock. Bring to the boil and simmer for 1¼ hours until the hare is cooked.

Duck cooked with vinegar
Vaathoo vindaloo

This is a classic southern Indian dish, using vinegar in the vindaloo style to counteract the greasiness of the duck. As with most of the Indian duck recipes, wild duck, especially wild mallard, is best.

1 duck weighing 900 g–1.2 kg/2–3 lb
100 g/4 oz ghee or 120 ml/4 fl oz cooking oil
2 large onions
4 cloves garlic
4 dried red chillies
4 cloves
4 cardamoms
2 teaspoons ground turmeric
2 teaspoons coriander seeds
1 teaspoon cumin seeds
2 teaspoons poppy seeds
2 teaspoons black pepper
4 tablespoons vinegar
1 teaspoon salt
600 ml/1 pint chicken stock
4 green chillies
50 g/2 oz desiccated coconut

Preparation time: 15 minutes
Cooking time: 1 hour 45 minutes

Wash the duck well and cut into 8 joints. Heat the ghee or cooking oil in a heavy saucepan. Fry the joints until they are sealed on all sides. Lift out with a slotted spoon and put to one side. Peel and thinly slice the onions and garlic and fry until they begin to soften. Crumble in the dried red chillies, cloves and cardamoms and continue to fry for a further minute.

Add the turmeric, coriander seeds, cumin seeds, poppy seeds and black pepper. Stir for a further 2 minutes and add the vinegar, salt and chicken stock. Bring to the boil and add the pieces of duck. Continue to simmer gently for 1 hour. Top and tail the green chillies and chop into 0.5-cm/¼-inch pieces. Add to the saucepan together with the desiccated coconut. Cook for a further 10–15 minutes until the duck is tender.

Above left to right: Madras anday and Vaathoo vindaloo; below: muyal

Duck with pistachios Vaathoo pista

ఞఞఞఞఞఞఞఞఞఞఞఞఞఞఞఞ

As with most Indian dishes made with duck, wild duck is best. You can also make this dish with small duckling, weighing about 1.5 kg/3 lb.

1 wild duck
50 g/2 oz ghee or 60 ml/2 fl oz
  cooking oil
2 medium onions
1 tablespoon coriander seeds
2 teaspoons cumin seeds
½ teaspoon powdered mace
1 teaspoon chilli powder
2 teaspoons black pepper
100 g/4 oz mashed potato
3 eggs
170 g/6 oz pistachio nuts
4 green chillies
1½ teaspoons salt
600 ml/1 pint chicken stock
2 teaspoons kewra water

Preparation time: 15 minutes
Cooking time: 1 hour 55 minutes

Wash the duck well, inside and out. Heat the ghee or cooking oil in a large heavy frying pan and gently fry the bird all over, turning it from time to time so that it begins to brown and some of the fat from the bird drips out into the frying pan. This should take 10–15 minutes. Remove the duck from the frying pan and put to one side.

Peel and coarsely chop the onions, fry in the remaining fat until they begin to soften, and then add the coriander seeds, cumin seeds, mace, chilli powder and black pepper. Stir for a minute and add the mashed potato, stirring in well until it has absorbed all the fat. Remove from the heat.

Hardboil the eggs, shell and chop them finely. Chop the pistachio nuts quite finely. Top and tail the chillies and chop. Mix the nuts and chillies into the potato and spice mixture. Add the eggs to the stuffing mixture

and stuff the cavity of the duck. Put the duck into a casserole with a well-fitting lid, sprinkle over the salt, pour over the chicken stock and the kewra water, cover the casserole and put into a preheated moderate oven, 180°C/350°F/Gas Mark 4, for 1 hour.

Then check to see whether the duck is cooked. Do this by pricking the breast to see if the juices run clear. If it is cooked, increase the heat of the oven to 200°C/400°F/Gas Mark 6, remove the lid from the casserole and move to the top shelf to brown the bird. Serve with rice to absorb the liquid from the duck.

From left to right: Vaathoo pista and Vaathoo.

Duck curry
Vaathoo

There are not many domestic ducks to be found in India but there are still plenty of wild ones. This recipe uses a quantity of vinegar and lemon juice to counteract the greasiness that is always found with wild duck.

To make a decent amount of this dish you really need to use two ducks as I have always found that by the time wild ducks are plucked and dressed there is not always a lot of meat on them.

2 wild ducks
50 g/2 oz ghee or 60 ml/2 fl oz cooking oil
2 large onions
4 cloves garlic
4 green chillies
1 × 8-cm/3-inch piece of fresh ginger
2 tablespoons ground coriander
1 tablespoon ground cumin
2 teaspoons ground turmeric
1 teaspoon chilli powder
1 teaspoon black pepper
100 g/4 oz tomato purée
100 g/4 oz desiccated coconut
300 ml/½ pint chicken stock
150 ml/¼ pint vinegar
2 lemons

Preparation time: 15 minutes
Cooking time: 1 hour 30 minutes

Cut each duck into 4 pieces. Trim away as much fat as you can from each of the portions. Heat the ghee or cooking oil in a heavy saucepan and fry the portions of duck until they are sealed. Lift out from the saucepan with a slotted spoon and put to one side. Peel and finely chop the onions and garlic, and fry them in the remaining oil.

Top and tail the green chillies and cut them into 0.5-cm/¼-inch pieces. Fry these with the onions and garlic for a further minute. Peel the piece of ginger, cut it into thin strips and add to the saucepan. Fry for a further 1½ minutes.

Then add the coriander, cumin, turmeric, chilli powder and black pepper. Spoon in the tomato purée and mix well. Liquidise the desiccated coconut with the chicken stock and add to the saucepan together with the vinegar.

Bring to the boil and add the duck pieces. Cover the saucepan and simmer gently for 40–50 minutes until the duck becomes tender. Squeeze in the juice from the 2 lemons and continue to cook for a further 10 minutes.

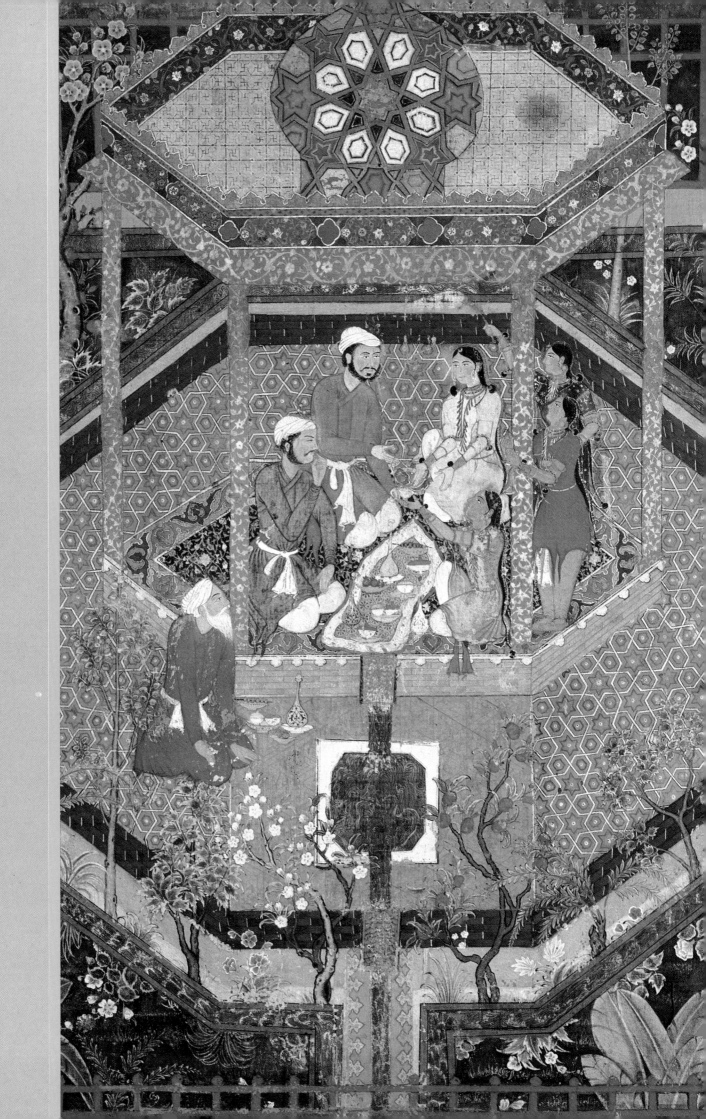

Chapter Three
Meat dishes of central
India

Today, the cooking of central India has absorbed a wide variety of cooking techniques. The main influence is the ancient Delhi style of cooking. As with Mogul cooking this laid great store on good ingredients and it is true to say that meat figures quite extensively in the dishes of this region.

With the cosmopolitan make-up of Delhi itself there were opportunities for all manner of meat dishes to develop, including those using beef. While the Hindus would not touch the beef for religious reasons there were plenty of Muslims and Christians who would.

Chicken with spices
Murgh masalewala

❧❧❧❧❧❧❧❧❧❧❧❧❧❧❧❧❧❧

This is a fairly complicated recipe requiring two sets of masala or spice mixtures. One is for the inside of the chicken and the second is for the outside. The chicken also has a stuffing, which you can vary to suit your taste. The stuffing used here is based on walnuts and eggs. You need to start the preparations the day before. If using a frozen chicken, make sure that it is completely thawed before starting on the cooking preparations.

1 × 1.5-kg/3–3½-lb chicken
10 cardamoms
10 cloves
½ teaspoon mace
½ teaspoon nutmeg
150 ml/¼ pint natural yogurt
1 teaspoon saffron threads
6 large onions
2 cloves garlic
50 g/2 oz ghee or 60 ml/2 fl oz
　cooking oil
2 teaspoons black pepper
3 teaspoons chilli powder
1½ teaspoons ground coriander
1 teaspoon ground turmeric
1 × 2.5-cm/1-inch stick of cinnamon
1 tablespoon vinegar
1 teaspoon salt
4 eggs
100 g/4 oz walnuts
1 × 5-cm/2-inch piece of fresh
　ginger
100 g/4 oz sultanas
2 green chillies

Preparation time: 30 minutes plus
　marinating overnight
Cooking time: 2 hours

First prepare the masala for the inside of the chicken. Remove the seeds from 6 of the cardamoms and put the seeds, together with 6 of the cloves, into a grinder. Grind together and mix in the mace and nutmeg. Transfer the mixture to a liquidiser or food processor. Add the yogurt and saffron threads and blend together for 1½ minutes. Wipe the chicken well and dry the insides with a tea towel. Rub the masala on the inside of the chicken.

Now make the masala for the outside of the chicken. Peel and finely chop 2 of the onions and the cloves of garlic. Heat the ghee or cooking oil

in a large frying pan and fry the onions and garlic until they begin to discolour. Add the remaining 4 cardamoms and 4 cloves, black pepper, chilli powder, coriander, turmeric and stick of cinnamon. Fry for a further 2 minutes and transfer to a liquidiser or food processor, together with the vinegar and salt. Blend all the ingredients together for 2–3 minutes. Put the chicken into a roasting pan and spoon the masala mixture over it, making sure all the outside is well coated. Cover loosely with aluminium foil and refrigerate overnight.

The next day prepare the stuffing. Take the remaining onions and peel and roughly chop them. Hardboil the eggs. Chop the walnuts and mix them together with the onions. Peel the ginger and chop it finely. Add to the stuffing. Fold in the sultanas. Shell and chop the eggs and mix into the stuffing. Top and tail the green chillies and cut them into 0.5-cm/¼-inch

From left to right: Murgh masalewala and Murgh dhansak.

pieces. Mix them into the stuffing. Push the stuffing into the cavity of the chicken and sew it up with clean cotton thread.

Preheat the oven to 180°C/350°F/ Gas Mark 4. Cover the chicken with its aluminium foil and roast in the oven for 1½ hours. Baste the bird from time to time. Remove the foil and increase the heat to 200°C/400°F/Gas Mark 6 to brown the chicken. Check to see that it is fully cooked by piercing the breast with a knife. If the juices run out clear, the chicken is ready to serve.

Chicken with lentils
Murgh dhansak

ಆಆಆಆಆಆಆಆಆಆಆಆಆಆಆಆಆ

Murgh Dhansak is one of the most popular dishes served in Indian restaurants and traces its origins to the Parsees or Zoroastrians, a religious group founded many thousands of years ago and for whom Dhansak is a speciality. Today, there are fewer than a million Parsees throughout the world. Being a Parsee can bring great financial benefits from within the religion. You need to start preparing this dish the day before.

1 × 1.5-kg/3–3½-lb chicken
100 g/4 oz brown lentils
100 g/4 oz green lentils
600 ml/1 pint water
225 g/8 oz aubergines
500 g/1 lb potatoes
3 large onions
225 g/8 oz spinach
6 green chillies
50 g/2 oz ghee or 60 ml/2 fl oz
   cooking oil
3 cloves garlic
1 × 5-cm/2-inch piece fresh ginger
10 cloves
10 cardamoms
1 × 5-cm/2-inch stick of cinnamon
2 bay leaves
1 teaspoon coriander seeds
½ teaspoon fenugreek powder
2 teaspoons ground cumin
½ teaspoon mustard seeds
2 teaspoons black pepper
2 teaspoons ground turmeric
1 teaspoon salt
1 heaped tablespoon chopped
   coriander leaves

Preparation time: 15 minutes plus
   soaking overnight
Cooking time: 1 hour 15 minutes

Mix the brown and green lentils together and wash them well. Leave them to soak overnight in plenty of water. The next day, skin and joint the chicken into 10–12 pieces. Drain the water from the lentils and put them into a saucepan together with the chicken pieces and cover with the water.

Remove the hard leaves from the aubergines and chop them into 2.5-cm/1-inch pieces. Peel the potatoes and chop them into pieces. Peel and chop one of the onions. Chop the spinach roughly and add it to the chicken. Add the potatoes, onions and aubergines.

Heat very slowly and cook gently just below boiling point until the potatoes begin to soften. When this happens, remove the chicken pieces, drain and put to one side. Increase the heat and bring the saucepan to the boil. Continue to cook until the lentils have completely softened.

Peel and roughly chop the second onion. Top and tail the green chillies. Pour the contents of the saucepan into a liquidiser and add the onion and green chillies. Blend together to make a sauce.

Peel the third onion and slice it thinly. Heat the ghee or cooking oil in a large saucepan and fry the sliced onion until it begins to soften. Peel the garlic and ginger and slice thinly. Add to the saucepan and continue to cook for a further minute.

Add the cloves, cardamoms, cinnamon stick and bay leaves and stir for a further minute. Then add the dry ingredients: the coriander seeds, fenugreek powder, ground cumin, mustard seeds, black pepper and ground turmeric. Cook for a further 2–3 minutes and pour in the mixture from the blender. Bring to the boil and add the chicken pieces. Simmer gently for about 20–25 minutes until the chicken is completely cooked. Stir in the salt and chopped coriander leaves and serve.

Delhi chicken curry
Delhi murgh

ళంళం ళంళం ళంళం ళంళం ళంళం ళంళం ళం

As chickens are so plentiful throughout India there are literally hundreds of recipes for chicken curry. What singles out the Delhi version is the use of large amounts of fresh ginger combined with the sweet and sour flavours of tomato purée and lemon juice. This mild curry is a refreshing dish and is very different from the standard chicken in thick brown sauce that is often served in the West as chicken curry.

1 × 1.5-kg/3–3½-lb oven ready
  chicken
100 g/4 oz ghee or 120 ml/4 fl oz
  cooking oil
1 large onion
2 cloves garlic
1 × 2.5-cm/1-inch stick of cinnamon
4 cloves
4 cardamoms
2 × 5-cm/2-inch pieces of fresh
  ginger
1 teaspoon chilli powder
2 teaspoons ground coriander
2 teaspoons ground cumin
1½ teaspoons ground turmeric
100 g/4 oz tomato purée
2 lemons
300 ml/½ pint chicken stock
2 teaspoons salt
1 teaspoon black pepper
1 tablespoon coriander leaves

Preparation time: 15 minutes
Cooking time: 1 hour

Skin the chicken and cut it into 10–12 joints. Heat the ghee or cooking oil in a large saucepan and gently fry the chicken joints until they are sealed. This is when the joints slightly change colour on the outside. Remove the chicken joints with a slotted spoon and put to one side. Peel the onion and garlic and slice very thinly. Fry these gently in the oil until they begin to soften. Now add the cinnamon, cloves and cardamoms and cook for a minute or so. Peel the pieces of fresh ginger and slice thinly. Add these to the saucepan and continue to cook for another minute or so.

Now add the chilli powder, coriander, cumin and turmeric. Cook for a further 2 minutes, then add the tomato purée together with the juice from the lemons. Stir in well to make

a smooth sauce, add the chicken pieces and the stock. Bring to the boil, cover the saucepan and simmer gently. Cook for between 30–45 minutes until the chicken is tender. It should be ready when the meat starts to fall off the bone. Just before serving sprinkle in the salt, freshly ground black pepper and the coriander leaves.

Chicken curry, as with any of the major curries, is very good for freezing. In fact, many people say it tastes better once it has been frozen and reheated. In any event, if there is any left over do not hesitate to put it in the freezer for use later.

Hyderabad chicken curry
Murgh hyderabad

ళంళం ళంళం ళంళం ళంళం ళంళం ళంళం ళం

Every major region in the Indian subcontinent boasts its own version of chicken curry. Hyderabad, naturally enough, considers its chicken curry to be the best. As this particular province of India is to the south of the subcontinent, as you might expect coconut features quite considerably in the recipe, and to make this dish properly you really do need to use fresh coconut.

Above: Murgh hyderabad; below left to right: Delhi murgh and Murgh palak.

1 × 1.5-kg/3–3½-lb chicken
1 medium onion
2 cloves garlic
100 g/4 oz ghee or 120 ml/4 fl oz
  cooking oil
6 cloves
6 cardamoms
½ teaspoon aniseed
1 × 5-cm/2-inch stick of cinnamon
1 teaspoon ground cumin
2 teaspoons chilli powder
2 teaspoons ground coriander
1 teaspoon ground ginger
2 teaspoons black pepper
2 teaspoons ground turmeric
100 g/4 oz tomato purée
300 ml/½ pint chicken stock
½ fresh coconut
2 teaspoons salt
1 teaspoon garam masala
1 lemon

Preparation time: 20 minutes
Cooking time: 1 hour 30 minutes

Skin the chicken and joint it into 10–12 pieces. Peel the onion and garlic and chop them finely. Heat the ghee or cooking oil in a heavy saucepan and fry the onion and garlic until they begin to soften.

Now add the cloves, cardamoms, aniseed and cinnamon. Next, add the ground cumin, chilli powder, coriander, ginger, black pepper and turmeric. Continue to stir for 2–3 minutes.

Reduce the heat and add the tomato purée to the spice and onion mixture. Then add the chicken joints. Increase the heat and pour on the stock. Bring to the boil and then add the fresh coconut meat, cut into thin slices.

Sprinkle in the salt and cover the saucepan. Simmer gently for 45–60 minutes until the chicken is tender. When the chicken is cooked sprinkle in the garam masala and the juice of the lemon.

Chicken with spinach Murgh palak

The combination of chicken and spinach is indeed a subtle blend of flavours. For this reason very minimum spicing is used so as not to mask the intrinsic flavour of the ingredients. I find this recipe is best with fresh spinach although you can use a frozen block of spinach.

1 × 1.5-kg/3–3½-lb chicken
50 g/2 oz ghee or 60 ml/2 fl oz
  cooking oil
1 large onion
3 cloves garlic
225 g/½ lb tomatoes
1 teaspoon ground coriander
1 teaspoon ground cumin
½ teaspoon chilli powder
½ teaspoon black pepper
4 cloves
4 cardamoms
300 ml/½ pint milk
1 teaspoon salt
750 g/1½ lb fresh spinach or 500 g/
  1 lb frozen spinach

Preparation time: 10 minutes
Cooking time: 1 hour

Skin the chicken and joint it. Heat the ghee or cooking oil in a large saucepan and fry the chicken until sealed on all sides. The chicken is sealed when it changes colour. Remove the joints with a slotted spoon and put to one side.

Peel the onion and garlic and slice thinly. Fry them together in the remaining ghee or oil until they begin to soften. Chop the tomatoes roughly and add these to the saucepan. Cook for a further 2–3 minutes until the tomatoes begin to break down. Sprinkle in the coriander, ground cumin, chilli powder and black pepper. Stir for a further minute or so. Add the cloves, cardamoms, chicken joints and milk. Bring to the boil and sprinkle in the salt. Simmer gently for a further 20 minutes. During cooking, keep the saucepan covered so as not to lose any moisture. If you are using fresh spinach, remove any hard stalks and shred it coarsely. If it is frozen, add the block of spinach to the saucepan. Continue to cook for a further 10–15 minutes until the chicken is tender.

Chicken with onions Murgh dopiazah

The word Dopiazah literally means 'two onions' and that is what this dish is all about. There is a saying in Indian cooking that when making a Dopiazah you should add as many onions as you think it needs and then add the same amount again. Only in that way, say the great chefs of India, do you get the correct flavouring of Dopiazah.

1 × 1.5-kg/3–3½-lb chicken
6 large onions
2 cloves garlic
2 green chillies
1 × 5-cm/2-inch piece of fresh
　ginger
2 lemons
100 g/4 oz ghee or 120 ml/4 fl oz
　cooking oil
2 teaspoons ground cumin
1 teaspoon ground coriander
1 teaspoon ground turmeric
1 teaspoon aniseed
1 teaspoon chilli powder
900 ml/1½ pints chicken stock
½ teaspoon saffron threads
1 teaspoon black pepper
2 teaspoons salt
150 ml/¼ pint natural yogurt
150 ml/¼ pint double cream

Preparation time: 15 minutes
Cooking time: 1 hour

Skin the chicken and cut it into 10–12 joints. Peel 3 of the onions and chop roughly. Peel the garlic and chop roughly. Top and tail the green chillies. Peel the ginger and cut into pieces. Put the onions, garlic, green chillies and ginger into a liquidiser or food processor and add the juice of 1 lemon.

Heat the ghee or cooking oil in a saucepan and fry the chicken joints until they are sealed on all sides. You can tell this when they change colour. Remove the joints with a slotted spoon and put to one side.

Take the remaining 3 onions and slice them fairly thickly into pieces about 0.5–1 cm/¼–½ inch thick. Fry these onions in the remaining ghee or oil until they just begin to soften. Then add the cumin, coriander, turmeric, aniseed and chilli powder. Stir for 2–3 minutes and add the chicken pieces and the stock.

Bring to the boil and cook for 2–3 minutes and then add the onion and chilli paste from the liquidiser. Stir this in well and simmer gently for 15 minutes.

Meanwhile, put the saffron threads into a cup and pour on enough boiling water to cover them. Leave for 10–15 minutes and then pour the water and the threads into the saucepan. Continue to cook the chicken for 30 minutes. Then check to see whether the chicken is tender. Sprinkle in the black pepper and salt and add the yogurt. At this stage the liquid should begin to thicken; if it is not thickening sufficiently, increase the heat to boil off any excess moisture.

Once the chicken is cooked, reduce the heat and stir in the double cream. Squeeze in the juice from the remaining lemon and serve.

Beef with onions
Gosht dopiazah

ꝗꝗꝗꝗꝗꝗꝗꝗꝗꝗꝗꝗꝗꝗꝗ

This is the beef version of the Chicken Dopiazah but it differs in the spicing; it is much hotter than the chicken version.

750 g/1½ lb lean braising beef
6 large onions
100 g/4 oz ghee or 120 ml/4 fl oz
  cooking oil
4 green chillies
2 cloves garlic
1 × 5-cm/2-inch piece of fresh
  ginger
2 lemons
1 teaspoon ground turmeric
1 teaspoon ground coriander
2 teaspoons ground cumin
3 teaspoons chilli powder
1 teaspoon black pepper
1 × 5-cm/2-inch stick of cinnamon
2 bay leaves
900 ml/1½ pints beef stock
3 teaspoons garam masala

Preparation time: 15 minutes
Cooking time: 1 hour 20 minutes

Trim off any excess fat from the beef and cut it into 4-cm/1½-inch cubes. Heat the ghee or cooking oil in a large saucepan and fry the cubes of beef gently until they are sealed on all sides. Judge this by the change in colour. Remove the pieces of beef with a slotted spoon and put to one side.

Take 3 of the onions, peel and chop them roughly. Put them into the liquidiser. Top and tail the green chillies and add to the onions. Peel and slice the garlic and add to the liquidiser. Peel the ginger and grate it finely into the liquidiser. Add the juice from one of the lemons and blend to make a fine paste.

Peel and slice thickly the remaining onions. Fry them in the ghee and when they begin to soften add the turmeric, coriander, cumin, chilli powder, black pepper, cinnamon and bay leaves. Cook for a minute or so and then add the beef. Stir for another 30 seconds and add the beef stock. Bring to the boil and simmer gently for 10 minutes.

Then add the onion paste from the liquidiser and continue to cook for 30–45 minutes until the beef starts to become tender. Add the garam masala and squeeze in the juice from the remaining lemon. Continue to cook, boiling off any excess liquid so that the beef is in a fairly thick sauce.

Above: Gosht dopiazah; below left to right: Murgh dopiazah and Bund gobi gosht.

Beef with cauliflower
Bund gobi gosht

ꝗꝗꝗꝗꝗꝗꝗꝗꝗꝗꝗꝗꝗꝗꝗ

Although beef is not generally eaten in India there are some Christian communities, especially Goa on the west coast, who will eat it on special occasions.

500 g/1 lb braising beef
1 small cauliflower
1 lemon
1 teaspoon salt
1 teaspoon black pepper
100 g/4 oz ghee or 120 ml/4 fl oz
  cooking oil
1 large onion
2 cloves garlic
1 × 5-cm/2-inch piece of fresh
  ginger
1½ teaspoons chilli powder
1 teaspoon ground turmeric
1 teaspoon ground cumin
150 ml/¼ pint natural yogurt
450 ml/¾ pint beef stock
2 teaspoons garam masala
1 tablespoon fresh coriander leaves

Preparation time: 25 minutes plus
  2 hours marinating
Cooking time: 1 hour

Trim any excess fat from the beef and cut into slices about 1 cm/½ inch thick. Lay the slices on a work surface and tenderise them by pounding with a tenderising hammer. Sprinkle over the juice of the lemon, salt and black pepper. Cover with cling film and leave to one side for 2 hours.

Heat the ghee or cooking oil in a saucepan and gently fry the beef on both sides until it changes colour. Remove from the saucepan with a slotted spoon and put to one side. Peel the onion and garlic and slice very thinly. Fry in the remaining ghee until they begin to soften. Peel the skin from the ginger and cut the flesh into thin slices. Add to the saucepan together with the chilli powder, turmeric and cumin. Fry for a further 2 minutes. Spoon in the yogurt and cook for 3–4 minutes so that the spices are well distributed in the yogurt. Cut away the florets from the cauliflower and add them to the saucepan, together with the beef stock. Add the beef and cook very gently with the saucepan covered until the beef is tender. Add the garam masala and coriander leaves and cook for a further 5 minutes.

Calcutta beef curry
Calcutta gosht

One of the most famous of all the beef curries, Calcutta Beef Curry is noted for its simple currying process and the addition of thick coconut milk to give it a distinctive flavour.

There are two schools of thought as to how one should make this dish. One calls for ground spices to be used, the other calls for whole spices to be used, which are 'bruised' just before cooking. In this recipe I am recommending using whole spices which are then crushed not powdered as I think it makes a more interesting dish.

500g/1 lb braising beef
50 g/2 oz ghee or 60 ml/2 fl oz
 cooking oil
1 medium onion
2 cloves garlic
3 teaspoons coriander seeds
1½ teaspoons cumin seeds
1 teaspoon black peppercorns
4 dried red chillies
1 × 5-cm/2-inch piece of fresh
 ginger
1 teaspoon ground turmeric
300 ml/½ pint beef stock
1 teaspoon salt
100 g/4 oz desiccated coconut
300 ml/½ pint water
1 lemon

Preparation time: 15 minutes
Cooking time: 1 hour 20 minutes

Trim any excess fat from the beef and cut into strips, about 1 × 4 cm/½ × 1½ inches. Put the beef to one side. Heat the ghee or cooking oil in a saucepan. Peel the onion and garlic and slice thinly. Add to the saucepan and fry until they begin to soften.

Meanwhile mix the coriander, cumin seeds, black peppercorns and chillies together with a mortar and pestle and pound them gently so that they are crushed not powdered. Add to the saucepan and cook for another minute. Peel the ginger, slice it into thin strips and add to the saucepan. Add the turmeric and stir for 1 minute.

Then add the beef, turning quickly to ensure the mixture is well dispersed throughout the beef. Pour on the beef stock, bring to the boil, reduce the heat and simmer for 15 minutes. Add the salt.

Combine the desiccated coconut with the water in a liquidiser, blending together for 2–3 minutes. Pour the coconut mixture into the saucepan and squeeze in the juice from the lemon. Bring back to the boil and continue to cook for approximately 40 minutes until the meat is tender.

If the sauce has not thickened by this stage then increase the heat to rapidly boil off some of the moisture.

Meatball curry
Kofta curry

Koftas are eaten throughout India but they are particular to the central part of the subcontinent from Delhi down to Jaipur and Nagpur. They can be made from any kind of minced meat, either beef or lamb or a combination of both. The skill is to combine aromatic spices with the meatballs themselves and put the root spices into the sauce. Hence you will find ground cloves and cardamoms in the Koftas, and turmeric and ginger included in the sauce mixture.

500 g/1 lb minced meat
1 medium onion
1 clove garlic
1 teaspoon black pepper
½ teaspoon ground cinnamon
½ teaspoon ground cloves
½ teaspoon cardamoms
1 teaspoon salt
1 egg
For the Sauce:
100 g/4 oz ghee or 120 ml/4 fl oz
 cooking oil
1 large onion
2 cloves garlic
2 teaspoons ground coriander
1 teaspoon chilli powder
1 teaspoon ground ginger
1 teaspoon ground cumin
1 teaspoon ground turmeric
600 ml/1 pint beef stock
1 lemon

Preparation time: 15 minutes
Cooking time: 1 hour 10 minutes

To make the meatballs, peel the onion and garlic and pass them, together with the minced meat, through the finest part of a mincer. Mix in the black pepper, cinnamon, cloves, cardamoms and salt and bind together with the egg. Form the mixture into balls about 4 cm/1½ inches in

diameter and fry gently in deep fat until they are brown on all sides. Lift out with a slotted spoon and put to one side to drain.

To make the sauce, heat up the ghee or cooking oil in a large saucepan. Peel and thinly slice the onion and garlic and fry until they begin to soften. Now add the remainder of the spices and cook for 4–5 minutes. Add the beef stock and squeeze in the juice from the lemon. Bring to the boil and gently lower in the meatballs. Simmer gently for 30–45 minutes, stirring carefully from time to time, being careful not to break up the meatballs.

Stuffed meatballs Kofta

ଶ୍ରୀଶ୍ରୀଶ୍ରୀଶ୍ରୀଶ୍ରୀଶ୍ରୀଶ୍ରୀଶ୍ରୀଶ୍ରୀ

This dish tends to be rather spicier than its Western counterpart, and is fairly hot.

From left to right: Calcutta gosht, Kofta and Kofta curry.

750 g/1½ lb minced meat
1 medium onion
1 clove garlic
1 × 2.5-cm/1-inch piece of fresh ginger
1 tablespoon chopped mint leaves
1½ teaspoons chilli powder
½ teaspoon ground turmeric
1 teaspoon ground coriander
1 teaspoon garam masala
1 teaspoon ground cumin
1 teaspoon black pepper
1 egg
75 g/3 oz mashed potato
1½ teaspoons salt
1 lemon

Preparation time: 30 minutes
Cooking time: 15 minutes

Peel and finely chop the onion and garlic. Peel the ginger and grate coarsely. Combine with the minced meat and mint leaves in a large bowl and mix in the chilli powder, turmeric, ground coriander, garam masala, cumin and black pepper. Beat the egg. Take the mashed potato and combine with half the egg and all the salt. Squeeze in the lemon juice and mix well into the potato mixture.

Divide the meat mixture up into round flat patties about 8 cm/3 inches across. Spoon a little potato mixture into each one. Draw the minced meat patty up around the potato mixture to form a ball. Beat the second half of egg again and dip each meatball into it. Deep fry the meatballs until golden brown.

Meat with bitter gourd
Keema karela

The bitter gourd is a strange-looking vegetable, looking like a thick French bean with a gnarled surface. It is bitter in flavour and that is one of the reasons it is used in this dish. However, it is generally considered to be far too bitter to be used as it comes, so a special technique is used to prepare the gourd. When buying bitter gourds make sure that they are quite firm and have not begun to soften. If they are soft then you will find that the inside will have a rather woolly texture.

750 g/1½ lb minced meat
1 lemon
1 teaspoon salt
1 teaspoon black pepper
500 g/1 lb fresh bitter gourds
1 large onion
50 g/2 oz ghee or 60 ml/2 fl oz
    cooking oil
1 teaspoon cumin seeds
1 teaspoon coriander seeds
1 × 5-cm/2-inch stick of cinnamon
1 teaspoon ground turmeric
1 teaspoon ground ginger
2 teaspoons garam masala
100 g/4 oz tomatoes

Preparation time: 1 hour
    30 minutes
Cooking time: 55 minutes

Put the minced meat into a bowl and squeeze on the juice from the lemon. Sprinkle in the salt and black pepper and mix well into the meat. Put to one side for an hour or so. Now prepare the karela or bitter gourd. Top the gourds, cutting about 3 cm/1 inch off the bottom end. Use this bottom end to rub against the cut surface of the karela in a circular motion and you will see that a kind of foam is created. This process serves to extract some of the bitterness from the bitter gourd.

Peel and thinly slice the onion. Heat the ghee or cooking oil in a heavy saucepan and fry the onion until it softens. Add the cumin seeds, coriander, cinnamon, turmeric, ginger and the garam masala. Fry for a further 2 minutes. Add the minced meat and fry gently until it starts to change colour. Cut the bitter gourds into slices about 0.5–1 cm/¼–½ inch thick and add to the saucepan. Cut the tomatoes roughly and add them to the saucepan. There should be no need to add any extra water as this is supposed to be a dry curry. If necessary add a little water to prevent the meat sticking.

Increase the heat very slightly, cover the saucepan tightly and allow it to steam cook. Stir the dish from time to time to ensure that the minced meat is well coated with the spice mixture and properly cooked. When all the meat has changed to a brown colour after about 45 minutes and the karela is soft, the dish is ready to serve.

Bombay lamb curry
Bombay gosht

Essentially this is a curry combining lamb, fresh tomatoes and yogurt. The idea is that it should be a fairly dry curry with the minimum amount of sauce.

500 g/1 lb shoulder of lamb, boned
1 large onion
1 clove garlic
100 g/4 oz ghee or 120 ml/4 fl oz
    cooking oil
1 teaspoon ground coriander
1 teaspoon ground turmeric
1 teaspoon ground cumin
1 teaspoon black pepper
1 tablespoon garam masala
2 green chillies
2 bay leaves
1 × 5-cm/2-inch stick of cinnamon
100 ml/4 fl oz natural yogurt
225 g/½ lb tomatoes
1 teaspoon salt

Preparation time: 10 minutes
Cooking time: 1 hour

Trim away any excess fat from the lamb and cut into 2.5-cm/1-inch cubes. Peel the onion and garlic and slice finely. Heat the ghee or cooking oil in a large saucepan and fry the onion and garlic until they soften. Now add the lamb cubes and fry with the onion and garlic until they are sealed on all sides. This is when the colour of the lamb changes from red to a buff colour. Remove the lamb cubes and put to one side.

Add the coriander, turmeric, cumin, black pepper and half of the garam masala. Stir together for 1 minute. Top and tail the green chillies, chop them into 0.5-cm/¼-inch pieces and add to the saucepan. Cook for a further 3 minutes. Add the bay leaves and stick of cinnamon and stir in the yogurt. Chop the tomatoes coarsely and add to the saucepan.

Bring to the boil and add the lamb. Simmer gently for 30–40 minutes until the lamb is tender. Five minutes from the end of cooking add the rest of the garam masala and the salt. If the curry appears too dry, add a little boiling water to help the cooking process along.

Lamb with almonds
Badam gosht

ψ֍ψ֍ψ֍ψ֍ψ֍ψ֍ψ֍ψ֍ψ֍ψ֍ψ֍

This is one of the rich and royal dishes of central India and uses the best and some of the most exotic ingredients. Almonds are always regarded as rather special in India and coconut milk is used to add to the richness. Start preparing this dish the day before.

750 g/1½ lb shoulder of lamb, boned
1 lemon
1 teaspoon salt
1 teaspoon black pepper
1 teaspoon saffron threads
300 ml/½ pint natural yogurt
½ fresh coconut
300 ml/½ pint boiling water
100 g/4 oz ghee or 120 ml/4 fl oz
    cooking oil
1 medium onion
6 cardamoms
6 cloves
1 teaspoon aniseed
1 × 5-cm/2-inch stick of cinnamon
1 × 5-cm/2-inch piece of fresh
    ginger
1 teaspoon chilli powder
50 g/2 oz sliced almonds

Preparation time: 2 hours
    30 minutes plus marinating
    overnight
Cooking time: 1 hour 15 minutes

Trim away any excess fat from the lamb and cut into 2.5-cm/1-inch cubes. Put the cubes into a large bowl and squeeze the juice from the lemon over the lamb and sprinkle on the salt and black pepper. Mix well in a bowl and leave for 2 hours in a refrigerator.

Meanwhile put the saffron threads into a cup and fill the cup with boiling water. Leave to stand for 20 minutes. Then mix the saffron water and the threads with the yogurt. Pour the yogurt over the lamb, mix in well and leave overnight in a cool place to marinate.

The next day, to make the coconut milk, grate the coconut meat into a liquidiser and add boiling water. Blend together to form a thick sauce. Pour the mixture into a double thickness of muslin stretched over a bowl and squeeze the milk out of the coconut pulp.

Heat the ghee or cooking oil in a large saucepan. Peel the onion and slice it thinly. Fry it gently until soft. Now add the cardamoms, cloves, aniseed and stick of cinnamon. Peel the ginger and grate it into the saucepan. Cook for 5 minutes and sprinkle in the chilli powder.

Then add the lamb together with its marinade. Continue to cook gently, turning the lamb from time to time. After 20 minutes add the coconut milk, bring the mixture back to the boil and simmer for about 30 minutes or so until the lamb is tender. Then add the almonds, stir in well, cook for a further 5 minutes and serve.

Above left to right: Keema karela and Badam gosht; below: Bombay gosht.

Lamb with potato
Aloo gosht

꒰꒱꒰꒱꒰꒱꒰꒱꒰꒱꒰꒱꒰꒱꒰꒱꒰꒱꒰꒱

This is very much a standard method of cooking meat in central India, whether it be lamb, goat or, in some cases, pork.

900 g/2 lb boneless lamb
100 g/4 oz ghee or 120 ml/4 fl oz cooking oil
1 large onion
2 cloves garlic
1 × 5-cm/2-inch piece of fresh ginger
2 teaspoons ground turmeric
1 teaspoon ground coriander
1 teaspoon black pepper
1 teaspoon ground cumin
6 cloves
6 cardamoms
2 teaspoons chilli powder
225 g/8 oz potatoes
300 ml/½ pint beef stock
2 teaspoons garam masala
1 teaspoon salt
100 g/4 oz tomatoes

Preparation time: 10 minutes
Cooking time: 1 hour

Trim any excess fat from the meat and cut it into cubes of about 2.5 cm/1 inch. Heat the ghee or cooking oil in a large, heavy saucepan. Peel the onion and garlic and slice them thinly. Fry for 2–3 minutes until they begin to soften. Peel the ginger and cut the flesh into thin strips. Add to the saucepan. Fry for a further 2 minutes.

Now add the turmeric, coriander, black pepper, ground cumin, cloves, cardamoms and chilli powder and cook for a further minute.

Peel the potatoes and cut them into approximately 2.5–4-cm/1–1½-inch pieces. Add to the saucepan together with the meat and the beef stock. Bring to the boil and simmer gently.

Cover the saucepan and cook for 20–25 minutes until the lamb and potatoes are tender. Sprinkle in the garam masala and salt, and add the tomatoes, peeled and roughly chopped. Cook for a further 5–10 minutes and serve.

Dry curry of lamb
Bhuna gosht

꒰꒱꒰꒱꒰꒱꒰꒱꒰꒱꒰꒱꒰꒱꒰꒱꒰꒱꒰꒱

This is one of the most popular dishes in Indian restaurants in the West, particularly with those who use the 'Three Pot' technique whereby the restaurant can maintain great long menus listing virtually every Indian dish in existence. Nearly all the curry dishes they serve come from one of three pots: one for chicken, one for lamb and one for beef, all precooked. Hence, if you order a Bhuna Gosht, some meat will be taken from the lamb pot, mixed in the frying pan with a certain combination of spices and then served. However, that is not the real way to make a Bhuna Gosht. Bhuna is basically a method of cooking lamb fairly quickly, using the minimum amount of moisture.

750 g/1½ lb shoulder of lamb, boned
50 g/2 oz ghee or 60 ml/2 fl oz cooking oil
1 medium onion
1 clove garlic
1 teaspoon chilli powder
2 teaspoons black pepper
2 teaspoons ground coriander
1½ teaspoons ground cumin
1 teaspoon ground turmeric
2 small tomatoes
1 teaspoon salt
150 ml/¼ pint beef stock
1 lemon
3 teaspoons garam masala

Preparation time: 10 minutes
Cooking time: 1 hour

Trim off any excess fat from the lamb and cut into 2.5-cm/1-inch cubes. Heat the ghee or cooking oil in a large saucepan. Peel and thinly slice the onion and garlic. Fry them gently until they begin to soften and add the chilli powder, black pepper, coriander, cumin and turmeric. Stir in well. Chop the tomatoes into quarters and add to the frying pan. Cook until they begin to soften. Then add the lamb and the salt. Pour in the stock and continue to cook very gently. Bring to the boil, turning the lamb. Squeeze in the juice of the lemon and simmer for a further 15–20 minutes. Then sprinkle in the garam masala. Turn the lamb well and continue to cook until it is tender. This should take a further 15–20 minutes.

Parsee stew
Parsee ka salan

꒰꒱꒰꒱꒰꒱꒰꒱꒰꒱꒰꒱꒰꒱꒰꒱꒰꒱꒰꒱

The Parsees are an ancient religious group, quite small in number, but very influential, not only in India but throughout the world. They have developed their own particular methods of cooking, independent of the rest of Indian cuisine. Much of their cooking emanates from the ancient kingdom of Persia – the country now called Iran.

900 g/2 lb boneless lamb
250 g/½ waxy potatoes
500 g/1 lb carrots
50 g/2 oz ghee or 60 ml/2 fl oz cooking oil
1 medium onion
1 teaspoon chilli powder
1 teaspoon black pepper
300 ml/½ pint stock
100 g/4 oz frozen peas
2 teaspoons chick-pea flour
1½ teaspoons garam masala
1½ teaspoons salt

Preparation time: 15 minutes
Cooking time: 40 minutes

Peel the potatoes and scrape the carrots. Cut the potatoes into smallish pieces about 4 cm/1½ inches across. Cut the carrots into fairly thick slices, about 1 cm/½ inch thick.

Heat the ghee or cooking oil in a heavy saucepan. Peel and slice the onion, fairly thickly, fry gently for 2–3 minutes and then add the potatoes and carrots. Fry for a further 2–3 minutes, then add the chilli powder and black pepper.

Trim away any excess fat from the lamb and cut into 2.5-cm/1-inch cubes. Add to the saucepan together with the stock. Bring to the boil and add the peas. Cook for 15–20 minutes with the saucepan tightly covered.

Then remove some of the liquid and mix it in a cup with the chick-pea flour to form a smooth paste. Add this paste to the saucepan, stir it in well and continue to cook until the sauce begins to thicken. Then sprinkle in the garam masala and salt and cook for a further 20 minutes. Check to see that the lamb is cooked, and serve.

Dry spiced liver
Masala kaleja

๛๛๛๛๛๛๛๛๛๛๛๛๛๛๛

Liver is not particularly popular in India but as you can imagine in a country where food is short, virtually every part of an animal tends to get used. As a result, quite sophisticated recipes have been developed. Masala Kaleja uses a good, thick spice paste to tenderise the liver before dry frying it. You need to start preparations the day before.

750 g/1½ lb lambs' liver
1 lemon
1 teaspoon salt
1 medium onion
1 clove garlic
1 × 5-cm/2-inch piece of fresh
   ginger
1 tablespoon vinegar
1 teaspoon ground turmeric
1 teaspoon chilli powder
1 teaspoon black pepper
Ghee or cooking oil for frying

Preparation time: 1 hour
   15 minutes plus marinating
   overnight
Cooking time: 15 minutes

Ask the butcher to slice the liver as thinly as possible. Slices about 0.5 cm/¼ inch thick are best. Arrange the liver slices in a flat dish and squeeze on the juice from the lemon. Sprinkle with the salt and put to one side for 1 hour.

Peel the onion and garlic and chop roughly. Put them into the liquidiser. Peel the ginger and grate it into the liquidiser. Add the vinegar, turmeric, chilli powder and black pepper. Liquidise together into a thick paste. You may have to scrape down the sides of the liquidiser several times with a spatula to ensure the paste is smooth. Spread the paste over the liver pieces and leave overnight in a cool place to marinate.

Next day fry the slices of liver gently in the minimum of ghee or cooking oil until the liver is cooked. The key to this dish is to fry the liver as slowly as possible so that it does not get tough.

From top to bottom: Aloo gosht, Bhuna gosht, Parsee ka salan and Masala kaleja.

Pork with eggs
Anday shikar

ҩѻҩѻҩѻҩѻҩѻҩѻҩѻҩѻҩѻҩѻ

Pork is not generally eaten in India for two reasons. Firstly, it is abhorred by Muslims, who regard the pig as unclean, secondly, even those of the majority who are permitted to eat pork regard it with a certain amount of scepticism due to the health dangers pork can bring when eaten in a hot country. Much of the pork on offer in India comes from wild boar, which are still hunted through the sugar cane plantations on horseback, with nothing more than lances. This is the famous 'pig sticking' of the British Raj. It is a dangerous sport that many would regard as cruel, although it has to be said that when armed with a lance on horseback the chances of falling off are great. Once off, the wild boar has more than an even chance of getting his own back!

750 g/1½ lb boneless pork
1 lemon
75 g/3 oz ghee or 90 ml/3 fl oz
    cooking oil
1 small onion
2 cloves garlic
1 × 5-cm/2-inch piece of fresh
    ginger
4 cardamoms
4 cloves
1 × 5-cm/2-inch stick of cinnamon
3 teaspoons ground coriander
1 teaspoon ground cumin
1 teaspoon ground turmeric
1½ teaspoons black pepper
2 dried red chillies
3 eggs
1½ teaspoons salt
1 tablespoon chopped coriander
    leaves

Preparation time: 10 minutes plus
    2 hours marinating
Cooking time: 1 hour 30 minutes

Trim off any excess fat from the pork and cut into 2.5-cm/1-inch cubes. Squeeze over the juice of the lemon and marinate for 2 hours or so.

Heat the ghee or cooking oil in a heavy saucepan. Peel the onion, slice it thinly and fry gently until it begins to soften. Peel the garlic, slice thinly and fry for a further 1½ minutes. Then peel the ginger, cut it into thin strips and add to the saucepan, together with the cardamoms, cloves and cinnamon. Stir in well for another

minute and add the coriander, cumin, turmeric, black pepper and dried red chillies. Stir in well until the chillies begin to break up. Cook gently for 2 minutes. Meanwhile hardboil the eggs.

Now add the pork and the salt and continue to cook for a further 2–3 minutes, stirring to ensure the pork is well coated with the spice mixture. Add enough boiling water just to cover the pork, cover the saucepan with a tight-fitting lid and simmer on a very gentle heat for 45 minutes. Shell the eggs and cut them lengthways into halves. As soon as the pork begins to become tender, gently lower the eggs into the curry mixture and continue to cook for another 15 minutes or so. Once the pork is tender, transfer to a serving dish, being careful not to break the eggs. Sprinkle with the coriander leaves and serve.

Roast duck with cashew nuts
Baduk

ҩѻҩѻҩѻҩѻҩѻҩѻҩѻҩѻҩѻҩѻ

This dish has found its way into the cooking of central India from the Christians of Goa and other parts of the west coast of India.

The cooking process is in two parts. The first part is to marinate the duck in a masala. Then it is cooked with a spice and cashew nut stuffing.

When cooking a duck it is important to remember that large amounts of fat will be lost from it. To cook the duck rest it on a rack or wire tray so that the fat runs away from it. You need to start the preparations the day before.

1 duck, approximately 2 kg/4 lb
2 lemons
4 teaspoons salt
2 teaspoons black pepper
50 g/2 oz ghee or 60 ml/2 fl oz
  cooking oil
1 medium onion
1 × 5-cm/2-inch piece of fresh
  ginger
2 teaspoons cumin seeds
1 teaspoon mustard seeds
½ teaspoon aniseed
12 cardamoms
1 × 5-cm/2-inch stick of cinnamon
12 cloves
2 teaspoons chilli powder
1 teaspoon ground turmeric
1 teaspoon coriander seeds
3 eggs
225 g/½ lb cashew nuts
3 tablespoons breadcrumbs
1 tablespoon honey

Preparation time: 15 minutes plus
  marinating overnight
Cooking time: 2 hours 30 minutes

Wipe the surface of the duck well
and prick all over with a fork.
Squeeze the lemon juice over and
inside the duck. Rub all over with the
salt and black pepper and leave
overnight in a cool place.

The next day, heat the ghee or
cooking oil in a frying pan. Peel and
finely chop the onion. Fry it in the
ghee until it begins to soften. Peel the
ginger, cut it into thin strips and fry
for 2 minutes. Then add the spices:
the cumin seeds, mustard seeds,
aniseed, cardamoms, cinnamon,
cloves, chilli powder, turmeric and
coriander seeds. Cook for a further
2–3 minutes. Hardboil the eggs.
Coarsely chop the cashew nuts. Shell
the eggs and mash them together
with the breadcrumbs and cashew

nuts. Add this mixture to the frying
pan and combine with the spices,
cooking very gently. Remove the
stuffing from the frying pan and stuff
the duck cavity. Sew the opening up
and place the duck on a wire tray or
rack in a roasting pan. Roast in a
preheated hot oven, 200°C/400°F/
Gas Mark 6.

After 20 minutes reduce the heat
to 180°C/350°F/Gas Mark 4. Turn
the duck over so that it is now
breast side down and cook for 45–50
minutes. Then, turn the duck the
right way up and continue to cook for
a further 45–50 minutes. Test to see
whether the duck is cooked by inserting a sharp knife into the breast;
if the juices run clear the duck is
ready to serve. Pour the honey over
the top of the duck and increase the
heat to 200°C/400°F/Gas Mark 6 and
crisp the duck skin for a final 5–10
minutes.

Chapter Four
Meat dishes of northern India

The meat dishes of northern India reflect the higher quality of meat available in this region. This quality stems from the kinder temperate climate which means that lush grass can grow on the hillsides and as a result good cattle can be raised. Much of the meat consumed is goat meat. However, in Pakistan where the Muslims, unlike the Hindus, do not revere the cow, beef is quite frequently used in some of the richer dishes, such as Pasanda. It has to be stressed, though, that for most people meat is still very much a great luxury even today.

Poultry, however, is certainly within the reach of many more people, even if restricted to a Chicken Biryani on a feast day. The abundance of poultry reflects the wheat culture of the north of India, where 'old world' traditional farming methods mean that there is plenty of corn left scattered around for chickens to scratch at. Indeed, it certainly could be argued that some of the best northern dishes are those made with chicken, developed to their heights by the Moguls. There are still records of great feasts where the number of chickens served would run into thousands. Pork is virtually unknown in the north of India and in any event if the pork were available the Muslims of course would not touch it, as it is against their religious beliefs. The spicing of the meat dishes of northern India is rather subtle, designed to bring out, rather than mask the flavour of the meat. Although many people in the north will eat rice with their meal, traditionally bread made from wheat flour in its various forms is the main carbohydrate accompaniment.

Chicken with yogurt
Murgh dahi

࿘࿘࿘࿘࿘࿘࿘࿘࿘࿘࿘࿘࿘࿘࿘

This is an interesting mild dish combining the subtleties of marinating with cooking processes involving a combination of frying and poaching. You can either use a whole chicken, which is the traditional way of making this dish, or chicken joints. I find that chicken joints are easier to deal with and they cook through far more quickly than a whole bird. Start the preparations the day before.

4 chicken joints or 1 × 1.5-kg/3–3½-lb
   chicken
4 green chillies
4 cloves garlic
1 × 8-cm/3-inch piece of fresh
   ginger
600 ml/1 pint natural yogurt
1 teaspoon paprika
1 teaspoon salt
1 large green pepper
100 g/4 oz ghee or 120 ml/4 fl oz
   cooking oil
100 g/4 oz chopped coriander
   leaves

Preparation time: 15 minutes plus
   marinating overnight
Cooking time: 45 minutes

Remove the skin from the chicken and cut the meat into joints. Using a very sharp knife make small cuts all over the pieces. Peel and roughly chop the chillies, garlic and ginger. Put into the liquidiser and add the yogurt, paprika and salt. Remove the seeds from the green pepper and chop roughly. Add to the liquidiser and process quickly. Once a smooth marinade has been achieved, pour this over the chicken joints. Cover the dish with foil or cling film and marinate overnight in a cool place, turning occasionally to ensure that all parts of the chicken are covered.

The next day, heat the ghee in a very heavy saucepan with a tight-fitting lid until it is very hot. Remove the chicken pieces from the marinade and add to the pan. Fry quickly for 30 seconds. Then add the marinade, cover the saucepan and continue to cook on a moderate heat for 10 minutes. Then, check the chicken, turning it and basting it with what remains of the sauce. Continue to cook in this way with the saucepan tightly covered until the sauce has virtually disappeared. Sprinkle on the coriander leaves and turn the chicken joints once or twice. Check that the chicken is cooked by inserting a sharp knife to release the juices. If they are clear the chicken is done. Serve immediately.

Royal chicken
Shahi murgh

࿘࿘࿘࿘࿘࿘࿘࿘࿘࿘࿘࿘࿘࿘࿘

Shahi Murgh literally translated means 'chicken for the King'. It owes its origin to Persia and as such contains some very typical Persian ingredients such as almonds. The essential nature of Shahi Murgh is to cook the chicken in aromatics, such as cloves and cardamoms. The result tends to be a rather scented dish.

1 × 1.5-kg/3–3½-lb chicken
1 clove garlic
1 green chilli
1 large onion
100 g/4 oz ghee or 120 ml/4 fl oz
   cooking oil
1 × 5-cm/2-inch piece of fresh
   ginger
10 cardamoms
10 cloves
1 teaspoon salt
1 dessertspoon natural yogurt
pinch of saffron
100 g/4 oz blanched almonds,
   sliced
100 g/4 oz fresh coconut, cut into
   thin slices
1 tablespoon chopped coriander
   leaves

Preparation time: 1 hour
   15 minutes
Cooking time: 1 hour

Skin and joint the chicken, cutting it into 8 joints. Peel and crush the garlic and rub over the chicken. Place to one side for an hour or so. Then, peel and chop the chilli and onion together into fairly fine pieces. Heat the ghee or cooking oil in a heavy saucepan and fry the chilli and onion mixture very gently for a minute or so. Peel and thinly slice the ginger and add to the saucepan, together with the cardamoms and cloves. Cook for another 2 minutes to release the scented oils of the cloves and cardamoms.

Now add the chicken and cook for a further 10 minutes, sealing each

Above: Shahi murgh; below left to right: Murgh dahi and Murgh ka salan.

side of the chicken pieces. Add the salt, yogurt and saffron, cover the saucepan and simmer for a further 45 minutes until the chicken is cooked.

The sauce for this should be fairly thick, if it appears too runny, then boil rapidly to drive off some of the water. Fifteen minutes before the dish is cooked, add the sliced almonds and the coconut. Sprinkle with the chopped coriander leaves before serving.

Chicken curry
Murgh ka salan

ቈቈቈቈቈቈቈቈቈቈቈቈቈቈቈቈቈቈቈ

Chicken curry is by far the most popular dish sold in Indian restaurants. What has always fascinated me is how in the early days of Indian food in the West, you were charged extra if you wanted to have Chicken Curry 'off the bone'. This mild but tasty recipe starts with a whole chicken. Of course, if you do not fancy jointing a chicken, then you can use chicken joints.

1 × 1.5 kg/3 lb chicken, oven-ready or boiling fowl
1 large onion
2 cloves garlic
100 g/4 oz ghee or 120 ml/4 fl oz cooking oil
5 teaspoons ground coriander
2 teaspoons ground turmeric
1 teaspoon ground ginger
½ teaspoon chilli powder
150 ml/¼ pint natural yogurt
150 ml/¼ pint water
2 teaspoons salt
1 teaspoon black pepper

Preparation time: 20 minutes
Cooking time: 1 hour 30 minutes

Skin and joint the chicken, cutting it up into 8 pieces, and place to one side. Peel and thinly slice the onion and garlic. Heat the ghee or cooking oil in a large saucepan and fry the chicken joints for a minute or so until they are sealed, then remove with a slotted spoon. In the remaining oil, fry the onion and the garlic. Cook for 5–6 minutes until the onion is soft, then add the spices.

Once the spices are well mixed in, add the chicken. Mix together the yogurt and the water and add to the pan. Add the salt and black pepper, cover the saucepan and simmer for about 1–1¼ hours until the chicken is cooked and falls off the bone. This dish has a fairly liquid curry sauce. Do not worry if the ghee floats to the top during the cooking, this is normal.

Chicken kebab Murgh tikka

Throughout the main cities of northern India, and in particular Pakistan, there are a number of outdoor stores which serve kebabs. Here, men sit crosslegged in their traditional casual dress of shirt and baggy trousers and in front of them are great long charcoal grills measuring up to 1.5 metres/5 feet long and about 30 cm/1 foot wide. These are filled with glowing coals and on the top are skewers of various kinds of kebabs. Two of the most popular are Tikka Kebab and Chicken Tikka. In the days before electricity these charcoal grills would have been fanned by someone sitting at one end of the grill with a huge flat fan or punkah fashioned from plaited banana leaves. Nowadays, this man is often replaced by a common electric fan. Such is the way of progress. Nonetheless, the flavour of the tikkas is just as good as it ever was and they make ideal barbecue food. Start the preparations a day or two before.

1 × 1.5-kg/3–3½-lb chicken
2 large onions
3 cloves garlic
2 tablespoons sesame seed oil
300 ml/½ pint natural yogurt
½ lemon
3 teaspoons ground coriander
1 teaspoon ground turmeric
1 teaspoon chilli powder
1 teaspoon ground ginger
1 teaspoon salt

Preparation time: 30 minutes plus
  1–2 days marinating
Cooking time: 15 minutes

Skin the chicken and remove all traces of fat. Remove the meat from the carcass, trying to keep the pieces as large as possible. The best way to do this is to cut the meat away in strips which can be folded onto the skewers when it is time to cook them. Peel and chop one of the onions finely. Do the same with the cloves of garlic.

Mix the sesame seed oil and the natural yogurt together in a liquidiser or food processor and add the juice from the lemon. Add the rest of the ingredients with the exception of the chicken and blend together for about 1½ minutes.

Lay the chicken pieces in one layer in a dish and cover with the marinade. Marinate for at least 24 hours and preferably for 48 hours. This should be done in a refrigerator. Check periodically to recoat any of the chicken that is left sticking above the level of the marinade.

When it is time to cook the Chicken Tikka, take the remaining onion, peel it and cut it into quarters. Remove each individual piece of onion and use these to separate each piece of chicken on the skewer. Put the chicken pieces on the skewers and cook over a slow charcoal grill until nicely done. It is important not to cook this dish too quickly otherwise it will be cooked black on the outside and still be raw on the inside. If a charcoal grill is not available, this dish can be made under an ordinary grill but it is really best served at a barbecue.

From left to right: Murgh tikka and Murgh tandoori.

Tandoori chicken
Murgh tandoori

Indian cooking really took off in the West with the advent of the Tandoori restaurants, which get their name from the word *tandoor*. This is the name given to the tall, cylindrical, clay oven used in many parts of India but particularly in the north and Pakistan. The idea of a tandoor is that it is preheated as a baker's bread oven would be to searingly high temperatures, usually using charcoal. Once the tandoor is up to temperature meat cooks very quickly inside, in a matter of minutes in fact. What happens is that the oven is so hot that as soon as any meat is placed inside it the outside of the meat immediately seals, thus ensuring that no further juices are lost. This means tandoori cooking tends to result in very tender and juicy meat. Of all the dishes, Tandoori Chicken is perhaps the most popular, often served as a starter in many Tandoori restaurants. To make this dish in the traditional fashion, it is customary to use poussins, which are small 350-g/ 12-oz chickens, usually cooked whole. Please note the colour of Tandoori Chicken varies enormously from bright red to bright orange. Using proprietary food colours, try and arrive at a colour which is somewhere in between the two. Remember, it's only colouring, it does not affect the flavour! Start the preparations the day before.

4 large chicken joints or 4 small
    poussins
2 teaspoons salt
2 teaspoons black pepper
$\frac{1}{2}$ lemon
450 ml/$\frac{3}{4}$ pint natural yogurt
150 ml/$\frac{1}{4}$ pint malt vinegar
1 large onion
2 cloves garlic
1 × 5-cm/2-inch piece of fresh
    ginger
4 teaspoons garam masala
1 teaspoon chilli powder
2 teaspoons paprika
$\frac{1}{2}$ teaspoon orange food colouring
$\frac{1}{2}$ teaspoon yellow food colouring

Preparation time: 1 hour 20
    minutes plus marinating
    overnight
Cooking time: 1 hour 30 minutes

Wash the chicken joints or poussins and remove all the skin (see page 17). If they still have complete wing tips and bottom feet joints on, remove these. Make two deep scores in the flesh of each joint or down the breast of each poussin with a sharp knife. Squeeze the lemon over the chicken joints or poussins, rubbing the juice well into the flesh. Sprinkle with the salt and black pepper and put to one side for 1 hour.

Then, put the yogurt and vinegar into a liquidiser and blend for 30 seconds. Peel and slice the onion, garlic and ginger, chop into small pieces and add to the liquidiser or food processor gradually, blending for a few seconds each time. Now add the spices and the food colouring and continue to liquidise for a minute or so until you have a very smooth sauce.

Arrange the chicken in a casserole or baking dish, and pour over the sauce. It is important that each joint or poussin is properly coated with marinade. Cover with cling film or foil and marinate in a fridge for at least 8 hours, preferably overnight.

From time to time using a spoon, recoat some of the pieces of chicken to ensure that they are fully marinated. Remove the cling film and cover with foil (if you have used foil to cover the chicken during the marinade process the same foil will do for the cooking process).

Cook for about 1$\frac{1}{2}$ hours in a moderate oven, 180°C/350°F/Gas Mark 4. The chicken will be cooked when a knife placed into the centre releases clear juices. If the juices are clouded, cook for a little longer. If the marinade separates during cooking, do not worry. After cooking, drain it off, liquidise it and serve it as a separate sauce.

Many people prefer to grill this dish with the chicken pieces or poussins cooked dry on a wire mesh. In my view, because this method of cooking Tandoori Chicken involves much cooler temperatures, the cooking takes longer and often the meat becomes too dry.

However, you can remove the foil from the top of the chicken joints or poussins for the final 20 minutes of cooking in the oven, and put the dish to the top of the oven to brown the chicken. If you like to have the chicken really black, then place it under a hot grill for the final 5 minutes.

Serve the joints on a bed of lettuce leaves and garnish with onion rings and wedges of lemon.

Chicken with cardamoms Murgh illaichi

ⲯⲟⲯⲟⲯⲟⲯⲟⲯⲟⲯⲟⲯⲟⲯⲟⲯⲟⲯⲟⲯⲟ

While it is true to say that spices provide the basis for flavouring in Indian food, the true heights of Indian cuisine are achieved through the use of what are known as the aromatics. These are the seeds, flowers and in some cases bark of various plants which, when fried in oil or roasted dry, release essential oils to give fragrance and flavour. Murgh Illaichi is one of the most popular dishes amongst the well-to-do. They have to be well-to-do to afford the cardamoms which are amongst the most expensive spices. However, you do not use very many in a meat dish. This recipe is also an introduction to the use of a masala. A masala is simply a name for a spice mixture, but it differs from a marinade in that it is much drier. Start the preparations the day before.

1 × 1.5-kg/3–3½-lb chicken
15 cardamoms
150 ml/¼ pint natural yogurt
1 × 5-cm/2-inch piece of fresh
    ginger
2 cloves garlic
1 teaspoon fennel seeds
1 teaspoon cumin seeds
1 teaspoon chilli powder
½ tablespoon salt
1 medium onion
100 g/4 oz ghee or 120 ml/4 fl oz
    cooking oil
pinch of saffron threads
1 × 5-cm/2-inch stick of cinnamon
6 cloves

Preparation time: 30 minutes plus
    marinating overnight
Cooking time: 1 hour

Peel the outer skins from the cardamoms. Put the yogurt in a liquidiser or food processor together with the seeds from the cardamoms. Peel the ginger and the garlic and cut up into small pieces. Add the ginger and the garlic to the liquidiser. Add the fennel, cumin seeds and chilli powder and liquidise for 1 minute until blended.

Wipe the surface of the chicken and make sure it is well dried. Rub over with the salt and leave to one side for 15 minutes. Then take the yogurt mixture and spread it all over the chicken, rubbing it well in. Put the chicken in the fridge and leave the masala to penetrate the flesh overnight.

Next day, finely chop the onion and heat the ghee in a frying pan. Fry the onion until it is soft. While this is happening, put the saffron threads into a cup and pour on enough boiling water to cover them. Once the onion is soft, break the cinnamon stick into small pieces and add to the frying pan, together with the cloves. Stir in well and cook for another 5 minutes. Take this mixture and spoon it into the cavity of the chicken. Pour the saffron threads, together with the water in which they have been soaking, over the top of the bird and cover tightly with aluminium foil. Cook in a preheated moderate oven, 180°C/350°F/Gas Mark 4, for about 40 minutes. Then remove the aluminium foil and place the bird to the top of the oven to allow it to brown. Check to see that the chicken is fully cooked by inserting a knife under the breast and if the juices that run out are clear, the chicken is cooked. If they are cloudy, it needs to cook a little longer.

Chicken biryani
Murgh biryani

When the great Mogul emperors wanted to put on a really lavish feast, great plates of Biryani, sometimes requiring two people to carry them, would be the centrepiece of the feast.

Naturally only the best Basmati rice would be used for the dish, but the real richness of the Biryani would be measured by all the other ingredients and in particular the amount of meat. Meat being a valuable commodity in a land where climate is not kind to animals, you could measure a man's wealth by the kind of meat dishes he served.

Whereas with a Pillao, meat and rice are cooked together, this is not necessary with a Biryani. Biryani is a good way of using up leftover meat, such as from Sunday chicken roast.

From left to right: Murgh illaichi and Murgh biryani.

500 g/1 lb chicken leftovers (slightly more or less does not matter)
225 g/½ lb Basmati rice
600 ml/1 pint chicken stock
1 small onion
50 g/2 oz ghee or 60 ml/2 fl oz cooking oil
1 clove garlic
2 teaspoons chilli powder
1 teaspoon ground cumin
2 teaspoons garam masala
1 teaspoon salt
50 g/2 oz sultanas
50 g/2 oz blanched almonds
orange food colouring
To garnish:
2 hardboiled eggs
2 tomatoes
1 green pepper

Preparation time: 10 minutes
Cooking time: 40 minutes

Separate the chicken meat from any bones and remove any fat or skin. Break the chicken up into fairly large chunks; I say break rather than cut – the idea is that the pieces should be large enough to still be recognisable as chicken by the time the cooking process is over.

Wash the rice well and drain. Put it in a saucepan and pour over the chicken stock, leaving to one side 2 tablespoons of stock for use later. Boil the rice for about 20 minutes until it is *al dente.*

Meanwhile, peel and slice the onion thinly. Fry it gently in the ghee or cooking oil in a large frying pan. Peel and slice the garlic and add that to the onion and cook for a further 2 minutes or so. Now add the spices – the chilli powder, cumin, garam masala and salt – and stir in well. Add the chicken to the curry sauce and stir well so that it is well coated. Now pour in the remaining 2 tablespoons of chicken stock and bring the mixture to a simmer.

The next stage involves combining the rice with the chicken and the sultanas and almonds. Once the two are combined, add a little orange food colouring to turn the whole mixture a bright orange. If the rice is too moist, boil rapidly, stirring the rice to prevent it from sticking.

Place the Biryani on a large dish and garnish with slices of hardboiled eggs, tomato and green pepper. To make slices of green pepper, cut off the top of the pepper and remove the seeds without breaking the outer skin. With a sharp knife cut the pepper into rings.

Chicken with dumplings Murgh maida

ఖ్రఖ్రఖ్రఖ్రఖ్రఖ్రఖ్రఖ్రఖ్రఖ్రఖ్రఖ్రఖ్ర

Dumplings are not something you come across very often in Indian cuisine. However, in parts of the north, particularly in areas where it gets quite cold, they are served in just the same way as dumplings are in the West, as a good, warming carbohydrate to fill you up. However, these dumplings are not made with ordinary wheat flour but with rice flour as befits a land of rice and paddy fields.

1 × 1.5-kg/3–3½-lb chicken
100 g/4 oz ghee or 120 ml/4 fl oz
    cooking oil
1 large onion
2 cloves garlic
4 teaspoons chilli powder
2 teaspoons black pepper
1 × 5-cm/2-inch stick of cinnamon
6 cloves
6 cardamoms
2 teaspoons ground turmeric
300 ml/½ pint chicken stock
1 teaspoon salt
170 g/6 oz rice flour
1 tablespoon garam masala

Preparation time: 15 minutes
Cooking time: 1 hour

Skin the chicken and cut it into 8 joints. Heat the ghee or cooking oil in a heavy saucepan and add the chicken pieces. Seal the meat by frying quite quickly in the oil and remove them with a slotted spoon. Place to one side. Peel and slice the onion very thinly and fry in the remaining oil until soft. Do the same with the cloves of garlic. Now add the chilli powder, black pepper, stick of cinnamon, cloves and cardamoms, together with the turmeric, stir in well and cook for a further 3 minutes. Return the chicken to the saucepan and add the chicken stock and the salt. Bring to the boil, reduce the heat, cover the saucepan and simmer for 20 minutes.

Meanwhile make the dumplings. Take the rice flour and add enough water and a pinch of salt to form a good dough. Break off small dumplings about 2 cm/¾ inch in diameter. After 40 minutes of cooking time, add the dumplings to the chicken, to-

gether with the garam masala. Be careful at this stage not to break the dumplings up as you put them in, but do ensure that they are immersed in the sauce. Cover the saucepan and continue to simmer for another 20 minutes until the chicken is tender.

Fried chicken livers Tali kaleja

ఖ్రఖ్రఖ్రఖ్రఖ్రఖ్రఖ్రఖ్రఖ్రఖ్రఖ్రఖ్రఖ్ర

Nowadays, most people do not bother to cook the livers that come with an oven-ready chicken and so many butchers do not include them with the chicken. However, it is possible to obtain chicken livers relatively cheaply, although you may have to put in a special request for them.

This particular recipe certainly is far tastier than the run-of-the-mill chicken-liver dishes. Liver does, in my view, need a certain degree of spicing to bring out its true flavour.

750 g/1½ lb chicken livers
100 g/4 oz ghee or 120ml/4 fl oz
    cooking oil
1 large onion
2 cloves garlic
1 teaspoon ground turmeric
1 teaspoon chilli powder
2 teaspoons ground coriander
120 ml/4 fl oz natural yogurt
1 teaspoon salt
1 tablespoon tomato purée
1½ teaspoons garam masala

Preparation time: 10 minutes
Cooking time: 25 minutes

Heat the ghee or cooking oil in a large saucepan. Peel and slice the onion very thinly and fry in the ghee until soft. Peel the garlic cloves and chop them finely. Add to the saucepan. At the same time, add the turmeric, chilli powder and ground coriander. Lower the heat and allow to cook gently for another 2 minutes.

Meanwhile, cut the chicken livers into halves, being careful to remove any stringy parts. Add them to the saucepan, increase the heat slightly and stir to ensure the livers are well coated with the spice mixture.

As soon as the livers have started to change colour, add the yogurt, salt and tomato purée, increase the heat and bring to the boil.

Then reduce the heat and simmer for about 15 minutes. After 10 minutes of cooking, add the garam masala and stir well in.

Indian Scotch egg Nargisi kofta

ఖ్రఖ్రఖ్రఖ్రఖ్రఖ్రఖ్రఖ్రఖ్రఖ్రఖ్రఖ్రఖ్ర

Nargisi Kofta is regarded as one of the more opulent of the Indian dishes that was particularly reserved for high days and holidays. This is the dry method of making Nargisi Kofta. There are methods which involve the cooking of the Koftas in a curry sauce. To my mind this is the more flavoursome of the two methods.

500 g/1 lb minced lamb
7 eggs
1 large onion
4 cloves garlic
50 g/2 oz ghee or 60 ml/2 fl oz
    cooking oil
1 teaspoon garam masala
1 teaspoon salt
1 teaspoon paprika powder
½ teaspoon nutmeg
3 teaspoons ground cumin
1 teaspoon black pepper
3 teaspoons ground coriander
cooking oil for deep frying

Preparation time: 20 minutes
Cooking time: 15 minutes

Hard boil 6 of the eggs. Place the seventh egg to one side. Peel the onion and garlic and slice thinly. Fry the garlic and the onion in the ghee or cooking oil. Once they are soft, remove and place in a liquidiser together with the rest of the ingredients except the meat. Liquidise for 1 minute and then add to the minced lamb. Mix well in and knead well until a very hard paste is formed.

Shell each of the hardboiled eggs and roll each one in the minced meat mixture to form an outer layer about 1–2 cm/½–¾ inch thick. Take the remaining egg and beat it well. Dip each Kofta in the beaten egg and deep fry them until dark brown.

Above: Tali kaleja; below left to right: Murgh maida and Nargisi kofta.

Roast lamb with spices
Raan

ఛ్ఛ్ఛ్ఛ్ఛ్ఛ్ఛ్ఛ్ఛ్ఛ్ఛ్ఛ్ఛ్ఛ్ఛ్

This is a triumphant dish specially designed for feast days and holidays. In the days of the Mogul emperors great legs of lamb were borne in by bearers at the height of the sumptuous feast. As with Murgh Illaichi, the recipe uses a dry masala to give a deep flavour to the meat before it is roasted.

1 leg of lamb (about 2.3 kg/5 lb in
    weight)
2 large onions
1 × 5-cm/2-inch piece of fresh
    ginger
5 cloves garlic
2 lemons
5 cardamoms
10 cloves
1 × 5-cm/2-inch stick of cinnamon
1 teaspoon ground turmeric
2 teaspoons ground cumin
2 teaspoons chilli powder
2 tablespoons salt
1 tablespoon pistachio nuts
1 tablespoon raisins
2 tablespoons yogurt
1 tablespoon honey

Preparation time: 15 minutes plus
    marinating overnight
Cooking time: 2 hours

This recipe calls for two applications of different masalas. To make the first one, peel the onions, ginger and garlic and squeeze the juice from the lemons. Put the onions, ginger, garlic, cardamoms, cloves, cinnamon, turmeric, cumin, chilli powder, salt and lemon juice in a liquidiser or food processor and process until a smooth paste is obtained. This may involve considerable scraping down of the sides but it is well worth it to get the mixture totally smooth.

Trim off any excess fat from the lamb and make a series of deep cuts with a sharp knife each side of the leg. Take the spice mixture and rub it all over the outer surface, making sure that it goes well into the slashes. This is important to allow the spices to penetrate properly into the meat. Leave to marinate overnight in the refrigerator, covered.

The next day, grind together the pistachio nuts, raisins, yogurt and honey. This is a far more liquid masala and needs to be dripped all over the leg of lamb. Place the lamb in a casserole large enough to contain all its juices and roast in a moderate oven, 180°C/350°F/Gas Mark 4, for up to 2 hours. Cover tightly with aluminium foil. After about 1½ hours, when the lamb begins to get tender, remove the foil and complete the roasting so that the masala becomes crisp on top of the lamb. If necessary, increase the oven temperature to 190°C/375°F/Gas Mark 5.

Lamb with yogurt
Roghan gosht

ఛ్ఛ్ఛ్ఛ్ఛ్ఛ్ఛ్ఛ్ఛ్ఛ్ఛ్ఛ్ఛ్ఛ్ఛ్

Roghan Gosht is perhaps the basis on which many of the so-called curries of northern India are made. This recipe involves lamb, although in many instances in the north, goat meat would be used. Goat meat is rather difficult to come by in the West and, in my view, it is usually rather tough. It does not benefit at all from the standard method of Indian butchery, which is to cut up the meat in chunks, irrespective of which part of the animal it has come from. If you use a good cut of lamb from the shoulder or leg to make Roghan Gosht, it is possible to make an even better dish than perhaps you would find in Northern India. Start the preparations the day before.

750 g/1½ lb lamb
1 lemon
2 teaspoons salt
450 ml/¾ pint natural yogurt
170 g/6 oz ghee or 175 ml/6 fl oz
    cooking oil
1½ large onions
2 cloves garlic
1 × 5-cm/2-inch piece of fresh
    ginger
2 teaspoons ground cumin
2 teaspoons paprika
1 teaspoon black pepper
100 g/4 oz tomato purée
1 teaspoon salt

Preparation time: 15 minutes plus
    24 hours marinating
Cooking time: 1 hour 50 minutes

Once you have pared away all the fat from the lamb, cut it into 2.5-cm/1-inch cubes and put it into a bowl. It is essential with this dish to make sure that the meat is very lean. Squeeze the juice from the lemon all over the meat. Rub in the salt and add the yogurt. Leave the meat to marinate for 24 hours. This is best done in the refrigerator with the bowl covered with foil or cling film.

To cook Roghan Gosht take a large, heavy saucepan or flameproof casserole and heat the ghee or cooking oil. Thinly slice the onions and fry them until soft. Peel and slice the garlic and add to the saucepan. Cook for a further 2 minutes. Peel the ginger and cut it into very, very thin strips, add to the saucepan and cook for a further 1 minute.

Now add the meat and reduce the heat so as to seal it on all sides. When this is done, remove the meat and add the rest of the spices and black pepper. Stir well, adding a little water at this stage if you find the dish has got too dry.

Cook for about 5 minutes and then add the meat with its yogurt, once again turning gently to ensure the meat is well coated with the spices. Then add the tomato purée and salt.

There should be enough moisture to ensure that while the curry is not very runny there is indeed a fair amount of sauce with it. If still more moisture is needed, add a little boiling water. Cover the saucepan and simmer for 1½ hours until the meat is tender.

From above: Shahi korma, Roghan gosht and Raan.

Royal lamb curry
Shahi korma

๛๛๛๛๛๛๛๛๛๛๛๛๛๛๛๛

This is one of the most exotic of the lamb dishes of India. It was originated for the Moguls and as befits its royal title includes some of the most exotic ingredients of Indian cooking: saffron, cardamoms and almonds. The korma is a good main dish for a dinner party.

900 g/2 lb lamb
300 ml/½ pint meat stock
1 × 5-cm/2-inch stick of cinnamon
2 bay leaves
1 small lemon
2 cloves garlic
15 cardamoms
15 cloves
1 tablespoon coriander seeds
100 g/4 oz ghee or 120 ml/4 fl oz
   cooking oil
1 large onion
2 teaspoons salt
2 teaspoons black pepper
150 ml/¼ pint natural yogurt
pinch of saffron
150 ml/¼ pint single cream
50 g/2 oz almonds
50 g/2 oz raisins

Preparation time: 15 minutes
Cooking time: 1 hour 40 minutes

Cut the lamb into 4-cm/1½-inch cubes and gently poach for 30 minutes in the stock, together with the cinnamon, bay leaves and juice from the lemon. Remove the lamb pieces with a slotted spoon and put to one side. Boil the remaining liquid rapidly to reduce its volume by about a half. Peel the garlic.

In an electric grinder put the cardamoms, cloves, coriander seeds and cloves of garlic. Grind these to a good paste, adding a little water if necessary.

Then heat the ghee or cooking oil in a large saucepan. Peel and thinly slice the onion and fry in the ghee for 3–4 minutes until it begins to soften. Add the cubes of lamb and fry quickly for a minute. Reduce the heat and add the concentrated stock and the spice paste. Bring back to the boil. Now add the salt and the pepper, stir in the yogurt and cook for 30 minutes until the meat is tender. After 20 minutes, add the pinch of saffron, stir in the cream and add the almonds and raisins.

Lamb pillao
Pillao gosht

This is quite simply pillao rice cooked with a little lamb. It has its origin more in the Arab world, where the idea of cooking meat together with rice stems from necessity as the nomads had to cook quickly and simply and with the minimum number of cooking pots.

750 g/1½ lb boned lamb
170 g/6 oz ghee or 175 ml/6 fl oz cooking oil
2 large onions
3 cloves garlic
4 teaspoons ground coriander
4 teaspoons ground cumin
4 cardamoms
1 bay leaf
1 lemon
300 ml/½ pint natural yogurt
225 g/½ lb rice
50 g/2 oz sultanas
50 g/2 oz blanched almonds

Preparation time: 10 minutes
Cooking time: 1 hour

Cut the lamb into cubes, removing any fat. Heat 100 g/4 oz of the ghee or 120 ml/4 fl oz of cooking oil in a large saucepan and fry the lamb to seal each piece on all sides. Remove the pieces of lamb from the pan and place to one side.

Peel the onions and garlic and thinly slice them. Add to the pan and fry for 3½ minutes. Add the coriander, cumin, cardamoms and the bay leaf and fry for a further 1 minute. Squeeze the juice from the lemon into the pan and then add the yogurt and pieces of lamb. Cover the saucepan and cook for 20 minutes.

Meanwhile, wash the rice well and drain as much water off as possible. Heat the remaining 50 g/2 oz of ghee or 60 ml/2 fl oz of cooking oil in a large pan and add the rice. Fry until it is well coated with the ghee or oil. Cover the rice with barely enough water to submerge it and cook for 10 minutes.

Now add the lamb, together with the sauce in which it has been cooking, mix in well, cover and continue to cook until the rice is soft. Then mix in the sultanas and blanched almonds, stirring gently to ensure they are well dispersed without crushing the rice.

Lamb with coconut
Shakotee

In this recipe coconut is used in two ways. First, thin slivers of cooked coconut are roasted to add as a garnish at the last minute and the rest of the coconut is used for the coconut milk. The combination of a good spicy lamb curry with coconut is something which has to be tasted to be believed.

900 g/2 lb lamb
1 large coconut
4 cardamoms
4 cloves
1 tablespoon coriander seeds
1 teaspoon cumin seeds
1 × 5-cm/2-inch stick of cinnamon
300 ml/½ pint hot water
2 lemons
2 teaspoons salt
2 teaspoons black pepper
100 g/4 oz ghee or 120 ml/4 fl oz cooking oil
2 large onions
3 cloves garlic
1 teaspoon ground turmeric
1 teaspoon ground ginger
2 dried red chillies

Preparation time: 30 minutes
Cooking time: 50 minutes

Extract the milk and break the coconut in two. Cut about a third of it into thin slivers and arrange them in a baking dish. Put the cardamoms, cloves, coriander and cumin, together with the cinnamon stick, into a second ovenproof dish. Put both dishes in a hot oven, 200°C/400°F/ Gas Mark 6, for about 20 minutes. Check from time to time to see that the coconut has not browned on just one side. Turn it until it is evenly brown on all sides. Put it to one side for garnishing later on.

Meanwhile, take the rest of the coconut and cut it into small pieces. Put any milk extracted from the coconut into the liquidiser and add the pieces of coconut, one at a time, liquidising between adding each one. Top up the liquidiser with the hot water. Liquidise. Cut the lamb into 2.5-cm/1-inch cubes, squeeze over the lemon juice from both lemons and then mix in the salt and black pepper. Put to one side.

Heat the ghee or cooking oil in a large saucepan. Peel and chop the

Left: Pillao gosht; above right: Shakotee; below: Mogli chops.

onions very finely and fry until soft. Chop and slice the cloves of garlic and add to the saucepan. Add the turmeric and ginger. Now, remove the spices from the oven and place between two sheets of greaseproof paper. Crush them with a rolling pin. Add these to the pan together with the dried red chillies and continue to stir. At this stage it is necessary to keep the heat very gentle. Now add the meat, turning it so that it is well coated with the spice mixture. Increase the heat and add the coconut milk to the sauce, bring to the boil and simmer for 30–45 minutes until the lamb is tender. Sprinkle on the browned coconut and serve.

Mogul lamb chops
Mogli chop

ଔଓଔଓଔଓଔଓଔଓଔଓଔଓଔଓଔଓଔଓଔ

This is another dish from the style of the Mogul emperors and very traditional, using yogurt to carry the flavour of the spice mixture into the chops. It is essential for you to use generous-sized lamb chops for this dish. Small, puny chops are hardly in the style of the Moguls! Start the preparations the day before.

4 lamb chops
1 small onion
2 cloves garlic
1 × 2.5-cm/1-inch piece of fresh ginger
300 ml/½ pint natural yogurt
1 tablespoon coriander leaves
2 teaspoons chilli powder
2 teaspoons garam masala
1 teaspoon salt
50 g/2 oz ghee or 60 ml/2 fl oz cooking oil

Preparation time: 10 minutes plus marinating overnight
Cooking time: 15 minutes

Peel the onion and garlic and chop them roughly. Peel the ginger and cut into strips and blend together with the onions and garlic, yogurt, coriander leaves and remaining spices in the liquidiser to obtain a smooth marinade. Take the lamb chops and prick them all over with a sharp fork. Pour the marinade over the chops and leave for 8 hours, preferably overnight, turning the chops now and again to ensure that they remain coated. (It is not necessary to get up in the middle of the night to do this!)

The next day, heat the ghee or cooking oil in a large frying pan and fry the chops, together with the marinade until they are cooked. It is important to do this slowly so that the lamb chops cook through gently.

Lamb kebab
Tikka kebab

In the city in Pakistan where I was born, Lahore, there is a famous bazaar known as Anarkali. By day, the bazaar is rather grubby and very bustling. But by night it seems to take on an almost fairytale image with hissing Petromax lamps illuminating all manner of stalls selling snacks. Among those snacks are the Tikka Kebabs, cooked in the same way as Seekh Kebabs, on great long charcoal grills, kept well-fanned by electric fans. This particular kebab recipe is one perfectly suited to any barbecue. I can highly recommend it. Start the preparations at least the day before. This dish can be kept in its marinade in the refrigerator for up to 10 days before cooking.

750 g/1½ lb lamb
1 lemon
1 large onion
2 cloves garlic
450 g/¾ pint natural yogurt
4 tablespoons malt vinegar
2 teaspoons garam masala
1 teaspoon paprika
2 teaspoons salt
1 × 5-cm/2-inch piece of fresh
    ginger

Preparation time: 15 minutes plus
    marinating overnight or longer
Cooking time: 15 minutes

Cut the lamb into 2.5-cm/1-inch cubes, being careful to exclude any fat. Cut the lemon in half and squeeze the juice over the pieces of lamb, mixing well to ensure they are all well coated. Peel the onion and cut it in two, put one half to one side and roughly chop the other half. Peel the cloves of garlic, put them together with the yogurt, vinegar and all the spices into a liquidiser. Remove the outer bark from the ginger and chop it into pieces. Add the ginger to the liquidiser. Liquidise for about 2 minutes until a smooth sauce has been made. Pour the sauce over the pieces of lamb, cover and place in a refrigerator for at least 24 hours. Check from time to time to see that all the pieces of lamb are well coated with the marinade.

When you are ready to cook the dish, thread the pieces of lamb onto skewers, separated by pieces of onion. Do this by taking the remaining half of onion, cutting it into two and removing each layer. Cook each skewerful of lamb cubes slowly over a barbecue or under a grill, being careful not to allow it to cook too quickly on the outside leaving the inside raw. Turn regularly.

Serve garnished with onion rings and wedges of lemon. Traditionally, this dish would be eaten with one of the Indian breads, such as naan or chapatti, and perhaps just a little mint chutney.

Minced meat kebabs
Husseini kebabs

This is very much a highly aromatic, spicy kebab served sometimes on its own as a snack and accompanied by cups of tea. It calls for a fairly complicated cooking process but the result I am sure you will agree, is well worth the effort.

500 g/1 lb minced meat, preferably
    lamb
2 green chillies
2 cloves garlic
1 × 2.5-cm/1-inch piece of fresh
    ginger
1 large onion
6 cloves
6 cardamoms
2 teaspoons desiccated coconut
25 g/1 oz blanched almonds
50 g/2 oz ghee or 60 ml/2 fl oz
    cooking oil
1 × 2.5-cm/1-inch stick of cinnamon
1 teaspoon ground turmeric
1 teaspoon ground coriander
1 teaspoon chick-pea flour
2 teaspoons salt
½ lemon
1 egg
oil for frying

Preparation time: 40 minutes
Cooking time: 15 minutes

Top and tail the green chillies and roughly chop them. Put the minced meat into a liquidiser and add the green chillies. Peel and chop the garlic and add to the liquidiser. Peel the outer bark from the ginger. Peel the onion and chop it roughly, together with the fresh ginger. Add the ginger and onion to the liquidiser and process for a minute or so. Although this might be difficult in

some cases because the mixture is too dry, it is important that no extra liquid is added at this stage.

Then, crush the cloves, cardamoms and almonds. In the case of the cardamoms, split open the green outer husk, remove the seeds, throw away the husk and place the seeds together with the cloves and the almonds between two sheets of greaseproof paper. Crush with a hammer or rolling pin. Heat the ghee or cooking oil in a large pan and fry the cinnamon, turmeric, coriander and chick-pea flour. Add the cloves, cardamoms, desiccated coconut and almonds. Cook for about 5–10 minutes, then add the meat mixture from the liquidiser. At this stage add the salt and the juice of the half lemon.

Cook for a further 15 minutes, until the minced meat has changed colour, then return the whole mix-

From left to right: Tikka kebab, Husseini kebabs and Masala chop.

Spicy lamb chops
Masala chop

વ્જીવ્જીવ્જીવ્જીવ્જીવ્જીવ્જીવ્જીવ્જીવ્જી

This is one of the ways in which sophisticated Indian people eat something approaching a Western meal. Lamb chops are traditionally served in the West with very little spicing on them, and usually little more added than salt and pepper! This would not do for the palate of the average Indian consumer, who is used to something a little more spicy; so the chops are prepared in a masala.

4 lamb chops
½ teaspoon chilli powder
½ teaspoon ground cumin
1 teaspoon ground turmeric
½ teaspoon ground mustard seeds
½ teaspoon black pepper
½ teaspoon salt
1 tablespoon vinegar
½ lemon
a little ghee or cooking oil for
   frying

Preparation time: 30 minutes
Cooking time: 15 minutes

Mix all the dry ingredients together with the vinegar to form a sauce. Squeeze in the lemon juice and rub the masala all over the chops on both sides. Leave for 20 minutes. Heat a little ghee or cooking oil in a frying pan and fry the chops on both sides until cooked.

ture to the liquidiser or food processor. Traditionally in India, this stage would involve putting the meat onto a large stone slab and pounding with another piece of stone until the whole mixture is a fine paste. The liquidiser should make things a whole lot easier! Once a fine paste has been achieved, form into oval kebabs about 8 × 5 cm/3 × 2 inches. Beat the egg and dip each kebab in the beaten egg and fry gently until brown on either side.

Mild beef curry
Pasanda

If Roghan Gosht is a favourite recipe for lamb or goat, then Pasanda is much preferred for the cooking of beef. This is almost exclusively a Moslem dish as the Hindus would not dream of eating beef. The key to making this dish work is the tenderising. It really is important that the meat is well pummelled before cooking. Start the preparations the day before.

750 g/1½ lb beef
1 lemon
2 teaspoons salt
600 ml/1 pint natural yogurt
170 g/6 oz ghee or 175 ml/6 fl oz
   cooking oil
2 medium onions
2 teaspoons ground turmeric
1 teaspoon ground cumin
2 teaspoons paprika
1 teaspoon chilli powder
3 teaspoons garam masala
1 × 5-cm/2-inch piece of fresh
   ginger
2 cloves garlic

Preparation time: 1 hour 10
   minutes plus overnight
   marinating
Cooking time: 1 hour 30 minutes

Slice the beef into 1-cm/½-inch thick pieces, lay the slices out on a hard surface and beat with a steak mallet. Squeeze the juice from the lemon over the meat and rub in the salt. Leave for 1 hour. Then mix with the yogurt, ensuring each slice is well coated, and lay the slices with all the yogurt in a large bowl. Cover and marinate overnight.

To cook Pasanda, take a heavy saucepan and heat the ghee or cooking oil. Peel and slice the onions thinly and fry until soft. Add all the spices except the garam masala. Peel and thinly slice the ginger and garlic. Add to the pan.

Once the spices and ginger have cooked for 5 minutes or so, add the slices of beef together with the marinade. Stir the marinade in well to ensure each slice is well coated with the spice mixture. Add a little water if too dry. Cover the saucepan and simmer for 1–1½ hours. After cooking for 45 minutes, add the garam masala and stir in well.

Beef in yogurt
Dahi gosht

This hot curry is another favourite dish from the north of India – again the use of yogurt is typical of the cooking that covers the great belt of land west from the Himalayas all the way to Arabia.

900 g/2 lb beef
4 cloves garlic
1 teaspoon coriander seeds
2 teaspoons chilli powder
2 teaspoons ground cumin
2 teaspoons black pepper
2 teaspoons salt
300 ml/½ pint natural yogurt
100 g/4 oz ghee or 120 ml/4 fl oz
   cooking oil
2 large onions
1 × 5-cm/2-inch piece of fresh
   ginger
4 cloves
4 cardamoms
4 green chillies
150 ml/¼ pint beef stock
50 g/2 oz desiccated coconut
50 g/2 oz ground almonds

Preparation time: 15 minutes plus
   marinating overnight
Cooking time: 1 hour

Trim off any excess fat from the beef and cut it into slices approximately 1 cm/½ inch thick. Peel the garlic and put it together with the coriander, chilli powder, cumin, pepper, salt and yogurt into a liquidiser. Blend until a smooth marinade has been made, adding a little malt vinegar if necessary to moisten the mixture. Arrange the slices of beef in a dish, cover with the spice yogurt and put to one side to marinate for at least 8 hours, preferably overnight.

The next day, heat the ghee or cooking oil in a large saucepan and thinly slice the onions and fry them for 5–6 minutes until soft. Peel the ginger and cut into small pieces. Add the cloves, ginger and cardamoms to the saucepan and cook for 1½ minutes or so to release the aromatic oils. Add the beef, together with the marinade, increase the heat and cook, turning the slices of beef so that they change colour on the outside. Top and tail the green chillies and chop them into small 0.5-cm/¼-inch pieces. Add to the saucepan and cook for a further 1 minute. Add

the beef stock, bring to the boil and simmer for 30 minutes. Stir in the coconut and almonds and simmer for approximately 15 minutes until the beef is tender.

Minced meat with peppers
Keema pimento

This must be one of the simplest of Indian dishes to make and it is often found in snack-bars throughout the whole of the Indian subcontinent. Many Indian office workers will have a kind of Keema Pimento sandwich where some of this dry curry will form the filling of perhaps half a piece of naan bread.

500 g/1 lb minced meat
2 green peppers
1 large onion
100 g/4 oz ghee or 120 ml/4 fl oz
   cooking oil
½ teaspoon cinnamon powder
1 teaspoon chilli powder
1 teaspoon ground cumin
1 teaspoon garam masala
2 teaspoons black pepper
2 teaspoons salt

Preparation time: 10 minutes
Cooking time: 25 minutes

Remove the stalks from the green peppers, cut them open lengthways and remove the seeds and pith. Cut each pepper into strips about 5 cm/2 inches long and 0.25 cm/⅛ inch wide.

Peel and thinly slice the onion. Heat the ghee or cooking oil in a frying pan and fry the strips of pepper for about 1 minute until they start to soften. Remove the pepper from the frying pan and fry the onion. Cook until it begins to soften and then add the rest of the ingredients with the exception of the minced meat.

Stir for a further 2 minutes until the spices have combined with the oil and onion and then add the minced meat, turning to ensure that it cooks evenly. When it has all changed colour, add the green peppers and cook for a further 2 minutes.

From left to right: Pasanda, Dahi gosht and Keema pimento.

Minced kebab
Seekh kebab

❦❦❦❦❦❦❦❦❦❦❦❦❦❦❦❦❦

Many people confuse this dish, thinking it is of some great religious significance. It has, though, nothing whatsoever to do with the Sikh religion except to say that Sikhs are very partial, along with many other people, to this particular dish.

To cook it properly you need a special kind of skewer which is rather like a fat knitting needle about 1 cm/½ inch in diameter, around which the minced meat mixture is squeezed. It is then cooked on a barbecue or charcoal grill.

Failing the special skewers, the dish can be made with solid pieces of Seekh Kebab although you have to cook it far more slowly if you do this.

500 g/1 lb minced beef
2 cloves garlic
1 medium onion
5 cardamoms
1 × 5-cm/2-inch piece of fresh ginger
½ lemon
2 teaspoons ground cumin
1 teaspoon black pepper
1 teaspoon salt
3 cloves
1 egg

Preparation time: 15 minutes
Cooking time: 15 minutes

Peel the garlic. Peel and finely chop the onion. Remove the seeds from the cardamoms and place the cardamoms in a liquidiser. Peel the ginger and cut into pieces. Add to the cardamoms, together with the garlic, juice of the half lemon, ground cumin, black pepper, salt and cloves. Liquidise together for about 1 minute.

Mix the spice paste on a board with the minced beef and add the onion. Knead the mixture until it is stiff, then add the egg, kneading well in. Squeeze pieces of the mixture around the skewers to form hollow kebabs about 10–15 cm/4–6 inches long each.

Cook over a high heat on a barbecue or under a hot grill. The idea of this dish is to cook it very quickly. However, if you cook the kebabs without skewers, you must slow down the cooking process to ensure even cooking throughout.

From left to right: Seekh kebab and Kharghosh ka salan.

Rabbit curry
Kharghosh ka salan

Rabbits are found throughout India, especially in the cooler northern climate, but they adapt well to the more arid parts of the country. In the West, rabbit is not particularly popular, but is enjoying something of a revival. Rabbit Curry should be a good introduction to this inexpensive meat and many people cannot tell the difference between Rabbit Curry and Chicken Curry.

1 rabbit
100 g/4 oz ghee or 120 ml/4 fl oz cooking oil
1 large onion
4 cloves garlic
1 teaspoon ground cumin
1 teaspoon ground coriander
2 teaspoons chilli powder
1 bay leaf
4 cardamoms
4 cloves
300 ml/½ pint chicken stock
2 teaspoons salt
100 g/4 oz tomato purée
4 teaspoons garam masala

Preparation time: 15 minutes
Cooking time: 1 hour 20 minutes

Wash the rabbit and joint it. To joint the rabbit, chop off the front legs and separate each leg by chopping through lengthways to make 2 joints. Divide the back section into 3 pieces by chopping crossways across the backbone. Divide each of these pieces into two. Divide the back legs and chop each leg into 2–3 pieces.

Heat the ghee or cooking oil in a frying pan and seal the rabbit joints fairly quickly, turning them constantly to ensure that all sides are sealed. Remove the joints and put to one side. Thinly slice the onion and fry it in the remaining ghee until soft. Peel and slice the garlic and add to the pan. Add the cumin, coriander, chilli powder and bay leaf, followed by the cardamoms and cloves. Mix in well and add the stock, together with the salt. Bring to the boil and stir in the tomato purée, reduce the heat and simmer for 1 hour until the rabbit is tender and tends to fall off the bone.

After 45 minutes, add the garam masala and stir in well. Check to see how thick the sauce is. The sauce should be fairly thick for this dish; if it is not, remove the cover from the pan and increase the heat to boil away any excess moisture.

Partridge
Teetar

ᰡᰡᰡᰡᰡᰡᰡᰡᰡᰡᰡᰡᰡᰡᰡᰡ

Towards the north of India and in Pakistan partridges are a particular delicacy. The Indian partridge is, if anything, slightly larger than its Western counterpart. You need to start the preparations the day before.

4 partridges
1 lemon
1 tablespoon salt
½ tablespoon black pepper
1 large onion
2 cloves garlic
100 g/4 oz ghee or 120 ml/4 fl oz
    cooking oil
5 cardamoms
5 cloves
2 teaspoons chilli powder
1 × 5-cm/2-inch stick of cinnamon
300 ml/½ pint natural yogurt
½ teaspoon saffron threads
150 ml/¼ pint single cream
5 cloves

Preparation time: 15 minutes plus
    marinating overnight
Cooking time: 1 hour 15 minutes

Have the partridges plucked and drawn and ask your game dealer or butcher to reserve the livers and hearts. Wash each bird well and leave to dry thoroughly. Cut the lemon into quarters and rub a quarter over each bird, squeezing the juice into the skin. Now rub over with half the salt and half the pepper. Marinate in a fridge overnight.

The next day, peel and finely chop the onion. Peel and thinly slice the garlic. In a large heatproof casserole heat the ghee or cooking oil and fry the onion until it begins to soften. Add the garlic, the remaining black pepper, the cardamoms, cloves, chilli powder and cinnamon. Stir in well and cook for a further 3 minutes. Now add the yogurt and remaining salt. Stir in and cook for a further minute. Remove from the heat and place the partridges in the casserole, the breast side uppermost. Spoon a little of the spice mixture over each bird, place the lid on the casserole and cook in a preheated oven, 200°C/400°F/Gas Mark 6, for 20 minutes.

Meanwhile place the liver and heart of each partridge into a liquidiser and add the saffron threads and cream. Liquidise for 2 minutes. Remove the casserole from the oven and pour this mixture over the top of the birds. Return to the oven and reduce the heat to 180°C/350°F/Gas Mark 4. After 30 minutes, remove the lid of the casserole and place the birds to the top of the oven and allow to brown for 10–15 minutes, basting now and again with the liquid in which they are cooking. Serve garnished with fresh onion rings.

Pheasant pillao
Jangli murgh pillao

ᰡᰡᰡᰡᰡᰡᰡᰡᰡᰡᰡᰡᰡᰡᰡᰡ

The pheasants one sees wandering around the estates of England trace their ancestry to a similar bird imported from the Indian subcontinent. Pheasants are to be found in many parts of India today, although not in the same quantities, as game shooting has not reached the same heights it has in the West. Nonetheless, this does make a rather exotic rice dish.

1 pheasant
2 large onions
2 cloves garlic
500 g/1 lb rice
225 g/½ lb green split lentils or
    mung dal
100 g/4 oz ghee or 120 ml/4 fl oz
    cooking oil
4 cloves
4 cardamoms
2 teaspoons sesame seeds
2 tablespoons ground coriander
2 teaspoons black pepper
1 × 5-cm/2-inch stick of cinnamon
150 ml/¼ pint natural yogurt
2 teaspoons salt

Preparation time: 10 minutes
Cooking time: 1 hour

Have the pheasant plucked and dressed for you and, if you can persuade the butcher, jointed. Keep some of the tail feathers for decoration. Peel and thinly slice the onions and garlic. Wash the rice and lentils and drain well.

Heat the ghee in a saucepan and seal the joints by frying them gently for about 2 minutes each. Drain and remove the pheasant from the saucepan and in the remaining ghee fry the onions until they are soft. Add the garlic, together with the cloves, cardamoms, sesame seeds, ground coriander, pepper and cinnamon. Cook for a further 3–4 minutes, then add the rice and mung dal. Stir in the yogurt and add sufficient water just to cover the rice and dal. Bring to the boil, add the salt and pheasant pieces, stir well and cover the saucepan. Cook very slowly until all the water has been absorbed and the rice is cooked.

Above: Teetar; below: Jangli murgh pillao.

Chapter Five
Fish dishes of Bengal
and Kerala

It may appear surprising combining the fish recipes of Bengal and Kerala as they are at opposite ends of India. On one hand you have Bengal which occupies much of the complex delta of the Ganges river as it flows into the Indian Ocean in the area now known as Bangladesh. On the other you have Kerala which is on the south-west coast of India, many hundreds of miles away, where predominantly the fish comes from the sea.

Although the cooking for the two areas has no doubt developed separately, nonetheless, because the ingredients and fish they have in common, many of the cooking techniques are the same.

One of the problems with writing fish recipes which are peculiar to a particular area is that many of the fish are not freely available in the West. However in these recipes I have tried to include fish which can be found easily in Western countries. If you have never tried an Indian fish dish then do experiment with one of these recipes. Traditionally in the West, fish cooking has always been rather bland with more flavour in the sauce than in the fish itself. With most of these recipes it is the fish that has the taste.

Fish curry
Muchli ka salan

This is a general recipe for currying any fish, mainly in the form of pieces or goujons. Any good white fish will do, cod in particular. However, this dish can be adapted to use mackerel, or any of the other cheaper fish that are on the market.

900 g/2 lb fillets of white fish
100 g/4 oz ghee or 120 ml/4 fl oz cooking oil
1 medium onion
1 clove garlic
1 teaspoon ground coriander
1 teaspoon ground cumin
1 teaspoon chilli powder
1 teaspoon black pepper
1 teaspoon fenugreek powder
2 tablespoons tomato purée
300 ml/½ pint boiling water
1 lemon
1 teaspoon salt

Preparation time: 10 minutes
Cooking time: 30 minutes

Heat the ghee or cooking oil in a large saucepan. Peel and finely chop the onion and garlic and fry them until they soften. Now add the coriander, cumin, chilli powder, black pepper and fenugreek powder and cook for a further 4–5 minutes. Stir in the tomato purée and then add the boiling water.

Cut the fish into small pieces, approximately 5 × 2.5 cm/2 × 1 inch, and drop these into the sauce. Bring to the boil, then reduce the heat to a gentle simmer and cook for about 15 minutes until the fish is cooked. Squeeze in the juice of the lemon and add the salt. Be careful not to overdo the stirring of this dish otherwise the fish will break up.

Fish with tomatoes
Meen tamatar

The use of tomatoes in fish cooking is well known throughout the world and in Indian cooking the reason for combining the two is the same as in the West, to use the sharpness of the tomatoes to counteract any oiliness in the fish.

900 g/2 lb fillets of white fish
50 g/2 oz ghee or 60 ml/2 fl oz cooking oil
2 teaspoons fenugreek seeds
1 × 5-cm/2-inch piece of fresh ginger
2 cloves garlic
2 teaspoons ground coriander
2 teaspoons ground cumin
1 teaspoon chilli powder
1 teaspoon black pepper
2 teaspoons ground turmeric
300 ml/½ pint natural yogurt
2 teaspoons salt
2 tablespoons vinegar
1 × 225-g/½-lb tin tomatoes
2 small lemons
1 tablespoon chopped coriander leaves

Preparation time: 10 minutes
Cooking time: 40 minutes

Heat the ghee or cooking oil in a saucepan and fry the fenugreek seeds gently. Peel and thinly slice the ginger and the garlic and add to the saucepan. Fry gently until they soften. Add the coriander, cumin, chilli powder and black pepper and cook for a further 1½ minutes. Stir in the turmeric, together with the yogurt, salt and vinegar. Continue to stir until the yogurt comes to the boil.

Add the tomatoes and bring to the boil once again. Cut the fish into pieces approximately 5 × 2.5 cm/2 × 1 inch. Add the fish to the saucepan and simmer gently for 30 minutes or so until it is cooked. Squeeze in the juice from the lemons, sprinkle with the chopped coriander leaves and serve. Be careful not to stir too much or else the fish will break down and become a mush. The sauce should be fairly watery.

Bombay fish curry
Bombay meen

Bombay Fish Curry is a name that appears on the menus of many Indian restaurants and there seem to be as many versions of it as there are restaurants. The bare essentials of this dish are coconut milk and dried chillies, to give it a really good kick!

900 g/2 lb fillets of white fish
100 g/4 oz ghee or 120 ml/4 fl oz cooking oil
1 medium onion
2 cloves garlic
2 dried red chillies
1 teaspoon mustard powder
1 teaspoon ground turmeric
2 teaspoons ground coriander
1 × 2.5-cm/1-inch piece of fresh ginger
300 ml/½ pint boiling water
50 g/2 oz desiccated coconut
2 teaspoons salt
1 lemon

Preparation time: 10 minutes
Cooking time: 40 minutes

Heat the ghee or cooking oil in a heavy saucepan. Peel the onion and garlic and chop finely. Cook them in the ghee until they are soft. Crumble the red chillies into the saucepan and add the remaining dry spices except for the salt. Peel the ginger and cut it into fine strips. Fry it for 2 minutes in the spice mixture. Now add the boiling water and the coconut. Add the salt and bring back to the boil.

Cut the fish into small pieces approximately 5 × 2.5 cm/2 × 1 inch and add the pieces as the sauce begins to thicken. Bring back to the boil and simmer gently for 15–20 minutes until the fish is cooked. Squeeze in the lemon juice and serve.

Above: Meen tamatar; below left to right: Muchli ka salan and Bombay meen.

Steamed fish with courgettes
Dum muchli

This is a very good recipe for combining white fish with some of the more tender vegetables. The idea is that the vegetables should take roughly the same time to cook as the fish and both be at their peak when served. Traditionally, when food is steamed in India it is done in a saucepan that has a concave lid. The saucepan is placed on a charcoal fire which is heated from below and when the steaming process is ready to start, the lid is put on and charcoal placed in it so that there is a heat source from above the food as well as below. In this way a layer of steam is maintained above the food in the saucepan, providing all-round cooking.

750 g/1½ lb fillets of cod or other white fish
225 g/½ lb courgettes
300 ml/½ pint natural yogurt
2 teaspoons chick-pea flour
2 teaspoons aniseed
1 tablespoon coriander seeds
½ teaspoon ground cinnamon
1 medium onion
4 cardamoms
4 cloves
½ teaspoon saffron threads
50 g/2 oz ghee or 60 ml/2 fl oz cooking oil
1 teaspoon salt
1 teaspoon black pepper
1 tablespoon chopped coriander leaves

Preparation time: 15 minutes, plus 2–3 hours for marinating
Cooking time: 25 minutes

Put the yogurt, together with the chick-pea flour, aniseed, coriander seeds and cinnamon into a liquidiser or food processor and blend together for 30 seconds. Peel the onion, chop it roughly and add to the liquidiser and blend in for a further minute. Remove the seeds from the cardamoms and add to the liquidiser together with the cloves. Add the saffron threads and liquidise together for 2–3 minutes until you have a smooth paste.

Wash the fish well, pat it dry and cut into small pieces, approximately 5 × 2.5 cm/2 × 1 inch. Lay the pieces in a dish and spread the mixture from the liquidiser over the fish. Cover the dish with aluminium foil or cling film and leave to marinate in a cool place for 2–3 hours.

Top and tail the courgettes and cut them into slices about 0.5 cm/¼ inch thick. Heat the ghee or cooking oil in a flameproof casserole and add the fish, together with the paste in which it has been marinating. Fry gently for a minute or so, and then add the courgettes. Sprinkle in the salt and black pepper, put the lid on the casserole and place in a preheated medium oven, 180°C/350°F/Gas Mark 4. Cook for 20 minutes until both the fish and the courgettes are tender. Serve sprinkled with the chopped coriander leaves.

From left to right: Dum muchli and Muchli ka tikka.

Barbecued fish
Muchli ka tikka

ೂೂೂೂೂೂೂೂೂೂೂೂೂೂೂ

Although this recipe is for bar-
becued fish, in actual fact it is far
easier to grill the fish rather than
cook it in the traditional way which
involves putting pieces of fish on
skewers. This is because fish easily
falls apart if it is overcooked. It can
still be cooked on a barbecue, although it is better to cook it as you
would a steak.

The recipe calls for a quantity of
fresh coriander, which should be
available from most Asian stores but
of course is much better and cheaper
if you grow it yourself by planting
coriander seed. Start the preparations the day before.

750 g/1½ lb fillets of white fish, sole
  or plaice
2 lemons
2 teaspoons salt
2 teaspoons black pepper
50 g/2 oz ghee or 60 ml/2 fl oz
  cooking oil
1 medium onion
1 clove garlic
1 × 8-cm/3-inch piece of fresh
  ginger
½ teaspoon ground turmeric
½ teaspoon chilli powder
170 g/6 oz fresh coriander leaves

Preparation time: 10 minutes, plus
  marinating overnight
Cooking time: 40 minutes

Wash the fillets of fish, and if they are
large cut them into pieces, approximately 15 × 8 cm/6 × 3 inches. The
size does not have to be too accurate,
it is a mere guide as quite naturally
the fillets will taper at one end. Lay
the fillets out in a dish, squeeze the
lemon juice over them, followed by
the salt and black pepper. Marinate
overnight in a cool place.

The next day, heat the ghee or
cooking oil in a large frying pan. Peel
the onion and garlic and chop very
finely. Fry both the onion and garlic
gently until they are soft. Peel and
chop the ginger finely. Add the turmeric, chilli powder and ginger to
the frying pan. Continue to cook for a
further 1 minute.

Chop the coriander leaves fairly
finely. Don't worry too much about
including some of the coriander
stalks but be sure to throw away any
brown parts of the stalks and leaves.
Add the coriander leaves to the frying pan, reduce the heat and continue to turn, using a flat wooden
spatula, until the leaves are well
coated with the spice mixture. This
should take between 5 and 10
minutes.

Remove the fillets from the marinade, lay them out flat and spoon a
little of the spice mixture onto each
fillet. Roll up each fillet and secure
with a cocktail stick. Cook slowly on a
charcoal barbecue ensuring that you
turn them to make sure they are
cooked evenly on all sides. The key
to this recipe is to ensure that the fish
do not cook too quickly. It is not
absolutely essential to use a charcoal
barbecue, they can be cooked
slowly under a grill but the flavour is
perhaps not so good.

Spiced fried fish
Muchli masala

In most forms of cooking, fish is generally prepared within hours of being caught. This recipe, however, calls for the fish to be marinated in a special masala or spice mixture. The principle of the recipe is twofold in India. One is to make pieces of otherwise uninteresting and tough fish quite tender and the other is to often cover up the lack of freshness in the fish. Needless to say, in your recipe the freshest fish possible will be used! Start the preparations the day before.

900 g/2 lb fillets white fish
1 lemon
1 teaspoon salt
1 teaspoon black pepper
3 cloves garlic
1 × 8-cm/3-inch piece of fresh ginger
150 ml/¼ pint natural yogurt
150 ml/¼ pint vinegar
2 teaspoons chilli powder
100 g/4 oz chick-pea flour
cooking oil for deep frying

Preparation time: 1 hour 20 minutes plus marinating overnight
Cooking time: 30 minutes

Cut the fillets of fish into large pieces up to 8 cm/3 inches across. Arrange them in a dish, squeeze the lemon juice over them, followed by the salt and black pepper. Leave to one side for 30–60 minutes. Peel the garlic and ginger, cut them into small pieces and liquidise together with the yogurt and vinegar. Add the chilli powder and blend into a fine sauce. Pour this over the fish and marinate overnight.

When you are ready to cook the fish, drain the marinade from the fish and return it to the liquidiser. Add the chick-pea flour and blend. If the sauce is too thick at this stage, add a little water to thin it down. The consistency should be that of a good thick batter. Dip each piece of fish in the batter and deep fry in cooking oil until golden brown on both sides.

Fishball curry
Muchli kofta

This is a very filling curry dish made from flaked fish. The skill with this dish is to ensure that when the curry is made the fishballs do not break up. This calls for careful handling and gentle cooking.

750 g/1½ lb fillets of white fish
300 ml/½ pint milk
300ml/½ pint water
1 medium onion
2 green chillies
100 g/4 oz mashed potato
3 teaspoons salt
1 egg
100 g/4 oz ghee or 120 ml/4 fl oz cooking oil
2 cloves garlic
1 × 5-cm/2-inch stick of cinnamon
4 cloves
4 cardamoms
2 teaspoons garam masala
2 teaspoons ground coriander
1 teaspoon ground turmeric
2 teaspoons ground cumin
2 bay leaves
1 lemon
300 ml/½ pint chicken stock
50 g/2 oz desiccated coconut

Preparation time: 30 minutes
Cooking time: 45 minutes

Poach the fillets for approximately 10–15 minutes on the top of the stove in the milk and water. Drain and pick over the flaked fish, remove the skin and any bones.

Peel the onion and chop it very finely. Top and tail the green chillies and chop finely. Combine the onion and green chillies together with the fish, mashed potato, 1 teaspoon of salt and egg to make a good firm paste. Form the paste into balls, approximately 2.5–4 cm/1–1½ inches in diameter. Fry gently in the ghee or cooking oil until sealed on the outside. Remove from the pan and put to one side to stand.

Heat the remaining ghee or cooking oil from the pan in a saucepan. Peel and slice the garlic thinly and fry gently until it begins to soften. Add the cinnamon, cloves and cardamoms and cook for 1 minute. Add the garam masala, coriander, turmeric, cumin and the bay leaves. Squeeze in the juice from the lemon. Add the chicken stock and the rest of

the salt and bring to the boil. Add the desiccated coconut and simmer for 20–25 minutes. Increase the heat to drive off some of the moisture.

As the sauce begins to thicken lower in the fishballs very carefully and cook for a further 5–10 minutes, stirring from time to time, but making sure the fishballs do not break up.

Above left to right: Muchli masala and Muchli kebab; below: Muchli kofta.

Fish patties
Muchli kebab

۞۞۞۞۞۞۞۞۞۞۞۞۞۞۞۞۞۞۞۞

There are many kinds of rather small, and quite often bony fish caught off the coasts of Kerala and in the delta of the Ganges in Bengal. The flesh is stripped from these fish and pounded into a paste, combined with spices and then fried. This is how the fish patty came into being in Indian cooking. This recipe is really an Indian fish cake. Traditionally in the West, haddock or cod would be used but it is possible to use a cheaper white fish.

500 g/1 lb fillets of white fish
300 ml/½ pint milk
300 ml/½ pint water
1 medium onion
2 green chillies
½ teaspoon ground ginger
1 teaspoon black pepper
1 teaspoon garam masala
1 tablespoon chopped coriander
   leaves
1 teaspoon salt
2 eggs
ghee or cooking oil

Preparation time: 30 minutes
Cooking: 15 minutes

Poach the fillets for approximately 15–20 minutes on the top of the stove in the milk and water. Drain and pick over the flaked fish to remove the skin and any bones. Using a fork, mash the fish to make a fine paste.

Peel the onion and chop it very finely. Top and tail the green chillies and cut into very small pieces, no more than 0.25 cm/$\frac{1}{16}$ inch thick. Combine the onion and green chillies with the fish and sprinkle in the ginger, black pepper, garam masala and coriander leaves. Sprinkle in the salt and break one of the eggs into the mixture. Combine together.

Divide the mixture and form into patties about 7 cm/2½ inches in diameter and 1 cm/½ inch thick. Beat the remaining egg and dip each patty in it. Fry lightly on both sides in ghee or cooking oil until golden brown.

Sole with saffron
Muchli safran

ቀቅቀቅቀቅቀቅቀቅቀቅቀቅቀቅቀቅ

This is an interesting Indian recipe. It differs from most methods of Indian cooking inasmuch as it uses the Western technique of poaching fish. But whereas fish in the West is poached in water perhaps flavoured with a little lemon juice, in India a mixture of yogurt and milk is used. The effect is a mild dish where the spices are used to provide nothing more than subtle hints of flavour. Start the preparations the day before.

500 g/1 lb fillets of sole or any
    other flat fish
1 lemon
1 teaspoon salt
$\frac{1}{2}$ teaspoon black pepper
150 ml/$\frac{1}{4}$ pint natural yogurt
150 ml/$\frac{1}{4}$ pint milk
$1\frac{1}{2}$ teaspoons fenugreek seeds
$\frac{1}{2}$ teaspoon saffron threads
1 teaspoon cornflour
1 clove garlic
1 tablespoon chopped coriander
    leaves

Preparation time: 10 minutes plus
    marinating overnight
Cooking time: 30 minutes

Wash the fish fillets and pat them dry with kitchen paper. Lay them on a plate, squeeze over the lemon juice and sprinkle on the salt and black pepper. Cover with cling film or aluminium foil and refrigerate overnight.

The next day, put the yogurt and the milk in a large saucepan, stir them together and warm gently. Grind the fenugreek seeds into a fine powder (alternatively use fenugreek powder although seeds are better and give a fresher flavour) and sprinkle them into the yogurt/milk mixture. Add the saffron. Increase the heat until the mixture begins to boil. Take a little of the milk mixture and mix with the cornflour to make a smooth paste. Add the paste to the saucepan and continue to stir. Peel the clove of garlic and chop it very finely. Sprinkle it into the milk/yogurt mixture and stir in well. Once the mixture begins to thicken, reduce the heat and add the fillets of fish, gently lowering them into the milk and yogurt mixture. Simmer gently until the fish is cooked. To serve, gently remove the fillets from the saucepan and put into a warm serving dish. Pour the sauce on top of the fish and sprinkle over the chopped coriander leaves.

Stuffed halibut
Tali muchli

ቀቅቀቅቀቅቀቅቀቅቀቅቀቅቀቅቀቅ

This recipe is often made with Pomfret, which is a fish that abounds off the west coast of India, but in Western countries halibut is more easily come by. Any flat fish can be used, the bigger the better. This recipe is for a fish about 900 g–1.2 kg/2–3 lb in size.

The cooking process is in two parts, the first is a sort of semi-marinating to rid the fish of some of its smell and flavour. The second process is frying. Fry the fish as gently as possible and try to have on hand two fish slices, and if possible an extra pair of hands to help you turn the fish in the final part of the process! Start the preparations the day before.

1 halibut, weighing 900 g–1.2 kg/
    2–3 lb
1 lemon
1 teaspoon salt
1 teaspoon black pepper
1 teaspoon chilli powder
100 g/4 oz ghee or 120 ml/4 fl oz
    cooking oil
1 tablespoon blanched almonds
1 tablespoon sultanas
1 large onion
225 g/8 oz potatoes
1 teaspoon garam masala
1 tablespoon chopped mint
1 egg
1 × 5-cm/2-inch piece of fresh
    ginger
1 green chilli

Preparation time: 20 minutes plus
    8 hours for marinating
Cooking time: 1 hour 15 minutes

Have the fish gutted and slit open to make almost 2 fillets. If you can persuade the fishmonger, ask him to remove the eyes, but not the head or tail. Wash the fish well in cold water and pat dry with kitchen paper.

Cut the lemon in half and rub it all over the fish, squeezing out the juice as you do so. Mix together the salt, black pepper and chilli powder and sprinkle over the fish, both inside and out. Cover the fish loosely with foil and put to one side in a cool place for about 8 hours, preferably overnight.

Heat the ghee or cooking oil in a large frying pan, big enough to take the whole fish. Gently fry the almonds and sultanas together, remove with a slotted spoon and put to one side. Peel and finely chop the onion, add half of it to the remaining ghee in the frying pan and fry until it begins to soften. Remove the frying pan from the heat and put to one side.

Peel the potatoes and boil in just enough water to cover them. When they are soft, drain and mash them with the garam masala, uncooked onion, mint and egg. Peel the ginger and chop it finely. Combine it with the mashed potato. Top and tail the green chilli and cut into small pieces about 0.5 cm/$\frac{1}{8}$ inch thick and add to the mashed potato mixture.

Put the frying pan, together with the precooked onion back on the heat. Add the potato mixture and gently fry. Remove the potato from the pan and stuff as much of it as possible into the cavity of the halibut.

Put the halibut into the frying pan and fry gently until it is cooked on one side, carefully turn it over, using two fish slices, and cook it on the other side until it is crisp. Depending on how absorbent the potatoes prove to be, you may need to add a little more ghee or cooking oil to help the frying process. Serve garnished with tomato slices.

Prawn curry
Jhinghe ka salan

This recipe is typical of dishes you will find served in Indian restaurants throughout the Western world. It is the basic recipe for currying prawns. Use frozen prawns as these are the easiest to deal with.

500 g/1 lb frozen prawns
100 g/4 oz ghee or 120 ml/4 fl oz
  cooking oil
1 large onion
1 clove garlic
1 teaspoon chilli powder
1 teaspoon fenugreek seeds
1 teaspoon black pepper
2 teaspoons ground cumin
1 teaspoon ground turmeric
2 teaspoons salt

Preparation time: 5 minutes
Cooking time: 15 minutes

Heat the ghee or cooking oil in a saucepan. Peel the onion and garlic and slice them thinly. Fry them gently until they begin to soften. Then add the chilli powder, fenugreek seeds, black pepper, ground cumin and turmeric. Cook for a further 2 minutes, and then add the prawns. There is no need to thaw out the frozen prawns as they will cook through quite adequately from frozen in this recipe. At this stage it is important not to turn the prawns too much or some of them will break up. Turn them gently until they are coated in the spice mixture, reducing the heat slightly if they begin to stick.

After they have cooked for a minute or so and once they begin to separate from each other, pour in a little boiling water – sufficient just to cover the prawns. Now sprinkle in the salt. Bring to the boil and simmer for about 10 minutes until the prawns are cooked. This sauce is fairly thin. If you require a thicker sauce, then increase the heat to boil off some of the liquid.

From above: Jhinghe ka salan, Tali muchli and Muchli safran.

Prawns in batter
Prawn pakora

This mild dish is normally served as a starter or a snack but can be used as a main dish accompanied by rice. The essential thing is to ensure that the Pakoras are eaten as soon as they are cooked, otherwise the batter becomes soggy and the prawns rather chewy.

500 g/1 lb prawns, peeled
300 ml/½ pint natural yogurt
170 g/6 oz chick-pea flour
2 teaspoons chilli powder
½ teaspoon mustard powder
1 teaspoon salt
½ lemon
1 medium onion
cooking oil for deep frying

Preparation time: 2 hours 15 minutes
Cooking time: 15 minutes

Put the yogurt into a large bowl and sift in the chick-pea flour. Use the back of a spoon to break up the chick-pea flour so that it passes through the sieve. As you add the flour to the bowl, beat the yogurt with a fork to make sure it is well mixed in. Now stir in the chilli powder and the mustard powder, together with the salt. Transfer the mixture to a liquidiser or food processor, squeeze in the juice from the half lemon and then grate in as much of the lemon peel as you can, making sure you do not grate in any pith. Liquidise for 1 minute. Peel and chop the onion and add to the liquidiser. Liquidise until the onion is combined with the batter. Put the batter into a bowl and cover with foil or cling film. Put into the refrigerator to chill for 2 hours.

Heat the cooking oil in a deep frying pan until some batter flicked into it immediately sizzles and rises to the surface of the cooking oil. Dry the prawns on kitchen paper and dip each one into the batter so it is well coated. Fry in the oil until golden brown. Lift out with a slotted spoon, drain on kitchen paper and serve hot.

Prawns with courgettes
Jhinghe karela

The skill of this dish is to ensure that the cooking time of the courgettes is carefully synchronised with that of the prawns. Use frozen prawns which have already been cooked and peeled. This dish is a disaster if it is overcooked so, if in doubt undercook the courgettes so that they retain their crunchiness and test the prawns frequently to check that they are cooked. This recipe is fairly hot.

500 g/1 lb prawns, cooked and peeled
500 g/1 lb courgettes
1 large onion
100 g/4 oz ghee or 120 ml/4 fl oz cooking oil
1 clove garlic
3 green chillies
1 × 5-cm/2-inch piece of fresh ginger
½ teaspoon chilli powder
1 teaspoon ground turmeric
½ teaspoon black pepper
1 tablespoon vinegar
1 tablespoon honey
1 teaspoon salt
2 teaspoons garam masala

Preparation time: 10 minutes
Cooking time: 40 minutes

Peel the onion and slice it thinly. Heat the ghee or cooking oil in a heavy saucepan and fry the onion until it softens. Peel and finely slice the garlic and top and tail the green chillies. Cut them into 0.5 cm/¼ inch pieces. Add the garlic and chillies to the pan. Fry for 1 minute. Peel and cut the ginger into thin strips. Add to the pan. Now add the chilli powder, turmeric and black pepper and cook for a further 2 minutes. Blend the vinegar and honey together and stir into the onion mixture. Bring to the boil.

Top and tail the courgettes and cut into slices about 0.5 cm/¼ inch thick. Add to the pan. Add up to 2 tablespoons of water, cover the saucepan and simmer for 10–15 minutes. As the courgettes begin to soften sprinkle in the salt and garam masala and add the prawns, cook for a further 5–10 minutes until the prawns are fully heated through and serve.

Spiced prawn pickle
Jhinghe ballachow

Although this is called a pickle it is really a dish in itself. It can be served as soon as it is prepared or preserved. This is not really a dish for those unused to Indian cooking as it is very hot and bitter. Some people may think it a waste to grind prawns into a pulp but you have to remember that along the coast of India where this dish originates, prawns are in plentiful supply. Try it as a starter with a few poppadums or as an accompaniment to curries. Start the preparations the day before.

500 g/1 lb peeled prawns
25 g/1 oz tamarind
2 tablespoons vinegar
2 cloves garlic
1 × 5-cm/2-inch piece of fresh ginger
2 dried red chillies
2 teaspoons salt
120 ml/4 fl oz sesame seed oil

Preparation time: 15 minutes plus overnight soaking
Cooking time: 10 minutes

Put the tamarind into a bowl, pour on the vinegar and leave to soak overnight. The next day, thaw the prawns fully if using frozen ones. Transfer the vinegar and tamarind into a mortar and grind the tamarind into the vinegar with a pestle to produce a thick pulp. Peel the garlic and peel and chop the ginger finely. Put the prawns into a liquidiser or food processor and add the dried red chillies, garlic and the fresh ginger. Sprinkle in the salt and blend so that the prawns are ground up with the other ingredients except the sesame seed oil to form a paste. During the blending, add the tamarind and vinegar mixture.

Heat the sesame seed oil in a heavy saucepan and fry the paste gently. The idea is to combine the oil with the paste to form a fairly liquid mixture. Cover the saucepan and simmer for 5–10 minutes. Allow to cool and either place into clean pickle jars to preserve or put into the refrigerator to chill and then serve.

Above: Jhinghe ballachow; below left to right: Prawn pakora and Jhinghe karela.

Prawns with spinach
Jhinghe saag

One of the classic Indian dishes to be served in Indian restaurants throughout the world is this unique combination of prawns and spinach. Spinach has quite a strong flavour compared with that of the prawns, but nonetheless they seem to complement each other very well. There are many recipes for Jhinge Saag, but I prefer this particular one, which you will find in most of the restaurants run by Bangladeshis in the West. The result is usually a fairly dry curry. You can measure the generosity of the restaurant by the amount of prawns it has in it compared to the spinach! This recipe calls for fresh spinach, although it is somewhat easier to make with a block of frozen spinach.

350 g/12 oz prawns, peeled
900 g/2 lb fresh spinach or a 500-g/ 1-lb block of frozen spinach
300 ml/½ pint water
75 g/3 oz ghee or 90 ml/3 fl oz cooking oil
1 medium onion
1 clove garlic
1 × 5-cm/2-inch stick of cinnamon
1 teaspoon ground cumin
½ teaspoon ground turmeric
1 teaspoon ground coriander
2 teaspoons chilli powder
1 teaspoon black pepper
100 g/4 oz tomato purée
1 teaspoon honey
1 teaspoon salt
1 teaspoon garam masala

Preparation time: 20 minutes
Cooking time: 30 minutes

Remove the stalks from the fresh spinach and chop the leaves coarsely. Put them into a large saucepan. Add the water and boil for 5 minutes until the spinach just begins to cook. Drain the water away and put the spinach to one side. If you are using frozen spinach, thaw it and then add it to the recipe when the part-cooked fresh spinach would be added.

Now heat the ghee or cooking oil in a saucepan, peel and slice the onion and garlic thinly and fry until they begin to soften. Add the cinnamon, cumin, turmeric, coriander, chilli powder and black pepper and cook for 2 minutes.

Add the tomato purée and honey and cook for a further minute, mixing in well. Add the salt and then the part-cooked fresh spinach or the block of frozen spinach. Stir well and as the spinach begins to get coated with the spice mixture, add the prawns. Continue to heat, stirring all the time and being careful not to break up the prawns.

Heat until everything is well heated through and the spices are well mixed in. Sprinkle in the garam masala and cook for a further 5 minutes. If you feel you need a little moisture to help the cooking process, then add a small amount of water, but remember this should be a very dry dish.

Prawn patties
Jhinghe kebab

Many people prefer to eat their prawns whole but if you try this recipe, where the prawns are ground up into a fine paste, I am sure you will agree it is an interesting way of cooking them.

500 g/1 lb prawns, peeled
1 medium onion
1 clove garlic
1 × 2.5-cm/1-inch piece of fresh ginger
2 green chillies
½ teaspoon chilli powder
½ teaspoon black pepper
½ teaspoon salt
1 teaspoon ground turmeric
2 eggs
ghee or cooking oil for frying

Preparation time: 15 minutes
Cooking time: 10 minutes

Thaw the prawns completely and, if necessary, peel them. Peel the onion, garlic and ginger. Top and tail the green chillies. Mix the prawns, onion, garlic, ginger and chillies together to a fine mixture in a food processor.

Mix in the remaining ingredients together with one of the eggs. Form the mixture into kebabs about 8 cm/ 3 inches across and 2.5 cm/1 inch thick. Beat the second egg and dip each kebab into it. Fry in the minimum of ghee or cooking oil until brown on both sides.

Prawns with coconut
Jhinghe ka patia

The standard Indian Prawn Curry is nothing special, but the Prawn Patia is really something! The addition of coconut and tomato purée makes this an almost opulent dish. This recipe uses fenugreek, which tends to absorb some of the sometimes unpleasant fishy odour of prawns.

From left to right: Jhinghe saag, Jhinghe kebab and Jhinghe ka patia.

500 g/1 lb frozen prawns,
  defrosted
1 lemon
1 teaspoon black pepper
100 g/4 oz ghee or 120 ml/4 fl oz
  cooking oil
1 medium onion
1 × 2.5-cm/1-inch piece of fresh
  ginger
6 cardamoms
1 teaspoon ground turmeric
1 teaspoon fenugreek seeds
2 teaspoons ground cumin
1 teaspoon ground coriander
100 g/4 oz tomato purée
2 teaspoons garam masala
1 teaspoon salt
50 g/2 oz desiccated coconut
1 tablespoon chopped coriander
  leaves

Preparation time: 5 minutes
Cooking time: 30 minutes

Put the prawns into a bowl and sprinkle with the juice from the lemon and the black pepper. Heat the ghee or cooking oil in a saucepan. Peel the onion, slice it thinly and fry it until it begins to soften. Peel the ginger and slice it thinly. Fry it for 1 minute. Add the cardamoms and cook for 2 minutes. Then add the turmeric, fenugreek seeds, cumin and coriander and cook for a further 2–3 minutes.

Now add the prawns, together with the lemon juice in which they have been soaking. Turn the prawns gently so they are evenly coated with the spice mixture, but not too roughly to ensure that they do not break up. Spoon in the tomato purée. Stir well and add sufficient boiling water just to cover the prawns in the saucepan. Increase the heat, bring back to the boil and cook for 5 minutes. Stir in the garam masala, salt and the desiccated coconut. Leave to cook for a further 10 minutes until the prawns are cooked through.

By this time, the sauce should begin to thicken. Pour into a dish and serve garnished with coriander leaves. If the sauce is not thick enough, then increase the heat at the end of the cooking and boil off any excess water.

Prawns with lemon and coconut Jhinghe sambal

While the vegetable sambals are best served as an accompaniment to a main dish this particular sambal is very good served as a starter. This recipe serves between four and six people adequately as a starter, and in any case it is a good snack just to have on its own.

500 g/1 lb peeled prawns
100 g/4 oz desiccated coconut
150 ml/¼ pint water
2 eggs
½ teaspoon ground ginger
1 teaspoon ground cumin
½ teaspoon ground turmeric
½ teaspoon black pepper
1 teaspoon salt
1 onion
1 clove garlic
1 green chilli
2 lemons
1 teaspoon salt

Preparation time: 30 minutes plus
  2 hours soaking

Put the desiccated coconut into a liquidiser and pour on the water. Liquidise together for 1 minute, and put to one side for 2 hours or so. Then hardboil the eggs, shell and put to one side. Mix together the ginger, cumin, turmeric, black pepper and salt and put to one side. Peel the onion and garlic and chop them finely. Top and tail the chilli and chop finely. Do not de-seed it. Mix the onion, chilli and garlic together well and squeeze in the juice of one of the lemons, adding the mixture of dry spices as you do so. Mix the sambal well.

Put the prawns into individual serving bowls and squeeze the juice from the other lemon on top. Heap the sambal and dressing on top of the prawns.

Liquidise again the coconut and water mixture and add a little salt. Pour this over the prawns and sambal mixture just before serving. Garnish with the slices of hardboiled eggs and serve.

Above left to right: Chinaconee mootay and Jhinghe bhajji; below: Jhinghe sambal.

Dry curry of king prawns Jhinghe bhajji

This is very much a fishermen's dish, prepared as they wait by their boats for a favourable wind. It is a very simple curry indeed involving the barest of ingredients. The idea is to add enough spice to the king prawns to give it interest.

12 frozen king prawns
1 medium onion
100 g/4 oz ghee or 120 ml/4 fl oz
  cooking oil
1 teaspoon ground cumin
2 teaspoons ground coriander
1 teaspoon ground turmeric
1 teaspoon chilli powder
½ teaspoon salt
½ teaspoon black pepper
1 teaspoon ground ginger
1 × 100-g/4-oz tin of tomatoes
  (optional)
1 teaspoon chopped coriander
  leaves

Preparation time: 15 minutes
Cooking time: 20 minutes

Thaw the king prawns and peel them. Peel the onion and slice it very thinly. Heat the ghee or cooking oil in a saucepan and fry the onion until it softens. Now add the cumin, ground coriander, turmeric, chilli powder, salt, black pepper and ginger, and stir over a gentle heat for 2–3 minutes.

Add the prawns to the saucepan, turning gently to ensure that they are coated with spice. After 2 minutes, add the tomatoes, together with any juice they might be in. (If you omit the tomatoes, add 2 tablespoons of boiling water.)

Cover the saucepan and turn the heat right down low to cook gently for 20 minutes or so. Shake the saucepan from time to time. Remove the lid from the saucepan. This curry should be quite dry, so if there is any excess liquid, increase the heat to boil off the moisture rapidly. Shake once again and sprinkle in the chopped coriander leaves as you do so.

Prawn curry with eggs Chinaconee mootay

This is a fairly typical dish from the west coast of India and it is found throughout the south of India as well. Normally, large king prawns are used, but in the absence of these, use ordinary frozen prawns.

350 g/12 oz frozen king prawns or
  ordinary frozen prawns, peeled
6 eggs
50 g/2 oz ghee or 60 ml/2 fl oz
  cooking oil
1 small onion
2 cloves garlic
1½ teaspoons chilli powder
1 teaspoon fenugreek powder
1 teaspoon ground coriander
2 teaspoons ground cumin
1 teaspoon black pepper
50 g/2 oz tomato purée
1 teaspoon salt
2 tablespoons boiling water
50 g/2 oz desiccated coconut
150 ml/¼ pint water
1 lemon
2 teaspoons garam masala

Preparation time: 25 minutes
Cooking time: 35 minutes

Hardboil the eggs and put to one side to cool. Heat the ghee or cooking oil in a large saucepan. Peel the onion and garlic and chop them very finely. Add to the ghee and cook until they begin to soften. Then add the chilli powder, fenugreek, coriander, cumin and black pepper. Stir well and reduce the heat to ensure the spices cook gently. Add the tomato purée and the salt. Now add the boiling water to thin down the sauce. Bring back to the boil and add the prawns. Turn them well to ensure that they are well coated.

Remove the shells from the eggs, cut them in half lengthways and arrange them in a large serving dish. Liquidise together the desiccated coconut and the water. Squeeze the lemon juice into the saucepan and continue to cook, sprinkling in the garam masala after 2 minutes. Pour the coconut and water mixture into the saucepan and cook again for a further 2 minutes or so. Simmer for another 10 minutes, pour the whole mixture over the eggs and serve.

Prawns with coconut and egg
Chinaconee meen

❖❖❖❖❖❖❖❖❖❖❖❖❖❖❖❖❖❖

This dish is normally only prepared on high days and holidays and it is very popular at the festival of the Coconut in Kerala when coconuts are thrown in the sea as an offering back to the God of the Sea for all the fish taken out during the past year.

225 g/½ lb prawns, peeled
1 fresh coconut
1 large onion
2 cloves garlic
100 g/4 oz ghee or 120 ml/4 fl oz cooking oil
1 × 5-cm/2-inch piece of fresh ginger
1 teaspoon chilli powder
1 teaspoon ground turmeric
1½ teaspoons ground coriander
2 bay leaves
100 g/4 oz tomato purée
300 ml/½ pint boiling water
1 tablespoon chick-pea flour
6 eggs
2 teaspoons black pepper
1 teaspoon salt

Preparation time: 10 minutes
Cooking time: 35 minutes

Make two holes in the end of the coconut and drain off any of the milk into a liquidiser. Break the coconut open and extract the meat. Divide the meat into two. Grate one half into the coconut milk and put the other half to one side. Blend the coconut meat and milk together into a thick paste. Add a little water if necessary. Peel the onion and garlic and slice thinly.

Heat the ghee or cooking oil in a large saucepan. Fry the onion and garlic in the ghee or cooking oil until they soften. Peel the ginger and cut into thin slices. Add to the pan. Stir for a further 1 minute, then add the chilli powder, turmeric and coriander and cook for 1 minute. Add the bay leaves and the tomato purée. Stir in well and add the boiling water.

Bring back to the boil, add the prawns and simmer gently for 10 minutes or so. Meanwhile hardboil the eggs. Cut the remaining coconut meat into thin slivers and add these to the saucepan. Remove a little of the liquid from the pan and mix it with the chick-pea flour to form a smooth paste. Add the black pepper and salt. Add the paste to the saucepan and stir it in well. Shell the eggs and cut them into halves lengthways. Take the coconut sauce from the liquidiser and add to the saucepan. Combine well by stirring gently. Arrange the eggs in a serving dish, pour over the curry and serve.

Spiced herrings
Choti muchli masala

❖❖❖❖❖❖❖❖❖❖❖❖❖❖❖❖❖❖

This recipe is an adaptation of one used for thousands of years by the fishermen of the Indian subcontinent but seldom seen these days. The idea was to cover the herrings in a thick layer of mud and the mud package was placed in the embers of a fire. There, the fish steamed gently until cooked. You can use aluminium foil to almost equal effect!

4 herrings, about 900 g/2 lb
2 teaspoons garam masala
1 teaspoon chilli powder
1 teaspoon ground coriander
1 teaspoon ground turmeric
1 teaspoon black pepper
1 medium onion
2 cloves garlic
1 lemon
2 teaspoons salt
50 g/2 oz butter

Preparation time: 15 minutes
Cooking time: 40 minutes

Mix the garam masala, chilli powder, coriander, turmeric and black pepper in a bowl. Peel the onion and garlic and chop them very finely. Combine with the spices to make a very dry paste. Wash the herrings well, removing any residual stomach parts in the cavity of each herring. Lay each herring in its own piece of foil large enough to be able to fold over and make a parcel.

Squeeze the juice of the lemon over the herrings and then sprinkle them inside and out with salt. Rub the spice mixture over the herrings and fill the cavity of each one with a little mixture. Cut the butter into four and place a piece on each herring, fold the foil into parcels and cook in a preheated moderate oven, 180°C/350°F/Gas Mark 4, for 30–40 minutes until the herrings are cooked.

Barbecued Bengal prawns
Jhinghe ka tikka

❖❖❖❖❖❖❖❖❖❖❖❖❖❖❖❖❖❖

Bengal prawns are the rather larger variety of prawn measuring 10–13 cm/4–5 inches long and up to 4 cm/1½ inches thick. The essential point is that they are fresh and that they are large, the larger the better. The prawns are usually bought pre-cooked by boiling but if they are not cooked, boil them first for 20 minutes. This dish can be cooked under a grill but it is really best to use a barbecue as the combination of the marinade and the flavour of the charcoal really makes this a tasty dish. Start the preparations the day before.

12 Dublin Bay prawns
1 lemon
1 teaspoon salt
1 teaspoon black pepper
1 teaspoon chilli powder
1 teaspoon garam masala
2 teaspoons fenugreek powder
450 ml/¾ pint natural yogurt
1 medium onion
1 × 5-cm/2-inch piece of fresh
   ginger
2 tablespoons vinegar
red colouring

Preparation time: 3 hours plus
   marinating overnight
Cooking time: 15 minutes

Remove the Dublin Bay prawns whole from their shells. Discard the claws and feet as you do so – these may be kept and used to make a prawn soup. There will be no claws if the prawns were bought frozen. Squeeze the lemon juice all over the prawns and leave to marinate for a couple of hours in the refrigerator.

Meanwhile, mix together all the dry ingredients with 2 tablespoons of the yogurt. Peel the onion and ginger and chop them coarsely. Put the onion and ginger together with the vinegar into a liquidiser and blend for 1 minute. Now add the rest of the yogurt and spice mixture and blend for a further 2 minutes until a smooth marinade has been obtained. Gradually add the food colouring to obtain a rich, red colour. Pour the mixture over the prawns and leave to marinate overnight.

The next day, when you want to cook the prawns, remove each prawn from the marinade and thread onto a thin skewer. The best skewers are the ones that are about 45 to 60 cm/18 to 24 inches long and have a flat blade. You will find that if you use round skewers the Dublin Bay Prawns will be difficult to turn. Cook

Above left to right: Chinaconee meen and Jhinghe ka tikka; below: Choti muchli masala.

gently over a barbecue to ensure that the fish is cooked properly throughout. The best way to do this is to cook them as far away from the heat as possible, finishing them off by putting them closer to the coals so that they get a little bit of charcoal black on them. It is essential to serve the prawns as they are cooked, otherwise they tend to shrink as they cool.

Mussel curry
Teesrio ka salan

ᘒᘒᘒᘒᘒᘒᘒᘒᘒᘒᘒᘒᘒᘒᘒᘒᘒ

Mussels abound in most parts of the world and in India, where food is generally short, they are much appreciated as nourishment which is there for the picking up off the seashore. Whereas the French tend to use herbs for flavouring their *moules à la marinière*, the Indians use a combination of ginger, cardamoms and cloves to make a piquant sauce as an accompaniment. Naturally enough, when buying mussels the old adage of eating them when there is an 'R' in the month is well worth following.

1.2 litres/2 pints fresh mussels
1 large onion
3 cloves garlic
100 g/4 oz ghee or 120 ml/4 fl oz cooking oil
1 × 8-cm/3-inch piece of fresh ginger
3 cardamoms
3 cloves
1 teaspoon black pepper
1 teaspoon ground turmeric
½ teaspoon coriander
1 teaspoon salt

Preparation time: 15 minutes
Cooking time: 30 minutes

Wash the mussels well in cold water and scrub away any loose barnacles that are attached to them. If the barnacles are 'welded' on, then do not worry about them. Cut off as many of the 'beards' as possible. Discard any mussels that are open at this stage as they will have died. Peel the onion and garlic and chop very finely.

Heat the ghee or cooking oil in a large saucepan and fry the onion and garlic. Peel and thinly slice the ginger and fry for 1 minute. Add the cardamoms, cloves, black pepper, turmeric and coriander. Stir well for a further minute or so and add the mussels.

Sprinkle over the salt and then add just enough water to almost cover the mussels. Increase the heat and bring the liquid to the boil. Cover the saucepan and cook for 15–20 minutes, shaking the saucepan from time to time. Discard any mussels that are still shut. Serve immediately with plenty of bread to soak up the juice.

Steamed mussels
Dum teesrio

ᘒᘒᘒᘒᘒᘒᘒᘒᘒᘒᘒᘒᘒᘒᘒᘒᘒ

The idea of this recipe from Kerala is to cook the shellfish as quickly as possible so that the shells open, and to cook them using the minimum of liquid. It can be adapted for any shellfish – even oysters!

1.2 litres/2 pints fresh mussels
100 g/4 oz ghee or 120 ml/4 fl oz cooking oil
1 large onion
1 clove garlic
1 × 2.5-cm/1-inch piece of fresh ginger
2 teaspoons ground coriander
1 teaspoon ground turmeric
1 × 5-cm/2-inch stick of cinnamon
2 teaspoons salt
1 teaspoon black pepper
3 lemons
2 tablespoons chopped coriander leaves
100 g/4 oz desiccated coconut

Preparation time: 10 minutes
Cooking time: 15 minutes

Heat the ghee or cooking oil in a heavy saucepan. Peel the onion and garlic, chop them finely and fry them until they begin to soften. Peel the fresh ginger and chop finely.

Add the ginger to the saucepan, together with the coriander, turmeric, cinnamon, salt and black pepper. Squeeze in the juice from 2 of the lemons and continue to cook for 2 minutes.

Wash the mussels well to remove any seaweed or other foreign matter. Scrub the beards and discard any mussels that are already open.

Add the mussels to the saucepan and cover with a tight-fitting lid. Increase the heat and shake the saucepan occasionally. Cook until all the mussels open. This should take about 10 minutes or so.

Transfer them into a warm bowl, throwing away any that have failed to open by this time. Squeeze the juice from the remaining lemon over the mussels and sprinkle on the chopped coriander leaves and desiccated coconut. Serve immediately while the mussels are still hot.

Crab curry
Kurleachi ka salan

Although this dish is called Crab Curry, it is more of a chowder or thick soup, except that there are no potatoes in the recipe. The recipe calls for 750 g/1½ lb of crab meat – this can be tinned or frozen – but both of these varieties tend to be rather expensive, so it is probably a good dish to try when you can buy some fresh crabs.

From left to right: Teesrio ka salan, Dum teesrio and Kurleachi ka salan.

750g/1½ lb crab meat or the meat from 4 freshly boiled crabs
1 lemon
1 teaspoon salt
1 teaspoon black pepper
1 fresh coconut
600 ml/1 pint boiling water
100 g/4 oz ghee or 120 ml/4 fl oz cooking oil
1 medium onion
2 cloves garlic
1 × 5-cm/2-inch piece of fresh ginger
2 teaspoons fenugreek seeds
2 teaspoons coriander seeds
1 tablespoon black peppercorns
1 teaspoon ground cumin
½ teaspoon ground turmeric
2 teaspoons chilli powder
2 tablespoons chopped coriander leaves

Preparation time: 3 hours
Cooking time: 30 minutes

Put the crab meat into a large bowl, break it up gently with a fork and squeeze in the juice from the lemon. Sprinkle over the salt and the black pepper and leave for 2 hours.

Meanwhile, make two holes in the coconut and drain any milk into a liquidiser or food processor. Break the coconut open and grate the meat of the coconut into the liquidiser. Blend for 2 minutes, adding the boiling water. Leave to stand for 1 hour. Then, squeeze the liquid out of the coconut pulp through a fine sieve or double thickness of muslin. Put this coconut milk to one side and reserve half of the remaining coconut pulp. Discard the rest.

Heat the ghee or cooking oil in a large saucepan. Peel the onion and garlic and chop finely. Peel and chop the ginger. Cook the onion and garlic for 2 minutes or so until it softens. Then add the ginger and continue to cook for a further 2 minutes. Add the fenugreek and coriander seeds, peppercorns, cumin, turmeric and chilli powder.

Now pour in the coconut milk, bring to the boil and simmer for 5 minutes. Add the crab meat, together with any lemon juice in which it has been marinating, and cook gently for a further 10–12 minutes. Be careful at this stage not to burn the curry. Add the reserved half of the coconut pulp, stirring in well to mix it throughout, the dish and cook for a further 2 minutes. Sprinkle in the chopped coriander leaves and serve.

Chapter Six
Vegetable dishes of
eastern India

Many of the vegetable dishes of eastern India are similar to those prepared in the south of the country. However, because in Bengal, the country now known as Bangladesh, the people are predominantly Muslim, there has not been over the years quite the same imperative to produce vegetarian dishes as in the south.

Eastern India specializes in a hundred and one different ways of cooking pulses or dals, everything from ordinary lentils to chick peas and they are an important staple food.

Curried banana balls
Kela kofta

Bananas abound in the Ganges delta and there are any number of recipes for using them, both ripe and unripe. This particular recipe is traditionally made with green bananas although you can make it with very hard underripe yellow bananas. This is a fairly rich dish using a lot of double cream but you will find that it is also quite filling.

500 g/1 lb underripe bananas
100 g/4 oz ghee or 120 ml/4 fl oz
    cooking oil
1 medium onion
1 clove garlic
1 × 10-cm/4-inch piece of fresh
    ginger
1 teaspoon chilli powder
$\frac{1}{2}$ teaspoon ground cumin
$\frac{1}{2}$ teaspoon ground coriander
1 teaspoon black pepper
$1\frac{1}{2}$ teaspoons salt
1 egg
100 g/4 oz tomato purée
2 tablespoons vinegar
1 tablespoon garam masala
300 ml/$\frac{1}{2}$ pint double cream

Preparation time: 10 minutes
Cooking time: 30 minutes

Boil the bananas in their skins for 10 minutes or so until the skins split. Peel the bananas and mash them to a pulp. Heat the ghee or cooking oil in a large, heavy frying pan. Peel and chop finely the onion, garlic and ginger and fry until soft. Sprinkle in the chilli powder, cumin, coriander and black pepper. Stir well and add the banana pulp and salt. Mix well and fry for 5–10 minutes.

If there is any excess oil at this stage drain this off (depending on how underripe the bananas are, more or less oil will be absorbed). Break the egg into the frying pan and mix in quickly with the pulp, before the egg has a chance to cook. Remove the mixture from the frying pan and allow to cool.

Meanwhile heat the tomato purée together with the vinegar. Bring to the boil and add the garam masala. Mix in well and cook for 2 minutes. Lower the heat and add the cream, stirring so it is well dispersed.

Shape the banana pulp into balls, about 2.5–4 cm/1–1$\frac{1}{2}$ inches in diameter, lower gently into the tomato purée and cook for 2–3 minutes until they are warmed through. Serve hot.

Peas with cream cheese
Matar panir

Cheese as it is known in the West is not very common in India: although it is true to say that a kind of Cheddar cheese is being produced for the Westerners living in India and has been available in the big cities for twenty years or so.

The only real cheese that can truly call itself Indian is a particular kind of cream cheese known as panir. This cheese involves a fairly laborious method of preparation but the result is well worth the effort. Panir is not only used in savoury dishes but is also the basis of a number of Indian pudding recipes.

From left to right: Kela kofta, Chotee gobi and Matar panir.

1.8 litres/3 pints milk
2 lemons
2 teaspoons salt
100 g/4 oz ghee or 120 ml/4 fl oz
    cooking oil
1 large onion
2 teaspoons ground cumin
1 teaspoon ground coriander
1 teaspoon ground turmeric
1 teaspoon chilli powder
1½ teaspoons black pepper
100 g/4 oz frozen peas

Preparation time: 4 hours
Cooking time: 25 minutes

Put the milk into a large saucepan and bring to the boil, stirring continuously. Once the milk has boiled, remove from the heat and allow to cool. Squeeze in the juice from the lemons so that the milk curdles. Allow to stand for 15–20 minutes. Take a double thickness of muslin and strain the curdled milk through the cloth, squeezing out the whey into a bowl. Put the whey to one side.

You are now left with the curds. Add the salt to this and mix well, keeping the curds still in a muslin cloth. Squeeze hard again. Cut open a clean plastic bag and lay it on the draining board of the kitchen sink, lift the curds in the muslin out of the bowl and place on the plastic. Lay

another piece of plastic on top and then last of all a large chopping board. Pile books on top of the board, to about 4.5 kg/10 lb weight, and leave for 2–3 hours so that the rest of the whey runs out and drains away and the panir is formed into a slab. You now have made Indian cream cheese.

Then heat the ghee or cooking oil in a heavy saucepan. Peel and slice the onion and fry until soft. Now add the cumin, coriander, turmeric, chilli powder and black pepper and stir for a further 2–3 minutes.

Add the frozen peas and stir well to mix in with the spice and onion mixture. Add 1 cup of the whey and bring to the boil. After 4–5 minutes, when the peas are cooked, take the panir and cut it into small pieces, about 2.5 cm/1 inch or so. Fry the panir gently with the peas, being sure not to break up the cheese. Cook for a further few minutes or so and serve.

Brussels sprouts Chotee gobi

Traditionally this dish is made with small cabbage, this is for no other reason than that quite often the cabbages grown in the Indian subcontinent, as with many other vegetables, tend to be rather smaller than the specialised vegetables grown in the West. As it is quite difficult to obtain very small cabbages, I have adapted this recipe for use with Brussels sprouts – the larger the sprouts, the better.

750 g/1½ lb Brussels sprouts
100 g/4 oz ghee or 120 ml/4 fl oz
    cooking oil
1 large onion
4 cloves garlic
1 teaspoon ground turmeric
1½ teaspoons chilli powder
1 × 5-cm/2-inch stick of cinnamon
2 teaspoons poppy seeds
2 teaspoons ground cumin
1 teaspoon sesame seeds
3 teaspoons ground coriander
300 ml/½ pint natural yogurt
2 lemons
2 teaspoons salt
2 teaspoons black pepper
2 tablespoons honey
2 tablespoons chopped coriander
    leaves

Preparation time: 10 minutes
Cooking time: 45 minutes

Wash the sprouts and trim away any outer leaves and hard parts of the stalk. Cut a cross in the top of each sprout and arrange stalk downwards in a large baking dish.

Heat the ghee or cooking oil in a large frying pan. Peel and thinly slice the onion and garlic. Fry until they are soft, then add the turmeric, chilli powder, cinnamon, poppy seeds, ground cumin and sesame seeds. Fry this mixture gently for a further 2–3 minutes and then stir in the ground coriander.

Transfer this mixture to a liquidiser and add the yogurt. Squeeze in the juice of the lemons. Add the salt and black pepper and blend together until a smooth liquid is obtained. Then spoon in the honey and liquidise again for a further 2 minutes. Pour this over the sprouts. Cover the baking dish tightly with aluminium foil and bake in a preheated hot oven, 200°C/400°F/Gas Mark 6, for 15–20 minutes.

After 15 minutes check to see how tender the sprouts are and spoon some of the spice mixture over the sprouts. Remove the aluminium foil and allow the sprouts to cook to completion. Sprinkle over the chopped coriander leaves and then serve.

Breakfast rice Kitcheree

❖❖❖❖❖❖❖❖❖❖❖❖❖❖❖❖❖❖

It is not hard to see how Kitcheree originated. Clearly some way was needed to use up rice left over from the previous night's supper to turn it into some kind of wholesome breakfast dish, and that is exactly what Kitcheree is.

Traditionally, in the days of the British Raj in India, Kitcheree would always be served with flaked fish, normally kippers, often brought out at some expense from Britain. However, the fish element of the dish was probably more to do with answering the need of the British army officers for kippers for breakfast than with the original recipe.

The original recipe combines rice with lentils. However, if you wish to have a Kitcheree with fish, use this recipe and add up to 170 g/6 oz of cooked flaked fish.

225 g/½ lb leftover boiled rice
170 g/6 oz green split lentils, either Mung or Egyptian
1 small onion
2 cloves garlic
50 g/2 oz ghee or 60 ml/2 fl oz cooking oil
10 cloves
10 cardamoms
1 × 5-cm/2-inch stick of cinnamon
2 teaspoons ground turmeric
2 eggs
1 teaspoon salt

Preparation time: 10 minutes
Cooking time: 45 minutes

Wash the lentils well and place in a saucepan; add just enough water to cover them. Cook them until they are soft. This should take about 15–20 minutes. Drain and put to one side. Peel and thinly slice the onion and garlic. Heat the ghee or cooking oil in a heavy saucepan and fry the onion and garlic until they soften. Add the cloves, cardamoms, left whole, and cinnamon and stir in well. Then add the turmeric, and cook for another minute.

Combine together the rice and lentils and add to the saucepan, turning all the time to help coat it with the spice mixture. Boil the eggs until they just start to go hard (between 4 and 5 minutes), shell them and chop them coarsely. Some of the yolk should still be runny. Add the chopped egg to the rice and lentils and combine it so that it mixes in well. Add the fish if using. Sprinkle in the salt and continue to cook for a further 5 minutes and serve.

Vegetable pillao Subsi pillao

❖❖❖❖❖❖❖❖❖❖❖❖❖❖❖❖❖❖

To the many vegetarians of eastern, and also southern, India the thought of eating any meat is alien for religious reasons. Vegetable Pillaos were developed by chefs for the great feast days, such as Diwali, the festival of lights, just as the great Lamb and Chicken Pillaos were developed in the north of India.

Quite often in Indian restaurants in the West, Vegetable Pillao is cooked in a rather different way, with the rice being made separately from a thick vegetable curry, which is then poured on the cooked rice at the last minute. This recipe calls for the rice and vegetables to be cooked together in the authentic Indian manner.

170 g/6 oz Basmati rice
170 g/6 oz carrots
1 small cauliflower
100 g/4 oz frozen peas
50 g/2 oz ghee or 90 ml/3 fl oz cooking oil
1 medium onion
6 cloves
6 cardamoms
1 × 5-cm/2-inch stick of cinnamon
2 teaspoons cumin seeds
1 teaspoon garam masala
1 teaspoon ground coriander
1 teaspoon chilli powder
1 teaspoon black pepper
600 ml/1 pint chicken stock
1½ teaspoons salt

Preparation time: 10 minutes
Cooking time: 45 minutes

Heat the ghee or cooking oil in a large, heavy saucepan. Peel and thinly slice the onion and fry in the oil until it is soft. Now add the cloves, cardamoms, cinnamon and cumin seeds and cook for 2–3 minutes. Add the garam masala, coriander, chilli powder and black pepper. Stir in well. Remove from the heat and put to one side.

Wash the rice well and pick it over to remove any foreign bodies. Scrub the carrots and cut them into strips about 5 cm/2 inches long by 0.5 cm/¼ inch thick. Remove the outer leaves from the cauliflower and cut into individual florets. Drain the rice and add to the spices, increasing the heat once again. Then add the carrots and cauliflower florets, stirring well to ensure the spice mixture is well dispersed with the vegetables. Pour in the chicken stock and salt, bring to the boil and simmer for 10 minutes. Then add the frozen peas and continue to cook for a further 10 minutes until the rice is cooked through. The idea is that this dish is cooked sufficiently for the rice to be *al dente*, leaving the vegetables fairly crisp.

From left to right: Kitcheree, Subsi pillao and Chawal safran.

Rice with saffron
Chawal safran

ቈቈቈቈቈቈቈቈቈቈቈቈቈቈቈቈቈቈ

This recipe is very similar to Saffron Rice, prepared in the north of India. The difference is that lentils are added. The lentils serve to bulk out the rice and give it extra flavour. This recipe uses ordinary pink split lentils. Use only the best Basmati rice as it is essential in this recipe that every grain is separate.

170 g/6 oz Basmati rice
50 g/2 oz split lentils
1 teaspoon saffron threads
75 g/3 oz ghee or 90 ml/3 fl oz
   cooking oil
1 medium onion
2 cloves garlic
1 × 5-cm/2-inch piece of fresh
   ginger
1 × 5-cm/2-inch stick of cinnamon
6 cloves
6 cardamoms
1½ teaspoons salt
50 g/2 oz sultanas

Preparation time: 15 minutes
Cooking time: 45 minutes

Wash the rice and lentils together, to ensure the rice separates when cooked. Do this thoroughly with at least three changes of water. Drain the rice and lentil mixture and put to one side. Put the saffron threads into a teacup and three-quarters fill the cup with boiling water. Leave to one side.

Heat the ghee or cooking oil in a heavy saucepan. Peel the onion and slice it thinly. Fry until soft. Peel and thinly slice the garlic and add to the saucepan. Peel the ginger and cut into very thin strips, fry for a further 2 minutes and add the cinnamon, cloves and cardamoms.

Now add the rice and lentils and turn constantly so that they become well mixed in with the ghee. Pour on sufficient boiling water to cover the rice and add the saffron, together with the water in which it has been soaking. Sprinkle in the salt.

Bring back to the boil, cover the saucepan with a tight-fitting lid and boil gently for 20 minutes or so until the rice is *al dente*. Strain off any excess water. Transfer the rice to a large serving dish and sprinkle on the sultanas before serving.

Bengal beans
Kabli chenna

Lentils are known in the West by a number of different names, Egyptian lentils, black-eyed peas, Bengal lentils or Bengal beans, and it is hard to tell whether the beans originated from Bengal or Egypt.

350 g/12 oz Bengal beans
100 g/4 oz ghee or 120 ml/4 fl oz cooking oil
1 medium onion
2 cloves garlic
1 × 5-cm/2-inch piece of fresh ginger
1 teaspoon coriander seeds
1 teaspoon fenugreek seeds
1 teaspoon ground turmeric
1 teaspoon ground cumin
1 teaspoon chilli powder
2 tablespoons vinegar

Preparation time: 10 minutes
Cooking time: 30 minutes

Wash the Bengal beans well in plenty of water, put into a saucepan and add just enough water to cover them. Bring to the boil, reduce the heat and cover the saucepan with a tight-fitting lid. Simmer gently until the beans are just starting to become tender adding more water if necessary.

Heat the ghee or cooking oil in a heavy saucepan. Peel and finely slice the onion, garlic and ginger and fry them until they soften. Then add the coriander and fenugreek seeds and continue to cook for a further 2–3 minutes. Add the turmeric, cumin and chilli powder. Stir well for another minute.

Drain the water from the beans and add the beans to the saucepan, turning well to ensure they are well coated with the spice mixture. Pour on the vinegar and continue to dry fry until the beans are completely cooked through.

Above left to right: Kabli chenna and Urd dal; below: Kathi dal.

Sour lentils
Kathi dal

This recipe uses a combination of white lentils and tamarind to give the dish its characteristic sour taste.

170 g/6 oz white lentils or urd dal
1 medium onion
2 cloves garlic
1 × 5-cm/2-inch piece of fresh ginger
1 teaspoon chilli powder
1 teaspoon garam masala
1 teaspoon ground turmeric
1 teaspoon black pepper
4 cardamoms
4 cloves
1 bay leaf
50 g/2 oz ghee or 60 ml/2 fl oz cooking oil
1 × 5-cm/2-inch stick of cinnamon
1 × 5-cm/2-inch piece of tamarind
1 teaspoon salt
2 tablespoons chopped coriander leaves

Preparation time: 10 minutes
Cooking time: 45 minutes

Wash the dal well and put into a saucepan. Cover with boiling water. Bring to the boil and simmer for 5 minutes. Leave the dal to one side.

Meanwhile peel the onion, garlic and ginger and mince them very finely. Combine them together with the chilli powder, garam masala, turmeric and black pepper.

Put the cardamoms, cloves and bay leaf onto a baking tray and place in a preheated hot oven, 200°C/400°F/Gas Mark 6, to roast for 10 minutes. When this is done remove the seeds from the cardamoms and crush the cloves. Grind these together with the bay leaf. Combine with the onion, garlic, ginger and spice mixture.

Heat the ghee or cooking oil in a large saucepan and fry the spice mixture for 1 minute, then add the cinnamon and partly cooked dal. Put the tamarind into a bowl, pour on 150 ml/¼ pint boiling water and leave to soak while the spice mixture is cooking gently. After 5 minutes, pour the tamarind water into the saucepan, squeezing any extra water from the tamarind pulp. Continue to cook until the dal is soft. Stir in the salt and chopped coriander leaves and serve.

White lentil curry
Urd dal

Various types of lentils are found throughout the Indian subcontinent but the white lentil is very common in the east.

The traditional Bengal way of cooking them is to cook them very slowly with a large amount of fresh ginger until they are soft but not squashy. You need to start preparing the lentils the day before.

170 g/6 oz white lentils or urd dal
75 g/3 oz ghee or 90 ml/3 fl oz
    cooking oil
1 clove garlic
1 × 8-cm/3-inch piece of fresh
    ginger
6 cloves
6 cardamoms
2 bay leaves
1 teaspoon ground turmeric
1 teaspoon chilli powder
1 teaspoon black pepper
2 teaspoons ground cumin
1 teaspoon ground coriander
3 teaspoons garam masala
2 teaspoons salt

Preparation time: 10 minutes plus
    overnight soaking
Cooking time: 45 minutes

Wash the lentils well, using at least 3
changes of water to remove any dust.
Pick the lentils over and remove any
blemished lentils or foreign objects.
Pour over enough water to cover the
lentils and leave to soak overnight.

The next day, drain away the water
and wash the lentils once again with
2–3 changes of water. Heat the ghee
or cooking oil in a saucepan. Peel
and thinly slice the garlic and fry for
1 minute. Peel the ginger and cut into
very thin strips. Add to the saucepan
and fry for a further 2–3 minutes.

Now add the cloves, cardamoms
and bay leaves. Stir for a further 30
seconds, then add the ground turmeric, chilli powder, black pepper,
cumin and coriander. Stir well and
add the lentils.

Reduce the heat at this stage and
using a spoon turn the lentils to mix
them in well with the spice mixture.
Add just enough water to cover the
lentils, bring to the boil and simmer
until the lentils are fully softened.
Sprinkle in the garam masala and
salt. Cook for a further 2–3 minutes,
stirring occasionally, and then serve.

Chick-pea curry Chenna dal

Chick peas are found throughout the Indian subcontinent. This recipe is a dry frying method, where the peas are soaked overnight and virtually fully cooked before finally being mixed with the spices. They are, I suppose, the Indian equivalent of baked beans. Start the preparations the day before.

225 g/½ lb chick peas
1 × 5-cm/2-inch stick of cinnamon
1 teaspoon salt
50 g/2 oz ghee or 60 ml/2 fl oz
  cooking oil
1 medium onion
2 cloves garlic
1 green pepper
4 dry red chillies
2 teaspoons ground turmeric
1 teaspoon fenugreek seeds
2 teaspoons ground cumin
3 teaspoons ground coriander
2 tablespoons tomato purée
4 cloves
4 cardamoms
2 teaspoons garam masala
2 tablespoons chopped fresh mint

Preparation time: 10 minutes plus
  overnight soaking
Cooking time: 2 hours 15 minutes

Wash the chick peas well, using at least three changes of water. Pick them over and remove any with blemishes. Cover well with cold water and leave overnight to soak.

The next day, wash the chick peas again and put into a saucepan with enough water to cover them.

Add the cinnamon and salt, bring to the boil, cover and simmer gently for 1½ hours until the chick peas are soft. Add extra water if need be to prevent them from sticking. Depending on the state of ripeness of the chick peas more or less boiling will be necessary to make them soft. Once the chick peas are soft, drain and put them to one side.

Heat the ghee or cooking oil in a heavy saucepan and peel and chop finely the onion and garlic. Remove the seeds from the green pepper and chop finely. Add the onion, garlic and pepper to the pan and fry for 2–3 minutes. Crumble in the dried red chillies and stir for a further 30 seconds. Add the turmeric, fenugreek seeds, cumin and coriander powder and stir in well. Now add the tomato purée, cloves and cardamoms. Stir well and continue to cook for a further 2 minutes.

Add the chick peas and a little boiling water, keep stirring and turning the chick peas until they are fully mixed with the spice mixture. After 10–15 minutes, add the garam masala and the chopped mint. Continue to stir and boil off any excess liquid to leave a very dry sauce with the chick peas. Serve piping hot.

Bengal beans Kabli chenna

This is a very good vegetarian dish, which is quite filling in itself as a main course. It can also be used as an accompaniment to virtually any of the curry dishes. You need to start preparing the beans the day before.

170 g/6 oz Bengal beans
50 g/2 oz ghee or 60 ml/2 fl oz
  cooking oil
1 large onion
1 clove garlic
1 × 2.5-cm/1-inch piece of fresh
  ginger
2 red chillies
1 teaspoon ground cumin
2 teaspoons ground coriander
1 teaspoon chilli powder
1 teaspoon ground turmeric
1 teaspoon black pepper
1 tablespoon tomato purée
1 lemon
2 tablespoons chopped coriander
  leaves
1½ teaspoons salt

Preparation time: 10 minutes plus
  overnight soaking
Cooking time: 1 hour 15 minutes

Wash the beans well in at least three changes of water, and soak overnight in plenty of water.

The next day, change the water and boil for 45 minutes until the beans are cooked through. Heat the ghee or cooking oil in a heavy saucepan. Peel and thinly slice the onion and garlic and fry until soft. Peel the ginger and cut into thin strips. Top and tail the chillies, add to the saucepan and continue to fry. Add the cumin, coriander, chilli powder, turmeric and black pepper.

Stir in well and cook for a further minute.

Drain the Bengal beans and spoon them into the saucepan, mixing in well to ensure that they combine with the spices. Now add the tomato purée and continue to cook for a further 10–15 minutes until the beans are warmed through. Squeeze in the juice of the lemon and combine the coriander leaves and salt. Cook for a further 2–3 minutes and serve.

Chilled banana spice Kela sambal

This is a very piquant dish often served as a main vegetable accompaniment to a meat curry. In Bengal very underripe bananas are used, the idea being not to have too much sweetness in the dish. The recipe combines bananas with fairly hot spices, and if you can manage the hotness the dish is well worth trying.

4 underripe bananas
2 lemons
2 green chillies (optional)
2 teaspoons chilli powder
1 teaspoon black pepper
1 teaspoon salt

Preparation time: 15 minutes plus
  1 hour chilling

Peel the bananas and cut them into very thin slices, no more than 0.25 cm/⅛ inch thick. Put the slices in a large bowl and squeeze over the juice from the lemons. Top and tail the chillies, finely chop them and mix with the banana slices. Mix together in another bowl the chilli powder, black pepper and salt, sprinkle over the bananas and chill for 1 hour before serving.

Above: Chenna dal; below left to right: Kabli chenna and Kela sambal.

Turnip curry
Selgum

Root vegetables, such as turnips, are not found all over India, but they are quite common in the wetter parts of eastern India. As with all turnip cooking in other parts of the world the secret, of course, is to cook them slowly so that they have an opportunity to become properly tender.

900 g/2 lb small, sweet turnips
50 g/2 oz ghee or 60 ml/2 fl oz
   cooking oil
1 large onion
1 teaspoon ground cumin
3 teaspoons ground coriander
1 teaspoon ground turmeric
1 teaspoon chilli powder
2 teaspoons sesame seeds
1 teaspoon poppy seeds
1 × 5-cm/2-inch piece of fresh
   ginger
300 ml/½ pint water
2 teaspoons salt
300 ml/½ pint natural yogurt
1 tablespoon chopped coriander
   leaves

Preparation time: 10 minutes
Cooking time: 1 hour

Peel the turnips, and cut into slices about 1 cm/½ inch thick. Heat the ghee or cooking oil in a heavy saucepan and lightly fry the turnips until they just begin to change colour on the outside. Lift out with a slotted spoon and put to one side.

Peel and thinly slice the onion and fry in the remaining oil. Then add the cumin, coriander, turmeric, chilli powder, sesame and poppy seeds. Peel the ginger and cut it into thin strips. Add to the frying pan and continue to cook for a further 4–5 minutes.

Now add the water, bring to the boil and add the salt and turnips. Continue to boil gently for 20 minutes and then stir in the yogurt. Cook for a further 10 minutes until the turnips are soft.

The sauce with this dish should be fairly thick, if it is still too liquid increase the heat to boil off the excess moisture. Sprinkle on the coriander leaves and serve.

Royal lentil curry
Shahi dal

This is a rather grand name given to what, for many, would be a very ordinary dish. However, among the poor of the eastern parts of India in Bangladesh, dal is very much part of a staple diet. Anything added to it to make it slightly different from the everyday meal is, of course, always welcome. This recipe has tomato purée and coconut to give it a lift. You need to start preparing the lentils the day before.

225 g/½ lb lentils
50 g/2 oz ghee or 60 ml/2 fl oz
   cooking oil
1 medium onion
2 cloves garlic
2 green chillies
4 cloves
4 cardamoms
1 × 5-cm/2-inch stick of cinnamon
2 tablespoons tomato purée
1 teaspoon salt
1 teaspoon black pepper
25 g/1 oz desiccated coconut

Preparation time: 10 minutes plus
   overnight soaking
Cooking time: 45 minutes

Wash the lentils well and leave to soak overnight. The next day, put into a large saucepan and add enough boiling water to cover the lentils. Return to the boil and simmer gently until they just begin to soften. Remove the saucepan from the heat and put to one side.

Heat the ghee or cooking oil in a large, heavy frying pan. Peel and thinly slice the onion and garlic and fry until they soften. Top and tail the green chillies and split lengthways. Add to the frying pan and cook for a further 30 seconds or so. Add the cloves, cardamoms and cinnamon and cook for another 2 minutes.

Add this mixture to the saucepan full of lentils and bring back to the boil. Stir in the tomato purée with the salt and black pepper. Cook until the lentils become the consistency of porridge, then stir in the desiccated coconut and serve.

Dry fried spinach
Tali saag

With vegetable cooking, fresh vegetables are naturally desirable, but for this recipe it is, in my view, better to use a block of frozen spinach as it makes the frying process that much easier.

500-g/1-lb block frozen leaf spinach
50 g/2 oz ghee or 60 ml/2 fl oz
   cooking oil
1 small onion
1 teaspoon ground ginger
1 teaspoon black pepper
½ teaspoon chilli powder
1 teaspoon salt

Preparation time: 30 minutes
Cooking time: 20 minutes

Remove the spinach from the freezer and put to one side to allow to soften for 30 minutes or so. Heat the ghee or cooking oil in a large frying pan. Peel and chop the onion finely and fry it gently for 1 minute. Then add the ginger, black pepper and chilli powder. Stir in well for a further 30 seconds.

Add the spinach, stirring so it breaks up. Keep turning it with a wooden spoon to ensure that it is well dispersed in the spice mixture. Sprinkle in the salt, continue to fry until the spinach is totally mixed in with the spices and onion and properly heated through. Serve immediately.

Dry spinach curry
Saag bhajji

This is a very simple dish and one that is whipped up in minutes. It owes its origin to the paddy-field workers in the east of India who traditionally are predominantly women. They are paid piece rates and so would want to spend as little time as possible preparing food. So, this quick method of preparing a vegetarian dish was invented, where the vegetables are literally fried very quickly in a sprinkling of spices.

500 g/1 lb fresh spinach
50 g/2 oz ghee or 60 ml/2 fl oz
   cooking oil
1 medium onion
2 cloves garlic
2 green chillies
1 teaspoon salt
1 teaspoon black pepper

Preparation time: 10 minutes
Cooking time: 15 minutes

Heat the ghee or cooking oil in a heavy saucepan. Peel the onion and garlic, chop them very finely and fry gently in the ghee until they just begin to turn colour.

Meanwhile prepare the spinach by trimming away any hard parts of the stalk and then chopping it very roughly. Top and tail the green chillies and cut into 0.5-cm/¼-inch pieces, add to the saucepan and continue to cook for a further minute. Then add the spinach, turning it constantly until it begins to cook down.

If necessary add a small amount of water, although the idea of this dish is that it should have no water whatsoever. The moisture of the vegetable itself should be sufficient. Sprinkle in the salt and black pepper and once the spinach is fully cooked through it is ready to serve.

Above: Tali saag; centre left to right: Saag bhajji and Shahi dal; below: Selgum.

Dry fried mushrooms
Mushroom bhagar

֍֍֍֍֍֍֍֍֍֍֍֍֍֍֍֍

If you are in the habit of serving mushrooms for breakfast try this recipe as an alternative to straight sautéing in butter. It calls for a little more preparation but the spicing, particularly with the addition of herbs such as thyme and sage, brings out the flavour.

225 g/½ lb button mushrooms
100 g/4 oz ghee or 120 ml/4 fl oz
    cooking oil
1 small onion
2 cloves garlic
1 teaspoon dried thyme
1 teaspoon dried sage
½ teaspoon ground cardamoms
1 teaspoon salt
½ lemon

Preparation time: 5 minutes
Cooking time: 10 minutes

Trim away any hard parts from the mushrooms, slice and put to one side. Heat the ghee or cooking oil in a heavy frying pan. Peel and chop finely the onion and the garlic and fry for 2–3 minutes until they soften, but do not allow them to brown. Stir in the thyme, sage and the ground cardamoms.

Add the mushrooms to the frying pan, stirring constantly to ensure that they are coated in the ghee or cooking oil. Sprinkle in the salt, then squeeze in the juice of the half lemon. Cook for a further minute and serve.

Steamed French beans
Dum ka subzi

֍֍֍֍֍֍֍֍֍֍֍֍֍֍֍֍

This is a very basic recipe designed to add the minimum of spices in order that the flavour of the beans themselves comes through. In India the steaming would traditionally be done by the so-called 'dum' method. This is where a saucepan with a close-fitting concave lid is placed on a charcoal fire, the beans dropped in and hot coals placed in the lid of it so that there is almost as much heat above the saucepan as there is below. In this way a layer of steam is kept above the beans to speed the cooking process.

500 g/1 lb French beans
1 teaspoon salt
1 × 8-cm/3-inch piece of fresh
  ginger
1 large onion
50 g/2 oz ghee or 60 ml/2 fl oz
  cooking oil
1½ teaspoons coriander seeds

Preparation time: 10 minutes
Cooking time: 25 minutes

Cut the beans crossways into 2.5-cm/1-inch pieces, sprinkle with the salt and put to one side. Peel the ginger and cut into thin strips. Peel the onion and chop it fairly coarsely. Heat the ghee or cooking oil in a saucepan and fry the onion and ginger gently until they are soft.

Pound the coriander seeds with a pestle in a mortar until they are broken up but not crushed totally into a powder. Add to the pan. Now add the French beans and enough water just to cover them. There should be as little water as possible in this recipe. If during the cooking process the beans dry out, then add a small amount of water to prevent sticking. Increase the heat until the liquid is boiling. Cover the saucepan and then reduce the heat to a gentle simmer. Cook for 5–10 minutes until the beans just begin to soften and then serve immediately.

Leeks with lime
Subzi nimboo

This is a very similar recipe to a French Vinaigrette, which is often served as a starter. The difference here is that lime juice is traditionally used, although if limes are not available, lemon juice may be substituted.

6 good-sized leeks
2 cloves garlic
300 ml/½ pint water
1 × 5-cm/2-inch stick of cinnamon
2 bay leaves
½ teaspoon saffron threads
1 teaspoon salt
2 tablespoons olive oil
½ teaspoon black pepper
½ teaspoon chilli powder
½ teaspoon mace
6 limes or 3 lemons

Preparation time: 10 minutes
Cooking time: 30 minutes plus 2
  hours chilling

Cut away most of the green leaves from the leeks, leaving just a little green at the top of the white part, and trim away the roots from the bottom of each leek. Peel the cloves of garlic and crush them, rubbing all over the leeks. Lay the leeks down in a large saucepan or frying pan and cover with water. Add the cinnamon and bay leaves, together with the saffron and salt. Bring to the boil and simmer for 15 minutes until the leeks are tender.

Remove the leeks from the liquid with a slotted spoon and put to one side. Boil the liquid to reduce its volume by half and allow to cool. Beat the liquid together with the olive oil, black pepper, chilli powder and mace. Squeeze in the juice from the limes or lemons. Arrange the leeks in a serving dish and pour the marinade over the leeks. Put into a refrigerator and chill for 2 hours before serving.

From left to right: Mushroom bhagar, Dum ka subzi and Subzi nimboo.

Chapter Seven
Vegetable dishes of
southern India

These are very much the vegetable dishes of the poor. The Hindus of the south for economic and religious reasons have built their whole cooking culture around the available vegetables. Predominately it is the pulses, the chick peas and the dals, in their numerous forms that make up the main dishes. These pulses vary from making simple soups to quite complicated dishes which incorporate meat combined with the dal to make the dish more filling. The vegetable cooking of the south also reflects the fact that rice is the predominant carbohydrate. Whereas in the north there are a number of methods of cooking rice which tend to be rather complicated, such as the Pilaus and the Biryanis, in the south most people prefer their rice plain boiled. It would be wrong not to count rice itself as a major vegetable in the cooking of southern India. Many dishes incorporate rice together with one or more dals to give it added flavour.

When it comes to spicing, the cooks of southern India aim to provide a flavour which creates a complete meal in itself. Therefore, the vegetable dishes of southern India are designed as dishes in their own right, rather than as accompaniments to meat as so many southern Indians from the cradle to the grave will eat nothing else but vegetables.

Vegetable curry
Subzi ka salan

This is a very basic recipe and can be adapted to all manner of vegetables. This version uses green beans, carrots and cauliflower. The essential point is to precook the vegetables so that they do not spend too much time in the cooking process and have their stuffing knocked out of them!

1 small cauliflower
225 g/½ lb carrots
225 g/½ lb French beans
100 g/4 oz ghee or 120 ml/4 fl oz
    cooking oil
1 large onion
2 teaspoons chilli powder
1 tablespoon ground cumin
1 × 5-cm/2-inch stick of cinnamon
½ tablespoon ground coriander
2 teaspoons ground turmeric
4 cloves
4 cardamoms
100 g/4 oz tomato purée
300 ml/½ pint chicken stock
2 teaspoons salt
2 teaspoons black pepper

Preparation time: 10 minutes
Cooking time: 25 minutes

Cut away the leaves of the cauliflower and break it up into florets. Scrape the carrots, top and tail the French beans and cut into bite-size pieces. Parboil all the vegetables together in a large saucepan.

Heat the ghee or cooking oil in a large saucepan and peel and slice the onion very thinly. Fry the onion gently until it softens, then add the chilli powder, cumin, cinnamon, coriander and turmeric. Cook for 2 minutes or so and add the cloves and cardamoms. Add the tomato purée, mixing in well, and cook for a further minute.

Drain the vegetables of their cooking water and add to the pan together with the chicken stock. Add the salt and black pepper, cover the saucepan and simmer for 10–15 minutes until the vegetables are cooked.

Above: Masoor dal; below left to right: Subzi ka salan and Bhindi bhajji.

Indian lentils
Masoor dal

The simplest way of cooking lentils is to boil them up with water to make a thick sauce reminiscent of Pease Pudding. This recipe, though, elevates the humble lentil to something rather more special, with the addition of coconut milk, desiccated coconut and the aromatics, cloves, cardamoms and cinnamon. Masoor is the name given to the dal most familiar to us, known here in the West as the pink split lentil.

225 g/½ lb pink split lentils or
    masoor dal
1 medium onion
2 cloves garlic
50 g/2 oz ghee or 60 ml/2 fl oz
    cooking oil
2 teaspoons ground coriander
2 teaspoons ground cumin
2 teaspoons ground turmeric
1 teaspoon chilli powder
4 cardamoms
4 cloves
1 × 5-cm/2-inch stick of cinnamon
1½ teaspoons salt
100 g/4 oz desiccated coconut
2 tomatoes

Preparation time: 10 minutes
Cooking time: 50 minutes

Wash the lentils well with plenty of water, put into a saucepan and add enough water to cover. Bring to the boil and boil gently until the lentils are soft.

Meanwhile, peel the onion and garlic and cut into thin slices. Heat the ghee or cooking oil in a frying pan. Add the onion and garlic and when they begin to soften, add the coriander, cumin, turmeric and chilli powder, mixing in well. Cook for 2 minutes, then add the cardamoms, cloves and cinnamon.

Now add the lentils together with any liquid they have been boiling in and stir rapidly to ensure the spices mix in well. Add a little more water if necessary. (This dish should be fairly liquid.) Add the salt and continue to cook for a further 5 minutes. Blend the desiccated coconut with 150 ml/¼ pint water in a liquidiser and add to the pan. Chop the tomatoes into quarters and add to the dal just before serving.

Okra curry
Bhindi bhajji

Okra or ladies' fingers are one and the same thing and the name depends on which part of the world you live in. It is a strange-looking lime-green vegetable, long and tapering. If you cut it crossways you reveal a perfect hexagon. I have always found it to be one of the most interestingly flavoured vegetables but only when it is cooked fresh.

Sadly, many Indian restaurants in the West insist on using the tinned version and I am afraid that the canning process often results in the

vegetable becoming very stringy. There should be no excuse nowadays for serving tinned okra as in most large cities the fresh vegetable is nearly always available. It is important, though, to ensure that you buy okra in peak condition. They should be firm to the touch and be free from blemishes. Okra that have been lying around for too long are soft and usually covered with black spots. The true test of freshness is when the pods snap open crisply.

One thing to watch out for when dealing with this vegetable is that its outer surface is covered with tiny needles almost invisible to the naked eye. If these needles are inadvertently rubbed into an eye they can be very irritating.

500 g/1 lb fresh okra
1 teaspoon salt
2 teaspoons black pepper
1 large onion
2 cloves garlic
100 g/4 oz ghee or 120 ml/4 fl oz cooking oil
2 teaspoons ground coriander
1 teaspoon ground turmeric
1 teaspoon chilli powder
1 teaspoon garam masala
50 g/2 oz tomato purée

Preparation time: 10 minutes
Cooking time: 20 minutes

Top and tail the okra and cut crossways into pieces about 1 cm/½ inch long. Sprinkle with the salt and black pepper. Peel the onion and garlic and slice thinly. Heat the ghee or cooking oil in a large saucepan and fry the onion and garlic until they soften. Add the coriander, turmeric, chilli powder and garam masala. Cook for a further minute, stirring well to ensure the spices do not stick to the bottom of the pan.

Now add the okra and cook for 3 minutes, turning the pieces gently to ensure they are well coated with the spices. It is important not to crush the okra at this stage. Add the tomato purée. This is supposed to be a dry curry but if it appears too dry, a little boiling water may be added to prevent the okra from sticking to the bottom of the pan. Cover the saucepan and simmer gently until they are cooked. Test for this by biting a piece. It should be soft but retain just a little of its crunch.

Mixed vegetable curry
Aviyal

A mixed vegetable curry is exactly what it says it is, a curry full of mixed vegetables, but in southern India this would often mean the inclusion of all kinds of exotic vegetables not normally available in the West. In this recipe I have included two of these, which with a little bit of searching you may be able to track down: drumsticks (which are just like beans) and bitter gourd, which is a long, thin vegetable with a very gnarled, dark green surface. If you cannot get these, then substitute French beans for the drumsticks and the equivalent weight of courgettes for the bitter gourd.

225 g/½ lb runner beans
225 g/½ lb carrots
2 green peppers
225 g/½ lb drumsticks or French beans
225 g/½ lb bitter gourd or courgettes
170 g/6 oz fresh coconut or 100 g/ 4 oz desiccated coconut
300 ml/½ pint water
100 g/4 oz ghee or 120 ml/4 fl oz cooking oil
1 large onion
2 cloves garlic
1 × 5-cm/2-inch piece of fresh ginger
1 teaspoon mustard seeds
2 teaspoons black pepper
3 teaspoons ground coriander
2 teaspoons ground turmeric
4 green chillies
4 teaspoons garam masala
2 teaspoons salt

Preparation time: 15 minutes
Cooking time: 30 minutes

Prepare the vegetables – string the runner beans and cut them crossways into pieces about 4 cm/1½ inches long. Scrape the carrots and cut these into sticks measuring 5 × 1 cm/2 × ½ inch. Remove the seeds from the peppers and cut these into large strips measuring 5 × 1 cm/2 × ½ inch. Top and tail the drumsticks or French beans and cut into 5-cm/2-inch pieces. Top and ta. the bitter gourd or courgettes and cut these into slices about 0.5 cm/¼ inch thick. Toss the vegetables together in a large bowl and cover with a minimum amount of water to prevent them drying out. Meanwhile put the coconut into a liquidiser, heat the 300 ml/½ pint of water to just below boiling point and pour into the liquidiser. Blend for 1 minute to produce a smooth liquid. Add a little more water if necessary.

Heat the ghee or cooking oil in a large, heavy saucepan (at least 2-litre/3–4-pint capacity). Peel the

Lentils with cauliflower
Gobi dal

While the various pulses are used very often on their own with the addition of perhaps a little spicing, there are curries that use lentils as a base and this is an example. The addition of cashew nuts, coconut and cauliflower serves to bulk it out into a very satisfying dish, perfect for vegetarians.

225 g/½ lb pink split lentils or masoor dal
1 small cauliflower
2 medium onions
100 g/4 oz ghee or 120 ml/4 fl oz cooking oil
1 teaspoon chilli powder
2 teaspoons black pepper
½ tablespoon ground cumin
½ tablespoon ground coriander
2 teaspoons ground turmeric
½ lemon
600 ml/1 pint chicken stock
50 g/2 oz desiccated coconut
½ tablespoon flour
1 teaspoon salt
100 g/4 oz cashew nuts

Preparation time: 5 minutes
Cooking time: 40 minutes

Wash the lentils well and drain off the water. Peel and finely chop the onions. Heat the ghee or cooking oil in a large saucepan and fry the onions. As they soften, add the chilli powder, black pepper, cumin, coriander and turmeric. Stir in well and cook for 30 seconds. Add the lentils. Stir well to ensure that each grain is coated and squeeze in the lemon juice.

Cut the cauliflower into small florets and add to the pan. Add the chicken stock and the desiccated coconut. Bring to the boil and simmer for 20 minutes. Mix the flour with some of the liquid to form a smooth paste and pour into the saucepan. Add the salt and cashew nuts. Cook for a further 5–10 minutes until the lentils have formed a thick sauce. This dish is a complete meal in itself when served with plain boiled rice.

Spiced cauliflower
Gobi musallum

This dish is found in one shape or another throughout the whole of India, but specifically in the west and the south. It uses cauliflower florets and the addition of tamarind and vinegar gives it the sourness which typifies this dish. It is also quite a spicy dish, so watch out!

1 large cauliflower
25 g/1 oz tamarind
300 ml/½ pint boiling water
50 g/2 oz ghee or 60 ml/2 fl oz cooking oil
2 teaspoons chilli powder
2 teaspoons ground coriander
2 teaspoons ground cumin
2 teaspoons ground turmeric
2 teaspoons black pepper
1 tablespoon vinegar
1 teaspoon salt

Preparation time: 2 hours
Cooking time: 30 minutes

Soak the tamarind husk in the boiling water and leave to soak for approximately 2 hours. Prepare the cauliflower by paring away all the outer green leaves, cut off the florets and discard the central stalk of the cauliflower.

Then heat the ghee or cooking oil and mix in the chilli powder, coriander, cumin, turmeric and black pepper. Stir for 2 minutes and then add the cauliflower florets, turning them gently to ensure that they are nicely coated with spice mixture. Squeeze the tamarind pulp over the water in which it has been soaking and discard. Pour the tamarind water into the saucepan and increase the heat. Now add the vinegar and salt and continue to cook very gently for about 15 minutes until the cauliflower is tender.

onion and garlic and slice them very thinly. Fry them gently in the ghee until soft. Peel the ginger and cut it into thin strips. Add to the saucepan, frying for another minute. Add the mustard seeds, black pepper, coriander and turmeric and stir for another minute.

You are now ready to add the vegetable which should be done a little at a time, turning them as you do so. When all the vegetables are in the saucepan and reasonably well coated with the spicy sauce, add the coconut purée, increase the heat and bring to the boil, cover the saucepan and simmer for 10 minutes.

Meanwhile, top and tail the green chillies and cut into pieces about 0.5 cm/¼ inch long. Add to the saucepan together with the garam masala and salt. Stir in well and simmer for a further 5 minutes. There should be not too much liquid with this dish; if there is, increase the heat to rapidly boil off the excess moisture.

From left to right: Gobi musallum, Gobi dal and Aviyal.

Marrow curry
Goodhi bhajji

This recipe is very much in the style of the classic vegetarian recipes of southern India, although the large marrows such as the type grown for prizes in the West are not usually readily available in India. This recipe can be used either for marrows or for courgettes; in any event, you want 1.3 kg/2½ lb of young marrows (preferably 2 small ones) or 1.3 kg/2½ lb of courgettes. The essence of this dish is not to overdo the spicing so you can actually taste the subtle flavour of the marrow itself.

1.3 kg/2½ lb young marrows or
    courgettes
120 ml/4 fl oz sesame seed oil
1 teaspoon mustard seeds
1 teaspoon ground turmeric
½ teaspoon chilli powder
½ teaspoon black pepper
1 teaspoon onion seeds
1 large onion
100 g/4 oz desiccated coconut
1 teaspoon garam masala
½ teaspoon salt

Preparation time: 10 minutes
Cooking time: 30 minutes

Prepare the marrow by scooping out the seeds and then peel away the outer skin. Cut into 4-cm/1½-inch cubes. If you are using courgettes for this, the preparation is slightly different: top and tail the courgettes and cut them crossways into 1-cm/½-inch thick slices.

Heat the sesame seed oil in a large saucepan until it just begins to smoke. Reduce the heat and add the mustard seeds, which will immediately splutter. Further reduce the heat and add the turmeric, chilli powder, black pepper and onion seeds. Stir for another 2 minutes or so on a gentle heat. Peel and thinly slice the onion and add to the saucepan to fry until just soft.

Now add the marrow and turn it gently so as not to break up the pieces. Continue to cook for a further 5 minutes, and sprinkle in the coconut, garam masala and salt. The idea of this dish is to cook it in whatever juice is available; however, if it seems a little dry and there is a danger of the marrow sticking (de-pending on their condition different marrows absorb large or small amounts of water), you can add a little water. Cover the pan with a tight-fitting lid and simmer very gently for about another 10 minutes until the marrow is cooked.

Above: Dum arvi; below left to right: Goodhi bhajji and Aloo bogar.

Steamed yam
Dum arvi

๙๏๙๏๙๏๙๏๙๏๙๏๙๏๙๏๙๏๙๏๙๏

Yams are more often associated with food of the Caribbean and African countries, however they are used in south India and in central India. To my mind, there is not a lot to recommend the yam as it is a rather starchy vegetable, far starchier in fact than the average potato. However, this is an interesting dish and if you have ever wondered how yams are cooked this is a recipe to try.

900 g/2 lb yams
170 g/6 oz ghee or 175 ml/6 fl oz
    cooking oil
1 large onion
1 × 8-cm/3-inch piece of fresh
    ginger
2 teaspoons ground coriander
2 teaspoons garam masala
1 teaspoon chilli powder
1 teaspoon black pepper
2 teaspoons ground turmeric
2 teaspoons salt
4 green chillies

Preparation time: 1 hour 40
    minutes
Cooking time: 1 hour 20 minutes

Wash the yams well and peel away their hard outer coating. Cut into pieces about 2.5–4 cm/1–1½ inches across and soak them in water for 1½ hours so that some of the excess starch floats away.

Heat the ghee or cooking oil in a large saucepan and fry the yam very gently so that the pieces just start to change colour on the outside. Remove the yam with a slotted spoon and place to one side. Peel and thinly slice the onion. Fry it in the remaining ghee. Peel the ginger and cut it into thin strips. Add it to the saucepan and continue to fry gently. As the onion begins to soften, add the coriander, garam masala, chilli powder, black pepper and turmeric.

Stir in well and after 2 minutes add the yam pieces, sprinkle in the salt and stir to ensure the yam is coated with the mixture.

Transfer the whole mixture to a warm casserole and put into a preheated oven (180°C/350°F/Gas Mark 4), with the casserole covered with aluminium foil. After 30 minutes, top and tail the green chillies and add to the casserole.

After a further 30 minutes, check to see whether the yams are tender. When they are, they are ready to serve. Some people like to serve them with butter on top. This helps to counter the extreme starchiness of this dish and it certainly does make it tastier.

Dry potato curry
Aloo bogar

๙๏๙๏๙๏๙๏๙๏๙๏๙๏๙๏๙๏๙๏๙๏

This is a recipe which is in general use throughout India but is very typical of the south in as much as it uses the bogar method of cooking: the quick frying of hot spices which are then combined with a vegetable. The method is favoured for vegetables because it allows all the flavour of the spices to be released without increasing the cooking time of the vegetables. This way the vegetables stay at their freshest. This recipe calls for the use of curry leaves and these are available at most Asian stores. As a substitute, you can use bay leaves. This is probably one of the hottest vegetarian dishes made in southern India, so beware!

900 g/2 lb potatoes
100 g/4 oz ghee or 120 ml/4 fl oz
    cooking oil
1 teaspoon ground cumin
½ teaspoon mustard seeds
5 curry leaves or bay leaves
6 dried red chillies
2 cloves garlic
2 teaspoons salt
½ teaspoon ground turmeric
2 tablespoons water
2 fresh green chillies

Preparation time: 15 minutes
Cooking time: 20 minutes

Peel the potatoes and cut them into 2.5-cm/1-inch cubes. Put into a saucepan, cover with water and boil for 10 minutes until they begin to soften. Drain and put to one side.

Heat the ghee or cooking oil in a heavy saucepan and add the cumin, mustard seeds, curry leaves or bay leaves and the dried red chillies, left whole. Cook for 2 minutes. Peel the garlic, thinly slice it and add to the saucepan. When it is brown add the potato cubes, salt, turmeric and the water. Cover the saucepan with a tight-fitting lid and allow to steam for 5 minutes or so. Top and tail the green chillies, cut into ½-cm/¼-inch pieces and sprinkle into the dish. As soon as the potato is fully cooked it is ready to serve.

Coconut curry
Narial ka salan

For this recipe it is essential to use fresh coconut which is quite common in the south of India. To check the freshness of a coconut, make sure that the eyes at the top of the coconut are intact and there is no trace of mouldiness around the top end of the coconut. It is also better but not essential that there is a little liquid left inside, although much of this can evaporate as the coconut is transported. To be sure, give the coconut a shake and if there is liquid inside and it looks fairly intact, then the chances are you will have a good one. This recipe is called Coconut Curry but it involves quite a lot of eggs, so it is really egg curry with coconut. However, the flavour is very good!

1 fresh coconut
4 eggs
1 lemon
2 large onions
100 g/4 oz ghee or 120 ml/4 fl oz
    cooking oil
1 teaspoon chilli powder
1 tablespoon ground coriander
2 teaspoons ground cumin
1 teaspoon black pepper
½ teaspoon saffron
1 teaspoon salt

Preparation time: 15 minutes
Cooking time: 25 minutes

Break open the coconut, remove the meat and cut it into thin slices. Squeeze the lemon juice over the coconut. Peel and chop the onions. Heat the ghee or cooking oil and fry the onions. As they soften, stir in the chilli powder, coriander, cumin and black pepper. Add the coconut meat and the saffron, stir in well, adding about 300 ml/½ pint of water and the salt.

Cover the saucepan and simmer for about 10–15 minutes until the coconut softens. Meanwhile, hard-boil the eggs, remove the shells and cut into wedges. Arrange on a serving plate and when the Coconut Curry is cooked, pour it over the top of the eggs.

Coconut with rice
Narial chawal

This is a good way of using coconut. It certainly makes a very different rice dish. Cooking it is fairly simple, once you have managed to break open the nut and extract the meat!

1 fresh coconut
500 g/1 lb Basmati rice
1 medium onion
100 g/4 oz ghee or 120 ml/4 fl oz
    cooking oil
2 teaspoons salt
1 teaspoon black pepper

Preparation time: 15 minutes
Cooking time: 25 minutes

Using a screwdriver or pointed implement, make two holes in the top of the coconut to drain out any milk that might be inside and keep this to one side. Break open the coconut and remove the meat. Divide the meat into two, chop one half roughly into pieces and blend together with the milk from the coconut in a liquidiser, adding more water if needed to make a fairly thick pulp. Grate the remaining coconut, using the largest side of the grater. Place the grated coconut to one side.

Meanwhile wash the rice well and remove any husks or stones. Peel and very finely chop the onion. Heat the ghee or cooking oil in a large saucepan and add the onion, cook for 2 minutes and then add the rice, drained of as much water as possible. Stir well to ensure each grain is well coated with the oil.

Now add the coconut milk mixture from the liquidiser and a sufficient amount of water just to cover the rice. Increase the heat and bring to the boil. Sprinkle in the salt and black pepper, simmer for 15 minutes, until the rice is *al dente*. Quickly mix in the rest of the grated coconut, keeping a little on one side to act as a garnish on top of the rice. You will note that the rice will stick together. Do not expect every grain to separate as this dish is designed to be rather more solid due to the presence of the coconut milk, binding the rice grains together. In any event, you will have a very good excuse for not having fluffy separated rice!

Cabbage cooked
with coconut
Cabbage foogath

A Foogath is a dish very typical of southern India. It is a sort of cooked mixed salad, although more recently individual vegetables have been given the Foogath treatment on their own. Quite often the vegetables are precooked and for that reason it is a very good recipe when you have leftovers. This recipe calls for half a cabbage, precooked by boiling, but if you are not using leftovers do ensure that if you start with a fresh cabbage you do not overcook it. Boil it but try to make sure there is some of the crunch left in it before starting on the Foogath process.

½ cabbage
90 ml/3 fl oz sesame seed oil
1 large onion
2 cloves garlic
1 × 8-cm/3-inch piece of fresh
    ginger
4 green chillies
1 teaspoon salt
1 tablespoon desiccated coconut

Preparation time: 5 minutes
Cooking time: 15 minutes

Cut away any bruised outer skin of the cabbage and cut it into small strips. Precook the cabbage by boiling it for 5 minutes. Heat the sesame seed oil in a large saucepan. Peel and thinly slice the onion, garlic and ginger and fry in the sesame seed oil until they begin to soften.

Top and tail the green chillies, cut into 0.5-cm/¼-inch pieces and add to the saucepan. Cook for a further 2 minutes and add the cabbage together with any small amount of liquid that might be left with it. Reduce the heat and turn the cabbage constantly to ensure that it is well mixed in with the spice mixture. Finally, sprinkle in the salt and desiccated coconut. Continue to cook until the cabbage is properly heated through.

Above left to right: Narial ka salan and Narial chawal; below: Cabbage foogath.

Sweet and sour cabbage
Khat meeti gobi

꘍꘍꘍꘍꘍꘍꘍꘍꘍꘍꘍꘍꘍꘍꘍꘍꘍

When you think of a sweet and sour dish in India it is very different indeed from the sweet and sour one used in Chinese cooking. Here, there is no thick, syrupy sauce to go with the dish, rather the sourness comes from the addition of vinegar and/or tamarind, with honey providing the sweetness. Honey in India comes from what is known as the Honey Fly, the literal translation of the Hindi word for bee.

½ large cabbage
50 g/2 oz tamarind
150 ml/¼ pint boiling water
50 g/2 oz ghee or 60 ml/2 fl oz
   cooking oil
1 teaspoon ground coriander
2 teaspoons garam masala
1 teaspoon black pepper
1 tablespoon vinegar
2 teaspoons salt
2 tablespoons clear honey

Preparation time: 35 minutes
Cooking time: 20 minutes

Soak the tamarind in the boiling water for 30 minutes. Meanwhile, cut away any bruised outer skin of the cabbage and cut the cabbage into very small strips. This may be done using a large coleslaw grater. Put the cabbage to one side.

Heat the ghee or cooking oil in a large saucepan and add the coriander, garam masala and black pepper. Stir in well and add the cabbage. Turn the cabbage so that the spice mixture is nicely distributed. Next, strain the tamarind water into the saucepan, add the vinegar and bring to the boil. Add the salt and the honey and stir well to ensure it is well coated. Cover the saucepan with a tight-fitting lid and simmer gently for about 10–15 minutes.

This dish is best when the cabbage is not fully cooked but still slightly crunchy. If you feel a little more water is needed then do not hesitate to add some, but remember that when properly cooked this dish should not be awash with water!

Rice with coriander and mint
Chawal dhania podina

꘍꘍꘍꘍꘍꘍꘍꘍꘍꘍꘍꘍꘍꘍꘍꘍꘍

As rice forms such a large part of the staple diet of most Indians, particularly in the south, there are a number of ways of trying to dress it up. Rice with coriander and mint is, to my mind, one of the most interesting flavours, combining the aromatic mint with the sharp, almost brackish flavour of the coriander. What is also interesting about this dish is the way in which the rice is half-cooked by boiling, then mixed with the spice mixture and yogurt and finished off. As with Coconut Rice, it is not too important that the grains of rice are separate in this dish, so it is a good recipe for beginners to the art of rice cooking.

225 g/½ lb Basmati rice
½ teaspoon saffron threads
100 g/4 oz ghee or 120 ml/4 fl oz
   cooking oil
1 × 5-cm/2-inch stick of cinnamon
4 cloves
1 × 8-cm/3-inch piece of fresh
   ginger
300 ml/½ pint natural yogurt
1 medium onion
2 tablespoons chopped coriander
   leaves
2 tablespoons chopped mint
2 teaspoons salt
2 teaspoons black pepper

Preparation time: 5 minutes
Cooking time: 30 minutes

Wash the rice well and cover with water in a heavy saucepan. Bring to the boil, adding the saffron threads. Boil rapidly for 10 minutes, remove from the heat and drain off the water.

Heat the ghee or cooking oil in a large saucepan until it begins to smoke, reduce the heat and throw in the cinnamon and cloves. Cook for about a minute. Peel the ginger and chop it very finely. Add to the saucepan and stir in well. Add the rice and stir in well, making sure that the grains are well coated with the mixture. Pour in the yogurt and mix in well. Peel and chop the onion. Add the coriander, mint, onion, salt and black pepper to the pan. Cover the

saucepan with a tight-fitting lid and increase the heat, shaking the saucepan constantly. As soon as all the excess liquid is absorbed, and the rice is cooked, the dish is ready to serve.

Above left to right: Khat meeti gobi and Chawal dhania podina; below: Chawal sambal.

Coconut salad
Narial sambal

❖❖❖❖❖❖❖❖❖❖❖❖❖❖❖❖❖❖❖❖❖

Sambals are found throughout the south of India and cover anything from a very simple preparation of vegetables and a few onions to a selection of mixed vegetables combined together with red chillies and lemon juice.

Coconut salad can be made with desiccated coconut or fresh coconut. It tends to be a little fiery, so this is not a dish for those unused to eating Indian food!

225 g/½ lb desiccated coconut or the flesh of 1 fresh coconut
2 large onions
2 teaspoons chilli powder
2 teaspoons black pepper
1 teaspoon salt
2 lemons
4 green chillies

Preparation time: 10 minutes plus 1 hour chilling

Peel the onions and chop them fairly finely. Mix together with the desiccated coconut or grated fresh coconut until they are well blended. During the mixing process sprinkle in the chilli powder, black pepper, salt and juice from the two lemons. Top and tail the green chillies and chop. Mix these into the dish. Chill for an hour or so in a refrigerator and serve.

Spiced aubergines Baigan masala

This dish calls for a little care in the cooking as the idea is to cook the aubergine with a combination of steaming and frying in as little liquid as possible, relying on the masala, which is the spice mixture, to bring out the flavour. It is a very interesting method of cooking and one well worth trying!

900 g/2 lb aubergines (the long variety)
1 lemon
2 tablespoons vinegar
2 teaspoons chilli powder
2 teaspoons ginger powder
2 teaspoons garam masala
2 teaspoons black pepper
1 teaspoon ground turmeric
50 g/2 oz desiccated coconut
100 g/4 oz ghee or 120 ml/4 fl oz cooking oil
1 medium onion
2 cloves garlic

Preparation time: 45 minutes
Cooking time: 30 minutes

Squeeze the juice of the lemon into a liquidiser and add the vinegar and chilli powder, together with the ginger, garam masala, black pepper, ground turmeric and desiccated coconut. Blend together for 1½ minutes to make a spicy, stiff masala. Meanwhile, prepare the aubergines by removing the hard, tough green leaves and cutting into slices about 1 cm/½ inch thick (there is no need to remove the outer skins or seeds). Lay the slices out in a dish and spread the masala over them. Leave for 30 minutes on one side for the spices to soak in.

Heat the ghee or cooking oil in a heavy saucepan with a close-fitting lid. Peel and slice the onion and garlic thinly and fry until soft. Now add the aubergines, together with any leftover masala. Cover the saucepan and cook on a very low heat for 20 minutes. As soon as the aubergines are tender they are ready to serve.

It is important during this cooking process to check every now and then to see that they have not dried out and if necessary turn them over, but do this gently so as not to break them up during the cooking.

Aubergines with tamarind Baigan bhagar

This is a dish with an interesting flavour. The idea of using the tamarind in this dish is to create a counterbalance to the flavour of the aubergines.

750 g/1½ lb aubergines
150 ml/¼ pint boiling water
50 g/2 oz tamarind
100 g/4 oz ghee or 120 ml/4 fl oz cooking oil
1 large onion
2 cloves garlic
1½ teaspoons chilli powder
2 teaspoons ground coriander
2 teaspoons ground turmeric
2 teaspoons mustard seeds
2 bay leaves
100 g/4 oz fresh coconut
2 teaspoons clear honey
1 teaspoon salt
2 teaspoons garam masala
2 green chillies

Preparation time: 2 hours
Cooking time: 35 minutes

Pour the boiling water over the tamarind husk and soak for 2 hours. Meanwhile, prepare the aubergines by trimming off the hard green leaves, cutting lengthways four times, then crossways to produce cubes measuring about 4 cm/1½ inches.

Heat the ghee or cooking oil in a frying pan and gently sauté the aubergine pieces for a minute or two. Remove them from the frying pan with a slotted spoon and place to one side. Peel and slice the onion. Fry the onion in the remaining oil until it is soft. Peel and thinly slice the garlic. Add to the frying pan, together with the chilli powder, coriander, turmeric and mustard seeds.

Transfer the mixture to a heavy saucepan and stir in the bay leaves and fresh coconut, cut into thin slices. Strain the tamarind water into the saucepan, leaving the pulp behind. Squeeze the pulp to extract the last drop. Now, stir in the honey and add the aubergines. Sprinkle in the salt, cover the saucepan tightly and simmer for 10-15 minutes until the aubergines are soft. Check from time to time to see that the dish is not sticking and turn the aubergines gently so as not to break them.

Five minutes into the simmering process, sprinkle in the garam masala and the green chillies, chopped into 0.5-cm/¼-inch pieces. Stir into the sauce. If necessary a little water may be added to increase the moisture level.

Parsee egg curry Ekoori

This recipe is for those who like an Indian version of scrambled eggs. Eggs are quite freely available in India although they tend to be rather small due to the poor conditions under which the poultry have to scratch around and find food. However, they are rather tasty; the whites tend to be much thicker than the whites of the average Western factory-farmed eggs.

6 eggs
1 medium onion
50 g/2 oz ghee or 60 ml/2 fl oz cooking oil
2 green chillies
2 teaspoons ground ginger
1 teaspoon ground turmeric
1 teaspoon black pepper
1 teaspoon salt
2 tablespoons chopped coriander leaves

Preparation time: 5 minutes
Cooking time: 10 minutes

Peel the onion and chop it finely. Heat the ghee or cooking oil in a large saucepan and fry the onion gently until it begins to soften. Top and tail the green chillies and cut into 0.5-cm/¼-inch pieces, add to the saucepan and continue to stir. Add the ginger and stir for 30 seconds.

Beat the eggs together with the turmeric, black pepper and the salt and then beat in the coriander leaves. Pour the mixture into the saucepan and mix in well with the onion. Continue to cook as for scrambled eggs, scraping the cooked eggs from the side and bottom of the pan constantly. Once the eggs are cooked they are ready to serve.

Above: Baigan masala; centre: Ekoori; below: Baigan bhagar.

Semolina with vegetables Uppama

❧❧❧❧❧❧❧❧❧❧❧❧❧❧❧❧❧

Uppama is a very interesting dish. I know there are many people with terrible memories of semolina from their schooldays, but this is a very good combination of spices, vegetables and semolina. What is more it makes a very filling dish. If it is a long time since you tried semolina give this one a try!

100 g/4 oz white lentils or urd dal
2 tablespoons sesame seed oil
1 teaspoon mustard seeds
1 medium onion
1 clove garlic
2 green chillies
100 g/4 oz semolina
4 carrots
2 medium tomatoes
1 × 8-cm/3-inch piece of fresh ginger
1 lemon
2 teaspoons salt
2 teaspoons black pepper
600 ml/1 pint water
2 tablespoons chopped coriander leaves

Preparation time: 10 minutes
Cooking time: 30 minutes

Wash the dal and shake free as much water as possible. Heat the sesame seed oil in a large, heavy saucepan until a single mustard seed dropped into it splutters. When this happens, add the rest of the mustard seeds and cook for 1 minute. Then add the dal (be careful the fat does not spit at you at this stage) and stir in well, ensuring the grains are well coated with the sesame seed oil. Reduce the heat and cook gently for 5 minutes or so.

Meanwhile, peel the onion and chop it finely. Add to the saucepan. Peel and thinly slice the garlic and add to the pan. Top and tail the green chillies and chop into small pieces. Add to the saucepan and sprinkle in the semolina, stirring constantly to ensure it is well dispersed throughout the dal. Scrape the carrots and cut them into rounds, about 0.25 cm/⅛ inch thick.

Chop the tomatoes roughly and add them, together with the carrots, to the saucepan, again mixing well. Peel the ginger and slice thinly into strips, add to the saucepan and continue to cook for another minute or so. Squeeze in the juice from the lemon and add the salt, black pepper and the water. Bring to the boil, reduce the heat and simmer for 10 minutes until the semolina begins to thicken. As soon as this happens the dish is ready to serve. Garnish with the chopped coriander leaves.

Fritters with yogurt Pakora ka raeta

❧❧❧❧❧❧❧❧❧❧❧❧❧❧❧❧❧

This is a very popular dish in the south of India and relatively simple to make. It is an interesting combination of the crisp spiciness in the pakora (which are the little batter balls made from gram flour) and the sharp coolness of yogurt. In my view, although the dish does keep for some time it is best when the pakoras have been freshly made and still retain some of their crispness; otherwise they tend to go soggy after prolonged immersion in the yogurt. The dish is a good accompaniment to any main course or as a starter.

900 ml/1½ pints natural yogurt
1 teaspoon dry mustard powder
1 teaspoon chilli powder
1 teaspoon salt
1 lemon
1 teaspoon vinegar
1 medium onion
170 g/6 oz chick-pea flour
oil for deep frying
paprika to garnish

Preparation time: 2 hours 15 minutes
Cooking time: 20 minutes

Put 300 ml/½ pint of the yogurt into a liquidiser and add the dry mustard powder, chilli powder and salt. Squeeze in the juice of ½ the lemon and the vinegar. Grate half of the lemon peel and put into the liquidiser. Liquidise into a smooth sauce and add to the chick-pea flour, blending well to form a rather thick batter. Cover the bowl and put into a refrigerator to stand for 2 hours.

To cook the pakoras, heat up some cooking oil in a deep or medium-deep frying pan. The oil is hot enough to cook the pakoras when a small quantity of batter dropped into the saucepan immediately sizzles and after a few seconds rises to the surface of the oil. When you have reached this temperature, spoon in little dollops of the mixture, about half a tablespoon at a time. Turn with a slotted spoon to ensure they are fried evenly on all sides. When they have browned nicely, remove them and place on kitchen paper to drain. When you have made the pakoras, carefully combine them with the remaining yogurt, sprinkle on a little paprika to garnish and serve.

Bananas with yogurt Kela ka raeta

❧❧❧❧❧❧❧❧❧❧❧❧❧❧❧❧❧

Bananas grow extremely well in much of the poor soil and monsoon climate that exist in many parts of southern India and so it is natural enough that they should be combined with yogurt to serve as a very good cooler to go with the hot and often fiery dishes of the south. Many people find this recipe a little too sweet but in my view the sweetness along with the coolness of the yogurt serves to act as a perfect foil for some of the hot spiciness of southern Indian curries.

4 bananas
½ lemon
300 ml/½ pint natural yogurt
50 g/2 oz desiccated coconut

Preparation time: 2 hours 10 minutes

Peel the bananas and cut them crossways into pieces about 1 cm/½ inch thick. Sprinkle with the juice from the half lemon and mix together with the yogurt in a serving bowl, topping with the desiccated coconut. Chill for about 2 hours and serve.

Above: Uppama; centre: Pakora ka raeta; below: Kela ka raeta.

Indian salad Chachumber

As throughout the world, salads in India generally consist of whatever salad vegetables are available at the time. There are various methods of making Chachumber, the most popular one involves simply a combination of tomatoes and fresh onions, with a little fresh ginger. But this recipe, however, includes lettuce and cucumber.

1 lettuce
2 teaspoons salt
2 teaspoons black pepper
1 large onion
2 lemons
1 × 5-cm/2-inch piece of fresh ginger
2 tablespoons vinegar
1 teaspoon ground coriander
1 teaspoon chilli powder
4 tomatoes
1 × 15-cm/6-inch piece of cucumber

Preparation time: 30 minutes

Remove the outer leaves from the lettuce, discarding any that are not perfect. Try to pull away as many leaves as possible and lay these, with the biggest leaves downwards, one upon the other, making about five or six layers. As you place each leaf, sprinkle on a little of the salt and black pepper. When you have about five or six together, roll them lengthways and with a sharp knife cut crossways. This is the easiest way of producing ready-seasoned rough-chopped lettuce

Peel and roughly chop the onion and mix together with the chopped lettuce. Squeeze the juice from the lemons. Peel the ginger and finely grate it. Mix together the lemon juice, vinegar, coriander, chilli powder and the remaining salt and black pepper. Add the grated ginger to the mixture. Put the mixture to chill in the fridge.

Cut the tomatoes and cucumber into 0.5-cm/$\frac{1}{4}$-inch slices. Take a large salad bowl and arrange a layer of chopped lettuce in the bottom of the bowl, then a layer of tomatoes and then cucumber. Repeat the layers and top off with the heart of the lettuce in the centre of the dish. Just before serving, sprinkle the ginger and vinegar mixture over the top of the dish.

Mixed chick-pea salad
Rajma chenna salat

This is very much one of the true vegetarian dishes of southern India. There are still millions of people in India who never eat meat on religious and economic grounds, although this is changing slowly, particularly in the big cities where there are modern influences. However, vegetarianism is still practised as a whole in most of the south of India, particularly by women, who on average take their religion far more seriously. For this reason all manner of methods have been used to create tasty, satisfying dishes.

This dish combines two types of pulses: black-eyed peas and chick peas, together with the more familiar red kidney beans. In their raw state, red kidney beans are very poisonous. This is because of a substance that exists in the outer skin of the bean. It is absolutely essential if you use raw kidney beans to make sure that they are cooked at a very high temperature (in boiling water) for at least 1 hour, preferably longer. For this reason I am suggesting that you use canned kidney beans, but ensure that in the canned state they have been fully cooked. There is no problem with the black-eyed peas or the chick peas, which should be cooked from their raw state, although this does mean starting the day before.

225 g/½ lb black-eyed peas
225 g/½ lb chick peas
1 medium size, 225–280 g/8–10 oz, can red kidney beans
1 clove garlic
1 tablespoon sesame seed oil
1 medium onion
1 teaspoon ground cumin
½ teaspoon ground coriander
1 teaspoon black pepper
1 teaspoon salt
2 green chillies
1 lemon
2 tablespoons chopped coriander leaves

Preparation time: 10 minutes plus overnight soaking
Cooking time: 2 hours 15 minutes plus 2–3 hours chilling

Mix the black-eyed peas and chick peas together and wash them well. Soak them overnight in enough water to cover them.

The next day, slowly bring them to the boil and simmer for about 2 hours until they become soft. It is important not to let them overcook as you do not want to end up with a thick, black-eyed pea mush! When they are cooked, drain off any excess water and place to one side.

Peel the clove of garlic and chop it finely. Whisk it together with the sesame seed oil. Peel the onion and chop it coarsely, put into a large salad bowl and pour over the garlic and oil mixture. Sprinkle in the cumin, coriander, black pepper and salt. Mix together well.

Top and tail the green chillies, cut into 0.5-cm/¼-inch pieces and add to the onion mixture. Mix well. Now add the chick peas and black-eyed peas, together with the kidney beans, drained of any liquid they may have had with them in the can. Mix in well, being careful not to crush the beans or peas, sprinkle over the juice from the lemon and finally the coriander leaves to finish off the dish.

Many people eat this as a main course in itself and it certainly is very filling. It is best to chill the salad for 2–3 hours before serving.

From left to right: Chachumber and Rajma chenna salat.

Chapter Eight
Vegetable dishes of
northern India

As with the meat dishes of northern India, the vegetable dishes of northern India reflect the temperate climate. Here green vegetables, such as broccoli, cauliflower and peas can be grown in abundance. Potatoes too are grown in the well-irrigated soil. The vegetables of northern India are used very much to reflect the high quality of meat available. Thus the spicing tends to be subtle and quite often the vegetables are mixed together to make one dish, such as potato with cauliflower.

Whereas in the south of India vegetables are designed to be a meal in themselves, vegetables in the north are very much an accompaniment.

Therefore the quantities served tend to be less.

In the north of India, the same rules apply to vegetable cooking as apply to the best of Western vegetable cooking, that is not to overcook them. Therefore, the best vegetable curries of the north are cooked with large pieces of the selected vegetable, cooked just long enough to make them palatable but so that they retain their crunchiness too. The vegetable that perhaps gains the most from the cooking technique used in the north of India is spinach. Cooked in the northern-Indian style with subtle spicing, it is a vegetable which few can fail to appreciate.

Rice
Chawal

✿✿✿✿✿✿✿✿✿✿✿✿✿✿✿✿✿✿

If you are going to cook Indian food to any great extent, then a knowledge of the gentle and noble art of rice cookery is essential! I know many people find this to be one of the great hurdles in their cooking. Rice cooking is very easy as long as you go about it in the right way. For many of the 550 million people living in India, rice is the one thing that keeps them going every day. An average Indian meal could well be summed up as a bowl of rice, a little dal made from lentils and perhaps a couple of green chillies just to add a bit of kick. That does not mean to say, however, that rice is not a tasty dish in itself. Cooked properly, many people would sooner have a bowl of good boiled rice in preference to chapattis or parathas.

The essential thing to remember when cooking rice is to choose the right variety. For many years in England rice was only used for making rice pudding, for which only sub-standard short grain rice was sold. This rice is very high in starch and consequently any attempt to boil it results in a solid mass which sticks together like wallpaper glue.

The best rice to accompany Indian food is undoubtedly, in my view, Basmati. This is very much the 'Prince' of rices and has a distinct flavour all its own. Failing that, long grain Patna rice is also acceptable. The key is the length of the grain. Only long grains ensure good fluffy separation of rice.

Once you have chosen the correct rice, the next thing to do is to make sure it is scrupulously washed before cooking. This is for two reasons. One is that rice quite often acquires all kinds of strange bits and pieces on its way from the paddy fields to your kitchen. Nowadays, rice that has been highly processed, and in some cases also pre-washed, is normally free from such impurities and foreign bodies. But if you buy loose rice you may well find it will have stones in and occasionally even the odd nail or two! This is, perhaps, inevitable bearing in mind the large quantities of rice involved and how it has to be stored once it is harvested. The other reason for careful washing is to remove the starchy powder that forms as the rice is in transit. The rice grains rub against each other and create quite a lot of rice powder. This, if allowed to remain, forms the basis of the glue that sticks rice together when it is cooked. However, if you want fluffy rice with the grains separated, then you must wash and wash again.

In practice this means putting the rice into a large saucepan and using up to ten changes of water until the water poured away is absolutely clear of any cloudiness caused by the rice powder. Having done all that, and, believe me, it really is necessary, the rice is ready for cooking. You should allow one cup of dry rice for each person. Place this in the bottom of a saucepan and add to it twice the volume of boiling water. Many people prefer to salt the water in which they cook rice. Personally I do not. I think rice is best cooked without any salt added. Bring the water back to the boil and cook for about 20–30 minutes until a grain of rice taken from the saucepan will be hard in the middle or *al dente* as the Italians call it. There is no hard and fast rule about the length of time this will take as it all depends on the relative dryness and hardness of the particular rice you are cooking.

As soon as the rice is *al dente*, drain off any excess water (there should not be too much of this) and transfer the rice into a casserole. Take a piece of double-thickness kitchen towel, moisten it and lay it over the top of the rice and place in a preheated hot oven, 180°C/350°F/Gas Mark 4. This allows any extra water to steam off. The rice should now be ready to serve.

Mango rice
Am chawal

✿✿✿✿✿✿✿✿✿✿✿✿✿✿✿✿✿✿

This is a very interesting rice dish and is one of the tastiest I have ever eaten. It combines the sweetness of mangoes with rice in a unique way. If you serve Mango rice you probably need not serve any other vegetable with the meat dish. Choose a mango that is very firm. It is best to buy one that is underripe rather than over-ripe.

50 g/2 oz chick peas or channa dal
225 g/½ lb Basmati rice
600 ml/1 pint water
1 large mango
100 g/4 oz ghee or 120 ml/4 fl oz cooking oil
1 teaspoon ground turmeric
4 cloves
4 cardamoms
2 teaspoons chilli powder
2 red chillies

Preparation time: 40 minutes
Cooking time: 30 minutes

Take the chick peas, wash well and soak in a cup of water for 30 minutes. Then, wash the rice and boil it together with the chick peas in the water until it is *al dente*. While this is happening, peel the mango and cut as many thin slices, about 1 cm/½ inch thick, away from the large flat stone in the centre as you possibly can.

Heat the ghee or cooking oil in a large frying pan and gently fry the turmeric, cloves, cardamoms and chilli powder for 2 minutes. Reduce the heat and add the pieces of mango. Fry these gently, trying to ensure that they do not break up too much. Now turn out the rice into a large bowl and mix in the mango pieces, together with the oil in which they have been cooking.

Once they are thoroughly mixed (again be careful not to crush the mango slices), chop the red chillies into 0.5-cm/¼-inch pieces crossways and top and tail them (be careful not to rub your eyes!). Sprinkle the red chilli pieces over the top of the rice and serve.

From above: Chawal and Am chawal.

Saffron rice
Kesari chawal

Saffron rice is exactly what it says it is; rice coloured with saffron. Saffron in itself has a slight fragrance but its main use is for colour. Saffron comes from the stamens of crocuses and it takes something like 75,000 crocus flowers to make 500 g/1 lb of saffron. That explains why it appears to be so expensive. However, relatively little saffron is needed to achieve very intense yellow colouring, In addition, when cooking Saffron rice turmeric is added and this not only enhances the colour but also adds more flavour. Many people confuse Saffron rice and Pillao rice. There is no doubt in my mind that if you want to bring out the total rice flavour then Pillao rice is the better bet. However, Saffron rice is more colourful!

500 g/1 lb Basmati rice
100 g/4 oz ghee or 120 ml/4 fl oz
    cooking oil
1 medium onion
1 clove garlic
1 teaspoon ground turmeric
1 teaspoon whole cumin seeds
½ teaspoon saffron soaked in a
    cupful of boiling water
1 teaspoon salt

Preparation time: 15 minutes
Cooking time: 30 minutes

Wash the rice again and again until it is totally free of rice dust. Drain and put to one side. Melt the ghee or cooking oil in a heavy saucepan with a close-fitting lid. Peel the onion and slice it thinly. Fry it in the ghee or cooking oil for about 5 minutes until it is soft and white. Peel and thinly slice the garlic. Add the garlic, turmeric and cumin seeds to the pan and mix in well.

Add the rice after a further 2 minutes and stir so that each grain is coated with oil. Now add the saffron together with the water in which it has been steeping. Add sufficient extra boiling water to cover the rice. Add the salt. Put the lid on the saucepan and simmer until the water is absorbed and the rice is *al dente*. If you find you have added too much water, simply drain it away at the end of the cooking process. Do not be tempted to overcook the rice just to absorb any extra water.

From left to right: Kesari chawal and Pillao.

Spiced rice
Pillao

Pillao rice is a dish that was especially developed by the chefs of the Mogul emperors. The emperors needed a dish that would serve great multitudes on feast days and special days of celebration. Clearly, to feed so many people required a dish that was not going to be too expensive but at the same time had an air of the exotic about it. So, Pillao rice was born and there are as many different recipes for Pillao rices of various sorts as there are Indian chefs.

The one point to be made is that Pillao rice is not fried rice, although a certain amount of frying of the rice does occur at the very beginning of the recipe. Fried rice itself is something restricted almost exclusively to the Chinese and in this case the rice is fried once it has already been boiled. The one thing especially advantageous about Pillao rice is that unlike boiled rice it is far less prone to sticking together. The oil keeps each grain separate. For this recipe it is important to use a heavy saucepan with a tight-fitting lid.

500 g/1 lb Basmati rice
170 g/6 oz ghee or 175 ml/6 fl oz
    cooking oil
1 medium onion
1 clove garlic
10 cloves
1 × 8-cm/3-inch stick of cinnamon
10 cardamoms
1 teaspoon salt
100 g/4 oz sultanas
50 g/2 oz blanched almonds

Preparation time: 15 minutes
Cooking time: 30 minutes

Heat the ghee or cooking oil. Peel and thinly slice the onion. Fry the onion in the oil until soft. Peel and thinly slice the garlic, and fry that together with the onion for a further 2 minutes. Now add the cloves, cinnamon and the cardamoms. Fry for a further minute over a gentle heat and add the rice. It is important that the rice is washed as well for this dish as you would for ordinary boiled rice. Attempt to drain as much water as possible from it.

Keep the heat low and continue to fry so that each grain of rice is coated with oil. Add the salt and cover the rice with boiling water. Bring back to the boil and then reduce the heat to a simmer. Cover the pan tightly and check every 5 minutes until the water has been absorbed by the rice and the rice is tender.

As soon as the rice is ready for eating, fry the sultanas and almonds in a little oil and mix into the rice. Traditionally, Pillaos are served with a decoration of finely beaten silver. But, you may omit this if you can't bear to see the family silver go under the hammer!

Spinach and potato chutney
Saag aloo

Spinach is quite highly regarded in India, particularly in the north, where among other things it is used to prepare the clay oven, known as the tandoor, before it is first used. Spinach leaves are rubbed over the inside of the oven when it is brand new to remove as much of the clay dust as possible and seal the inner surface in readiness for the extreme heat to which it will be subjected.

500 g/1 lb spinach
500 g/1 lb waxy potatoes
1 large onion
1 clove garlic
50 g/2 oz ghee or 60 ml/2 fl oz cooking oil
½ teaspoon ground coriander
1 teaspoon paprika
2 cardamoms
1 teaspoon ground ginger
1 teaspoon black pepper
1 teaspoon salt

Preparation time: 10 minutes
Cooking time: 40 minutes

Wash the spinach well and then put into a large saucepan. Just cover with water and bring to the boil. Meanwhile, peel and cut the potatoes into 2.5-cm/1-inch cubes and add to the saucepan. Simmer the spinach and potatoes for about 10–15 minutes until the potatoes begin to soften. Now drain the saucepan of water and place the spinach and potato mixture to one side.

Peel and thinly slice the onion and garlic. Heat the ghee or cooking oil in another saucepan and add the onion and garlic and cook for 2 minutes. Then add the spices but not the salt. Stir for a further minute and add the potato and spinach mixture. Combine this gently with the spice mixture, making sure not to crush the potatoes. Add the salt, adding slightly more or less according to taste. Allow to simmer very slowly for a further 10 minutes. The idea is that all the spice mixture should be easily absorbed into the vegetables.

This dish should be very dry and it should not be necessary to add any extra water as the spinach holds quite a lot of water itself.

Tomato curry
Tamatar ka salan

The tomatoes found in northern India are rather different from those found in the West, they tend not to be so nicely rounded and are more similar to the Italian style of plum tomatoes. For this reason canned tomatoes are best for this dish. However, you can, of course, use fresh tomatoes of the equivalent weight. This is a very good vegetarian dish with rice.

A large can of tomatoes – approximately 600 g/20 oz
50 g/2 oz ghee or 60 ml/2 fl oz cooking oil
1 large onion
1 clove garlic
2 green chillies
1 × 5-cm/2-inch piece of fresh ginger
1 teaspoon mustard seeds
1 bay leaf
1 teaspoon chilli powder
2 teaspoons ground coriander
1 teaspoon ground turmeric
1 tablespoon desiccated coconut
1½ teaspoons salt

Preparation time: 10 minutes
Cooking time: 45 minutes

Drain the juice from the can of tomatoes and reserve it. Cut the tomatoes into halves. Heat the ghee or cooking oil in a large saucepan. Peel and slice the onion and garlic. Top and tail the chillies and slit lengthways. Peel and slice the ginger into thin strips and cook gently with the onion and garlic in the ghee or cooking oil until soft. Add the mustard seeds. Now stir in the spices, except the salt, and continue to cook for a further 2 minutes.

Add the tomatoes, bring the dish back to the boil and add sufficient tomato juice to make a moist but not over-wet curry. Sprinkle in the desiccated coconut and the salt, cover the saucepan and simmer for about 30 minutes. If you are using fresh tomatoes, then increase the cooking time to 45 minutes. During the cooking, check to see whether the moisture has evaporated and that the tomatoes are not sticking to the bottom of the saucepan. If you feel that the dish needs a little more juice, then add more of the reserved tomato juice.

Carrots with cashew nuts
Gajjar bhajji

Cashew nuts themselves have a distinctive flavour and when combined with carrots the result is quite a different dish. This should turn out to be a dry curry and is good for accompanying those meat dishes which contain a lot of curry sauce, such as Raghan Gosht, Pasanda and Nargisi Kofta. This is a very nutty dish but it is authentic Indian cooking. If you prefer, use only 170 g/6 oz cashew nuts.

500 g/1 lb carrots
1 large onion
100 g/4 oz ghee or 120 ml/4 fl oz cooking oil
1 × 5-cm/2-inch piece of fresh ginger
1 teaspoon garam masala
1 teaspoon chilli powder
1 teaspoon flour
225 g/½ lb cashew nuts
150 ml/¼ pint chicken stock
1 teaspoon salt
2 tomatoes

Preparation time: 10 minutes
Cooking time: 25 minutes

Scrub the carrots and cut them lengthways into fairly thick strips. Peel and slice the onion. Heat the ghee or cooking oil in a large saucepan and fry the onion and carrots. Peel the ginger and cut into lengthways strips. Add the ginger, garam masala and chilli powder to the pan. Continue to stir and add the flour. As the mixture thickens, add the cashew nuts, stock and salt.

Bring to the boil and simmer with the pan covered for about 20 minutes until the carrots are fully soft. If they soften sooner than this, they are ready. Chop the tomatoes coarsely and add to the pan. Cook for a further 3–4 minutes and serve. The curry should have a fairly thick sauce but if it is not thick enough, rapidly boil it to drive off any excess water.

From above: Tamatar ka salan, Saag aloo and Gajjar bhajji.

Lentils with spinach
Palak dal

The combination of spinach and lentils makes a very good dish indeed. This recipe calls for frozen spinach but fresh spinach could be used just as easily. Instead of 225 g/½ lb of frozen spinach, substitute 500 g/1 lb of fresh spinach. Again, use the common red split lentil.

225 g/½ lb red split lentils
300 ml/½ pint water
225 g/½ lb frozen spinach or 500 g/ 1 lb fresh spinach
1 medium onion
1 clove garlic
1 teaspoon ground ginger
1–2 teaspoons chilli powder
1 teaspoon salt
2 tablespoons natural yogurt

Preparation time: 10 minutes
Cooking time: 50 minutes

Wash the lentils well and place in a heavy saucepan. Cover with the water. Meanwhile, if using frozen spinach, remove from the freezer and allow the block to begin to thaw. (Complete thawing is not necessary, this will be achieved when the spinach is added to the lentils at a later stage.) If using fresh spinach, wash well and chop finely. Peel the onion and garlic and coarsely slice them. Add to the lentils. Cover and bring to the boil, then add the ginger, chilli powder and the salt and simmer gently.

Cover the saucepan and allow to simmer until the lentils break down and turn into soup. Once this has been achieved, boil off any excess water so that quite a thick sauce is made. Add the spinach. If this is not totally thawed out by now do not worry, continue to cook until the spinach is thawed and totally mixed in with the lentils. Finally, add the yogurt and stir well in. Cook for a further 3 minutes and serve.

From above: Palak dal, Murgh piaz and Tarka dal.

Onions stuffed with chicken
Murgh piaz

This is a dish which has relatively recent origins and it is one which is considered to be an Indian way of cooking Western food. Nonetheless, it is a good combination of flavours.

4 large onions
225 g/½ lb cooked chicken (make do with leftovers from a roast!)
1 medium onion
50 g/2 oz uncooked Basmati rice
1 teaspoon ground turmeric
½ teaspoon chilli powder
½ teaspoon black pepper
1 teaspoon salt
150 ml/¼ pint chicken stock

Preparation time: 30 minutes
Cooking time: 55 minutes

Top and tail the onions and very carefully peel away the outer brown skin. Put into a large saucepan and cover to two-thirds with water. Gently simmer the onions for about 30 minutes until they begin to soften. It is important not to overcook the onions at this stage. Meanwhile, take the medium-sized onion, peel it and cut into quarters and, together with the chicken, pass it through a fine mincer.

Wash the rice well and mix it into the chicken and onion mixture. Sprinkle in the spices and salt. Mix well. When the large onions are cooked, push out the middle section of each onion, leaving four or five outer layers intact. This needs some care, but once the innermost layer of onion has been removed the others will come easily. Arrange the onions in a baking dish and spoon in the chicken mixture. Cut the onion removed from the centre sections into long strips and sprinkle over the top of each onion. Pour over the stock.

Tightly cover with aluminium foil and put into a preheated moderate oven, 180°C/350°F/Gas Mark 4. Simmer very gently for about 45 minutes or so. In this time the rice in the mixture should have absorbed any moisture and should be cooked. Once the rice is cooked, remove the foil and increase the heat to 200°C/400°F/Gas Mark 6 and put the onions to the top of the oven to brown.

Lentils with a spicy topping
Tarka dal

Apart from rice the other main staple food of most Indians are the dals. These are made from grams or pulses all related to the pea family and there are literally hundreds of different types.

There are three or four in common use; ordinary red lentils, which are used extensively in the West and in the past were the basis of Pease pudding, mung dal, urd dal (this is used mainly in making poppadums) and channa dal. One of the simplest dals to make is straightforward Tarka dal which is made using the red split lentils. The Tarka part of it comes from the topping that is poured over the dal once it is cooked.

225 g/½ lb red split lentils
1 small onion
50 g/2 oz ghee or 60 ml/2 fl oz cooking oil
2 cloves garlic
1 teaspoon ground turmeric
2 green chillies
600 ml/1 pint water
1 teaspoon salt
1 tablespoon sesame seed oil
1 teaspoon cumin seeds

Preparation time: 15 minutes
Cooking time: 45 minutes

In transit, grams and pulses suffer from the same problems as rice. They become powdery and it is essential to remove this powder before cooking. The best way to do this is to wash them as you do rice. Put the lentils into a large saucepan and give them several changes of cold water. Once you have done this they are ready to be cooked.

Peel and thinly slice the onion. Melt the ghee or cooking oil in a heavy saucepan and fry the onion for about 3 minutes. Now peel and slice one clove of garlic and fry that too. Mix in the turmeric and add the lentils. Reduce the heat immediately and stir quickly to ensure the lentils are coated in the oil.

Take the green chillies and top and tail them. Cut into 0.5-cm/¼-inch pieces crossways. Please remember not to wipe your eyes with your hands as the juice from the green chillies can prove very irritating. Add to the pan. Once the lentils have been frying for about a minute, cover with water, bring back to the boil, add the salt and boil until the lentils break down into a mush. If you recognise this dish as being very familiar and similar to Pease pudding that is because that is exactly what it is, Pease pudding – Indian style. What singles it out is the next part. Once the dal is made it should be nice and smooth (add more water if necessary) and you are ready to add the Tarka.

Heat the sesame seed oil in a small frying pan. Sesame seed oil is used because it can be heated to a much higher temperature than other oils. This recipe calls for the oil to be heated until it is smoking. Peel the other clove of garlic and slice it as thinly as possible. When the sesame seed oil is smoking, throw the garlic and cumin seeds into the oil (watch out that it doesn't spit) and fry very quickly. The garlic will turn almost instantly brown and then black. Once this happens immediately transfer the dal into a serving dish and pour the Tarka on the top. Again watch it does not spit. Serve immediately.

Okra with potatoes Aloo bhindi bhajji

Okra is available throughout the world, but for some reason very little Western cooking has made use of this particular vegetable. When buying okra the secret is to ensure that they are fresh and not overripe. You can spot the ones that have been lying around too long by the fact that they will be soft and also beginning to blacken excessively.

Be careful when handling okra not to rub your eyes, as they have tiny little needles on their outer surface which will sting immensely if they get in your eyes.

225 g/$\frac{1}{2}$ lb okra
225 g/$\frac{1}{2}$ lb waxy potatoes
1 medium onion
75 g/3 oz ghee or 90 ml/3 fl oz
   cooking oil
1 teaspoon chilli powder
1 teaspoon ground turmeric
1 teaspoon garam masala
1 teaspoon ground cumin
1 teaspoon black pepper
1 teaspoon salt
1 tablespoon chopped coriander
   leaves

Preparation time: 10 minutes
Cooking time: 40 minutes

Peel the onion and slice it thinly. Heat the ghee in a large heavy saucepan and fry the onion until brown. Meanwhile, peel the potatoes and cut them into slices. When the onions are soft, add the potato slices to the saucepan and fry gently. It is important to fry them gently so that they cook evenly. Remember you are not making chips!

Meanwhile, prepare the okra by cutting away the stalk and the tail of each one and cut them into slices about 1 cm/$\frac{1}{2}$ inch long crossways. Now sprinkle in the spices except the salt. Turn the potato slices and onion gently to mix the spices thoroughly with the oil and vegetables. Now add the okra and again mix in well but gently, making sure not to break up the potato or okra unnecessarily.

At this stage there should be enough moisture to continue to cook the okra. If you feel it is a little too dry, add some water. Add the salt. Cover the saucepan and simmer for about 20 minutes until the okra are soft but not too soft. They should retain some of their crunch. Serve, garnished with chopped coriander leaves sprinkled over the top of the dish.

Potato and cauliflower curry Aloo gobi

Although rice is the main carbohydrate ingredient of Indian cooking, potatoes are eaten to a small extent in the Indian subcontinent, although nothing like the quantity consumed in the West. It is also relatively unusual to find cauliflowers in all parts of India which is why this particular recipe tends to be restricted to the rather more temperate northern region, where they can be grown in a climate that sometimes approaches that of southern Europe. The dish itself is fairly dry and quite spicy.

1 small cauliflower
900 g/2 lb waxy potatoes
100 g/4 oz ghee or 120 ml/4 fl oz
   cooking oil
2 onions
1 teaspoon chilli powder
$\frac{1}{2}$ teaspoon ground ginger
2 teaspoons ground coriander
450 ml/$\frac{3}{4}$ pint water
2 teaspoons salt
1$\frac{1}{2}$ teaspoons garam masala

Preparation time: 10 minutes
Cooking time: 35 minutes

Wash the cauliflower and trim away any leaves. Cut into florets. Peel the potatoes and cut them into 2.5-cm/1-inch cubes. Heat the ghee or cooking oil in a large saucepan. Peel and slice the onions and fry them gently for 2–3 minutes. Add the chilli powder, ginger and coriander and stir for a further 1 minute.

Add the potatoes and cauliflower and, using a wooden spoon, gently turn them so that they are coated by the spice and oil mixture. Now add the water and salt and bring to the boil. Cover the saucepan and simmer gently for 20 minutes until the potatoes and cauliflower are soft. It is important not to overcook this dish because the idea is to have discernible pieces of cauliflower and pota-

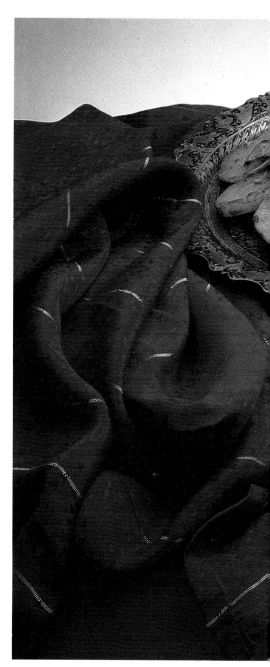

Above left to right: Aloo bhindi bhajji and Aloo chop; below: Aloo gobi.

toes without them becoming mushy.

As soon as the potato and cauliflower are cooked, add the garam masala and simmer for a further 5 minutes. If there is too much water left over reduce this by boiling rapidly.

Potato chops
Aloo chop

This recipe is very popular in many parts of India, particularly with the middle classes, who regard it as being a Western dish and therefore something which every well-to-do family should serve from time to time. It is quite tasty and a great alternative to the standard way of serving potatoes in the West, so why not give it a try. This recipe should make about 12 potato chops depending on how large you make them.

1.2 kg/3 lb floury potatoes
1 large onion
2 cloves garlic
75 g/3 oz ghee or 90 ml/3 fl oz cooking oil
½ teaspoon ground ginger
1 teaspoon garam masala
1 teaspoon ground turmeric
1 teaspoon ground coriander
350 g/12 oz minced meat
100 g/4 oz tomato purée
2 teaspoons salt
2 teaspoons black pepper
1 dessertspoon chopped mint
1 egg
100 g/4 oz breadcrumbs

Preparation time: 10 minutes
Cooking time: 50 minutes

Peel the potatoes and boil them in salted water until cooked. Mean-while, peel and finely chop the onion and garlic. Drain the water from the potatoes, add the onion and garlic and mash until very smooth.

Heat the ghee or cooking oil and fry the ginger, garam masala and all the other spices except the salt and pepper for 2 minutes. Now add the minced meat and fry this until cooked. Add the tomato purée, frying for a further 3–4 minutes. Add the salt and black pepper. Remove from the frying pan and add to the mashed potato, together with the chopped mint, mixing in well.

Form the mixture into lamb chop or patty shapes. Beat the egg and dip each chop into the egg, coat with breadcrumbs and shallow fry in the minimum of oil for a few minutes until golden brown.

Yogurt cooler
Raeta

Raeta is one of those dishes essential to virtually any Indian meal. It is the 'fire-extinguisher' that many people find necessary when they are eating a hot meal. Raeta is simply yogurt with the odd vegetable in it. The Raeta I prefer is one made with cucumber. No cook in India would dream of buying their yogurt from a shop. It is so easy to make and of course so much cheaper that virtually all yogurt now is made at home, and there is a difference in flavour too!

5-cm/2-inch piece of cucumber
600 ml/1 pint natural yogurt
1 teaspoon salt
1 teaspoon paprika
1 tablespoon chopped fresh mint

Preparation time: 15 minutes plus
　　2 hours chilling

Take the cucumber and cut lengthways into long strips. This is the traditional way of cutting cucumber for Raeta. You will sometimes come across Raeta with the cucumber cut into cubes or large chunks but narrow strips is the best way to use it as this ensures the yogurt can be easily mixed in with the Raeta. Take the yogurt and with a fork beat in the salt and half the paprika. Now gently combine the cucumber strips with the yogurt. Pour into a serving bowl and sprinkle the remaining paprika and mint on the top, to garnish. Chill in the fridge for 2 hours and serve.

Aubergines and
tomatoes
Baigan tamatar

Many people believe the French invented the combination of aubergines and tomatoes and it is certainly true to say that ratatouille has found a place for itself in haute cuisine. However, Indian chefs independently spotted this flavoursome combination although they give it a much simpler name, Baigan Tamatar – Aubergines and Tomatoes.

A note on buying aubergines: always choose firm ones with shiny skins. They vary in colour from almost white to black. The best ones I have found are those which are a deep purple colour. For this dish it is better to use the longer rather than the short, squat variety of aubergine.

750 g/1½ lb aubergines
100 g/4 oz ghee or 120 ml/4 fl oz
　cooking oil
2 medium onions
1 clove garlic
1 teaspoon chilli powder
1 bay leaf
1 × 5-cm/2-inch stick of cinnamon
2 teaspoons ground coriander
1 teaspoon salt
1 teaspoon black pepper
750 g/1½ lb tomatoes
4 tablespoons tomato purée

Preparation time: 20 minutes
Cooking time: 25 minutes

Take a heavy saucepan and, using a gentle heat, warm the ghee or cooking oil. Meanwhile, peel and slice the onions thinly and fry them in the ghee for 2–3 minutes until they are soft. Peel and slice the clove of garlic and add to the onions, together with the chilli powder, bay leaf, stick of cinnamon, coriander, salt and black pepper. Stir from time to time to make sure all the spices are mixed in well with the oil.

Immerse the tomatoes in some boiling water so that the skins split and they are easy to peel. While this is happening, remove the dark leaves from the aubergines and cut each aubergine into four, lengthways and then, keeping the aubergine assembled, cut crossways to produce 2.5-cm/1-inch cubes of aubergine. Return to the tomatoes and peel and

quarter them. Add the tomatoes to the saucepan and stir in. Bring to the boil, adding a little water if necessary, and stir. The tomatoes should break down into a pulp.

Now add the aubergines and turn them so that they are quickly coated by the mixture. Add the tomato purée and a little water just to make sure the mixture does not stick to the pan. Cover the saucepan and simmer for about 30 minutes until the aubergines are tender. It is important not to overcook this dish as the idea is that whilst the tomatoes are broken down into a pulp, the aubergines still remain in their cubes, so they should be cooked until they are just tender and no more. The sauce should be reasonably thick and not too liquid. If there appears to be too much water at the end of cooking, boil this off rapidly. Serve hot.

From left to right: Raeta, Baigan tamatar and Baigan bhugia.

Dry cooked aubergines Baigan bhugia

ଔଦ୍ଦୌ ଔଦ୍ଦୌ ଔଦ୍ଦୌ ଔଦ୍ଦୌ ଔଦ୍ଦୌ ଔଦ୍ଦୌ

This particular dish uses aubergines cooked in a simple but for some people quite difficult way. The idea of Bhugia is to cook the vegetable with as little moisture as possible. This means that all the essential flavour of the vegetables is concentrated, but of course it does mean that it has to be watched closely when cooking so as not to dry it out or, worse still, to burn it!

500 g/1 lb aubergines
100 g/4 oz ghee or 120 ml/4 fl oz
    cooking oil
1 large onion
2 teaspoons salt
2 teaspoons paprika
100 g/4 oz tomato purée
3 green chillies
2 teaspoons garam masala

Preparation time: 15 minutes
Cooking time: 25 minutes

Heat the ghee in a heavy saucepan. Peel and thinly slice the onion and fry until soft. Cut off the dark green leaves of the aubergines and cut lengthways several times and then crossways to form 1-cm/½-inch cubes. Add the salt and paprika to the saucepan and stir well in. Add the diced aubergines and tomato purée and keep stirring to ensure that the aubergines are well coated. The heat should be medium to high for this, but make sure you continue to turn the aubergines to prevent them sticking to the saucepan. If necessary add a little water.

Top and tail the green chillies and cut them into 0.5-cm/¼-inch pieces. Be careful when handling green chillies as their juice can sting very badly if you rub it in your eyes. Make sure you wash your hands immediately after handling them. Add the chillies to the saucepan and stir in. Cover the saucepan and reduce the heat so that the aubergines simmer gently for 5 minutes or so. Now add the garam masala, stir once again and cook for a further 15 minutes until the aubergines are just soft.

As you can imagine, with 3 green chillies, this is a fairly hot dish. If you don't fancy anything quite as hot as this, then you can cut down or even omit the green chillies completely.

Stuffed aubergines Keema baigan

ఞఞఞఞఞఞఞఞఞఞఞఞఞఞఞఞఞఞ

For this dish it is better to use short, squat aubergines as they lend themselves better to being stuffed than the long variety. Whatever the shape of aubergine you buy, they must be firm and have shiny skins.

2 large aubergines
100 g/4 oz carrots
75 g/3 oz ghee or 90 ml/3 fl oz cooking oil
1 large onion
100 g/4 oz peas
170 g/6 oz tomatoes
1 teaspoon paprika
1 teaspoon salt
1 teaspoon black pepper
1 × 2.5-cm/1-inch piece of fresh ginger

Preparation time: 20 minutes
Cooking time: 40 minutes

Remove the green leaves from the base of each aubergine. Cut each one lengthways in half and boil in about 1.2 litres/2 pints of slightly salted water for 10–15 minutes. Meanwhile, scrape, wash and dice the carrots. With a slotted spoon, remove the aubergine halves from the pan and scoop out the pulp of the aubergines, being careful not to puncture the skin as you do so. Put the skins and the pulp to one side.

Heat the ghee or cooking oil in a large frying pan. Peel and chop the onion and fry until soft. Add the peas and carrots to the frying pan. Keep the heat fairly gentle so that the vegetables cook slowly but thoroughly. Now mash the aubergine pulp roughly with a fork and add to the frying pan, together with the peeled and quartered tomatoes. Add the paprika, salt and black

From left to right: Keema baigan, Karela, Goodhi bhajji and Pimento keema.

pepper and stir well in.

Take the piece of ginger and peel away all the outer brown bark. Cut the ginger into very thin strips and add these to the frying pan. The idea is not to overcook the ginger, so at this stage the vegetables should be ready. Arrange the four halves of the aubergines on a baking tray and spoon in the cooked mixture. Put the aubergines in a preheated moderate oven (180°C/350°F/Gas Mark 4) and bake for 25 minutes until they are golden brown.

Preparation time: 10 minutes
Cooking time: 15 minutes

Wash the courgettes well and top and tail them. Cut them into slices about 0.5–1 cm/¼–½ inch thick. Heat the ghee or cooking oil in a frying pan and gently fry the courgette slices for a minute or so and place them to one side. Peel and slice the onion and fry in the remaining ghee. If the courgettes are particularly dry, you may have to add a little more ghee or cooking oil.

Once the onions are soft, add the spices, salt and black pepper. Then cook the mixture for 2–3 minutes. Add the courgette slices, tossing them well to ensure they are fully coated. Lightly sprinkle the desiccated coconut over the dish, cook for a further half minute and serve.

Marrow curry
Goodhi bhajji

Marrows are particularly popular in northern India. One of the reasons for this is that they grow easily in the more temperate climate of the north. You will notice that for this dish the amount of spices has been cut right down. This is because the flavour of the marrow is so delicate and any overspicing would completely kill it. Similarly, it is important not to overcook this dish.

1 marrow, between 500–750 g/
   1–1½ lb
1½ teaspoons salt
1 onion
100 g/4 oz ghee or 120 ml/4 fl oz
   cooking oil
½ teaspoon garam masala
½ teaspoon chilli powder
½ teaspoon ground turmeric
½ teaspoon curry powder

Preparation time: 10 minutes
Cooking time: 15 minutes

Peel the marrow and cut it in half lengthways. Remove all the seeds. Now cut it into 4-cm/1½-inch cubes, put to one side and sprinkle with the salt. Peel the onion and slice it thinly. Fry it in the ghee until it is soft but not brown. Add the rest of the spices and stir well in. Add the pieces of marrow and turn them gently to coat them with the ghee or cooking oil. Be

careful not to mash them as you do this. Cover the saucepan and cook very gently for about 10 minutes. This curry should be fairly dry but if you find it sticking to the pan, then add a small amount of water to ease the cooking process.

Stuffed peppers
Pimento keema

This is very much a dish cooked by the Indian middle classes, who regard it as a suitable dish for those who wish to emulate Western customs. It seems that stuffed peppers appear in one form or another throughout the world, but this recipe has, as you might expect with an Indian recipe, just a little more spice to add to the interest.

4 green peppers
1 medium onion
50 g/2 oz ghee or 60 ml/2 fl oz
   cooking oil
225 g/½ lb minced meat
1 teaspoon garam masala
1 teaspoon chilli powder
1 teaspoon salt
1 teaspoon black pepper

Preparation time: 10 minutes
Cooking time: 40 minutes

Wash the peppers and then with a sharp knife cut around the stalk where it joins the pepper and remove this. Cut out the inner seeds, making sure the pepper remains in one piece. Place the peppers to one side.

Peel the onion and chop it very finely. Heat the ghee or cooking oil in a frying pan. Mix the onion with the minced meat, garam masala, chilli powder, salt and black pepper and gently fry this mixture in the oil. As soon as the meat begins to turn colour, remove the mixture from the heat and stuff each pepper.

Place the peppers upright in a baking dish and cover tightly with foil, having drained any oil from the frying pan into the dish. It is essential to cover the dish tightly with foil so that none of the moisture escapes. Cook in a preheated moderate oven, 180°C/350°F/Gas Mark 4, for about 30 minutes until the peppers are tender.

Spiced courgettes
Karela

Courgettes are quite often used in India as are their near relatives, the various bitter gourds. This is an interesting recipe as it calls for very subtle cooking of the courgettes. They must be gently fried, not overcooked so, although you will taste the spices, you will still taste the essential flavour of the courgettes themselves.

500 g/1 lb courgettes
50 g/2 oz ghee or 60 ml/2 fl oz
   cooking oil
1 medium onion
1 teaspoon chilli powder
1 teaspoon salt
½ teaspoon black pepper
2 teaspoons desiccated coconut

Chapter Nine
Puddings and fruits

There are a myriad of different puddings and desserts served throughout the Indian subcontinent. Some of them have particular regional associations, others are found wherever you go, some though more frequently in the cities than in the country areas. Most Indian puddings seem to consist of two ingredients – sugar and milk. Indian chefs over the centuries have developed techniques of concentrating milk, by boiling it often for several hours at a time and some of the more traditional recipes start, for example, with 14.5 litres (24 pints) of milk! This would make approximately 900 g (2 lb) of sweetmeat. Clearly there are few cooks, no matter how keen, in the West who would be prepared to or have the time to go in for this amount!

With these recipes I have tried to use certain shortcuts and modifications to make the cooking easier without marring the final product, for example quite often dried milk powder can be used instead of large quantities of fresh milk. Similarly with the sugar. Traditionally in the Indian subcontinent a rough, raw sugar known as ghur is used to sweeten most dishes. Being relatively unrefined, this has the advantage of having plenty of flavour. I certainly would not recommend using ordinary white granulated sugar for any of these recipes but soft brown sugar is quite acceptable as is honey. Both of these will be found in the following recipes. Cooking Indian sweets is not the easiest of tasks and it calls for a good deal of concentration and commonsense. If a recipe looks as if it is too dry and is going to stick to the bottom of the saucepan, then a little milk can be added. Similarly, do not be put off a recipe if you do not have one of the special ingredients, such as pistachio nuts. Substitutes can often be made, such as finely chopped almonds or even unsalted cashews. Indian sweets are an acquired taste, but once you have acquired it you will have, believe me, great difficulty in losing your taste for these sweetmeats.

No Indian meal would really be complete without fresh fruit in one form or another. In tropical climates found in most parts of the Indian subcontinent there are any number of different exotic fruits to be enjoyed. Some of these, including the banana, coconut and pineapple, we are familiar with in the West. However, there are some fruits which are more rarely found in the West and this section will, I hope, enable you to be able to buy some of the more unusual fruits such as mangoes, lychees and guavas, when you see them for sale, fresh in the fruiterers or supermarkets.

Ground rice pudding Phirni

This recipe calls for the use of powdered rice but in my view it is best to start off with whole grain rice and grind it up yourself. Therefore this recipe uses the techniques of soaking the rice overnight, then forming a rice paste as the basis for the dish. Its flavour is very similar to an aromatic blancmange.

50 g/2 oz rice
1.2 litres/2 pints milk
170 g/6 oz soft brown sugar
25 g/1 oz pistachio nuts
25 g/1 oz blanched almonds
3 or 4 drops of kewra water

Preparation time: 10 minutes plus overnight soaking
Cooking time: 45 minutes

Wash the rice well and pick it over to remove any impurities. Cover the rice with water and leave overnight to soak. The next day, strain half the water away and grind the rice with the remaining water. This is best done in a liquidiser.

Put the milk and sugar into a large saucepan and bring to the boil, stirring to dissolve the sugar. Then add the rice mixture and continue to boil gently until the mixture begins to thicken.

Chop the pistachios and almonds and add them to the milk. The almonds and pistachios should not be chopped too finely. Cover the saucepan and cook for a further 30 minutes on a very low heat. Shake in the kewra water and pour the mixture into individual serving bowls. Allow to cool and put into a refrigerator to chill.

Vermicelli Sewain

Vermicelli is not very widely eaten in the Indian subcontinent but there are one or two dishes that are associated with feast days. In particular Sewain is associated with the Moslem holy days known as Eid. Traditionally on these days people visit family and friends and take with them gifts of sweetmeats and puddings.

225 g/½ lb vermicelli
100 g/4 oz ghee or 120 ml/4 fl oz cooking oil
10 cloves
10 cardamoms
1.2 litres/2 pints milk
170 g/6 oz soft brown sugar
100 g/4 oz chopped almonds
50 g/2 oz sultanas
3 teaspoons rose water

Preparation time: 10 minutes
Cooking time: 50 minutes

Heat the ghee in a heavy saucepan and add the cloves and the seeds from the cardamoms. Throw away the outer husk of the cardamoms. Stir well and fry gently for 2–3 minutes to release the aromatic oils into the ghee. Then add the vermicelli, being careful not to allow it to break up. As it absorbs the oil it will soften and slide into the saucepan. Fry for 2–3 minutes. Then add the milk. Bring to the boil and simmer gently and add the sugar, stirring gently so it dissolves.

It is important throughout this dish not to be too rough with the stirring otherwise the vermicelli will break up. Continue to cook for 15–20 minutes until the vermicelli becomes soft. Stir in the almonds and sultanas and cook for a further 5 minutes. Shake in the rose water and as the sauce begins to thicken remove from the heat, allow to cool, pour into a large bowl and chill before serving. This dish can also be eaten piping hot.

From above: Khir, Sewain and Phirni.

Indian rice pudding Khir

This is the one dish where you do not have to worry about the quality of the rice used. This is because the rice is cooked and cooked until it breaks down into a thick, creamy sauce. An aromatic flavour is obtained by using kewra water, an extract of a cactus plant, and a few drops of it give a scented aroma to any sweet dish. As a substitute, if you cannot get hold of kewra water use rose water in similar quantities.

50 g/2 oz rice
1 × 5-cm/2-inch stick of cinnamon
4 cloves
1.2 litres/2 pints milk
100 g/4 oz soft brown sugar
4 cardamoms
50 g/2 oz raisins
25 g/1 oz chopped almonds
a few drops of kewra or rose
  water

Preparation time: 10 minutes
Cooking time: 1 hour 30 minutes

Wash the rice well and pick it over to remove any impurities. Put into a saucepan and pour in enough water to cover the rice. Bring to the boil and add the cinnamon and cloves. continue to boil for 20 minutes until the rice is fully soft, then pour off the water and add the milk and bring to the boil once again.

Stir in the sugar. Remove the outer husk from the cardamoms and add the cardamom seeds to the saucepan. Continue to boil gently, stirring the milk to stop the rice sticking to the bottom of the saucepan. When the mixture begins to become thick (this should take about 45 minutes) add the raisins and chopped almonds. Cover the saucepan and simmer on a very low heat for a further 30 minutes. Shake in a few drops of kewra water or rose water and pour into small serving dishes. Allow to cool and then chill in a refrigerator before serving.

Cream cheese balls
Rasgullah

৬৬৬৬৬৬৬৬৬৬৬৬৬৬৬৬

This is one of the great Mogul sweet dishes and calls for a fairly lengthy preparation. Most of this is taken up with the preparation of the cream cheese or panir as it is known in India. In this recipe I have used cream cheese, which can be easily bought in the West. However, should you want to make it yourself then instead of 225 g/½ lb of cream cheese, gently boil 2.5 litres/4 pints of milk for 40 minutes and curdle it with lemon juice. Strain the curds through a double thickness of muslin and leave overnight to remove all the moisture.

225 g/½ lb cream cheese
50 g/2 oz semolina powder
25 g/1 oz almonds
25 g/1 oz pistachios
350 g/12 oz sugar
1 × 5-cm/2-inch stick of cinnamon
4 cloves
4 cardamoms
300 ml/½ pint double cream
2 teaspoons kewra water

Preparation time: 15 minutes
Cooking time: 1 hour 30 minutes
    plus chilling

Put the cream cheese in a large chilled bowl, sprinkle in the semolina and knead well to ensure it is well mixed. It is important to keep the bowl fairly cold otherwise the cream cheese will tend to melt. Form the cream cheese and semolina mixture into balls about the size of a golf ball. Chop the almonds and pistachios and add a pinch of nuts to each of the balls, pressing it into the middle and then re-forming into balls.

Heat 900 ml/1½ pints of water in a heavy saucepan and add the sugar together with the cinnamon, cloves and cardamoms. Bring to the boil and boil rapidly for 15–20 minutes until the mixture forms a syrup. Lower the balls into the syrup and poach them for 1 hour. Remove from the heat and stir in the double cream and the kewra water. Traditionally rasgullahs are served chilled, although they can be eaten hot. They will keep in a refrigerator for up to a week.

Ice cream
Kulfi

৬৬৬৬৬৬৬৬৬৬৬৬৬৬৬৬৬

Throughout the Indian subcontinent there are the Kulfi vendors. They are often to be seen cycling around the major cities on tricycles fitted with boxes containing all manner of ices. Kulfi is the name given to virtually any kind of ice that contains an element of cream in it. Because no artificial gelling agents are used the ices tend to melt very quickly. Therefore they have to be kept in a freezing mixture of chopped ice and salt. For this reason Kulfis are traditionally frozen in cone-shaped zinc containers. These containers are rather difficult to come by in the West but any container suitable for freezing will do.

600 ml/1 pint gold top milk
3 tablespoons honey
450 ml/¾ pint double cream
50 g/2 oz chopped almonds
½ teaspoon almond essence

Preparation time: 10 minutes
Cooking time: 15 minutes plus
    freezing

Heat the milk until it boils and continue boiling to reduce it to about 450 ml/¾ pint. Lower the heat and stir in the honey and cream. Continue to stir over a gentle heat, reducing the volume to two-thirds. Stir in the almonds and almond essence. Pour the ice cream into one large container for freezing or into individual bowls. Allow to cool to room temperature and then put into a freezing compartment. Check the ice cream from time to time and when it is on the point of freezing, use a fork to whip the ice cream. Freeze again until solid.

Coconut cake
Narial ka halwa

ಧಿಹಿಧಿಹಿಧಿಹಿಧಿಹಿಧಿಹಿಧಿಹಿಧಿಹಿಧಿ

This is an excellent recipe for using fresh coconut, although desiccated coconut can be substituted.

1 fresh coconut or 170 g/6 oz
   desiccated coconut
150 ml/¼ pint boiling water
50 g/2 oz butter
2 egg yolks
170 g/6 oz soft brown sugar
1 teaspoon mace
1 teaspoon ground cinnamon
2 teaspoons ground nutmeg
50 g/2 oz chopped almonds
50 g/2 oz chopped cashew nuts

Preparation time: 15 minutes
Cooking time: 25 minutes

Drain any liquid from the coconut and put to one side. Break the shell open and grate the meat coarsely into the goblet of a liquidiser. Add the liquid from the coconut, together with the boiling water. If using desiccated coconut you may need to add a little extra water. Liquidise together for 1 minute. Strain through a double thickness of muslin to produce a thick coconut milk. Squeeze the coconut to extract the last drops of moisture. Put the milk to one side.

Melt the butter in a heavy saucepan and fry the grated coconut gently until it begins to brown. Beat in the egg yolks together with the brown sugar and a little of the coconut milk to prevent the mixture sticking. Continue to stir and add the mace, cinnamon and nutmeg, mixing in well. Cook for a further 2–3 minutes. Add the rest of the coconut milk. Bring the mixture to the boil.

When the mixture has thickened to

From left to right: Rasgullah, Kulfi and Narial ka halwa.

the consistency of porridge, add the almonds and cashew nuts. Cook for a further 10 minutes until the mixture is ready to set. Spoon into a greased baking tin, level the surface with the back of a spoon and set to one side to cool. When cold cut into squares and serve. Coconut Cake will keep for 2–3 weeks in an airtight tin.

Coconut pudding
Beveca

ৡ৽ৡ৽ৡ৽ৡ৽ৡ৽ৡ৽ৡ৽ৡ৽ৡ৽ৡ৽ৡ৽

This is a very traditional southern Indian recipe and is another classic use of coconut. It is essential to use a fresh coconut for this recipe. Test for this by shaking the nut to ensure there is liquid inside and check the eyes of the nut to ensure they are clean and undamaged.

1 coconut
2 tablespoons rice flour
2 tablespoons honey
2 eggs
1 teaspoon rose water
1 teaspoon caraway seeds
50 g/2 oz sliced almonds

Preparation time: 15 minutes
Cooking time: 1 hour

Pierce the coconut, extract the liquid to one side. Break open the nut, extract the meat and grate it finely. Put the coconut meat together with the liquid from the coconut into the goblet of a liquidiser. Liquidise for 2–3 minutes. Pour the mixture through a double thickness of muslin and squeeze out the thick coconut milk into a bowl. You should now have 300 ml/½ pint of this liquid.

Sieve the rice flour into the coconut milk and pour into a large saucepan. Bring slowly to the boil and stir in the honey. Beat in the eggs and rose water and continue to boil gently until the mixture begins to thicken. Grease a baking dish lightly with butter. Pour the mixture into the dish and sprinkle the caraway seeds and sliced almonds over it. Place in a preheated moderate oven, 180°C/350°F/Gas Mark 4, and bake for 20–30 minutes until golden brown. Serve piping hot.

Sweet dumplings in syrup
Gulab jamun

ৡ৽ৡ৽ৡ৽ৡ৽ৡ৽ৡ৽ৡ৽ৡ৽ৡ৽ৡ৽ৡ৽

Gulab Jamun are quite often offered in Indian restaurants in the West. Sadly, however, they are invariably served cold, having been cooked up to 2–3 days earlier. By this time, they will have lost much of their essential flavour. This flavour comes from a rare combination of cream cheese and condensed milk. Traditionally this would be made by boiling several pints of milk for hours on end until virtually all the liquid has evaporated. The following recipe uses full cream baby milk powder and to my mind the results are just as good.

100 g/4 oz cream cheese
50 g/2 oz full cream dried baby milk
50 g/2 oz self-raising flour
900 ml/1½ pints water
500 g /1 lb sugar
4 cloves
4 cardamoms
1 × 2.5-cm/1-inch stick of cinnamon
a few drops of kewra water
vegetable oil for deep frying

Preparation time: 10 minutes
Cooking time: 45 minutes

Put the cream cheese in a bowl and sift into it the milk powder and flour. Knead together, adding a little liquid milk to form a hard paste. Heat the water in a saucepan and add the sugar. Bring to the boil stirring so that the sugar dissolves. Add the cloves, cardamoms and cinnamon. Boil for 20 minutes to reduce the liquid, making a thin syrup.

Return to the hard paste and form into small balls about 2 cm/¾ inch in diameter. Heat some clean cooking oil in a deep fryer. When a small amount of dough dropped into the oil sizzles and immediately floats to the surface of the oil it is the correct temperature. Fry the balls until they are golden brown. Remove, drain well and drop them into the syrup. As the balls cool (after about 5 minutes), sprinkle on the kewra water and serve.

Fritter whirls in syrup
Jallebi

ৡ৽ৡ৽ৡ৽ৡ৽ৡ৽ৡ৽ৡ৽ৡ৽ৡ৽ৡ৽ৡ৽

There is always to be found a Jallebi stand in all the bazaars of the Indian subcontinent. Here two or three men sit around a huge open vat of hot oil, squeezing in swirls of batter from forcing bags. These swirls of batter immediately sizzle and when golden and crisp are lifted out by another man. They are then plunged into a sweet, aromatic syrup, and then immediately drained, to be served to the waiting customers. By night the Jallebi stands are lit by hissing Petromax lamps and the combination of light and smell creates an almost fairytale atmosphere.

170 g/6 oz flour
150 ml/¼ pint yogurt
½ teaspoon saffron threads
1 teaspoon dried yeast
500 g/1 lb sugar
900 ml/1½ pints water
4 cloves
4 cardamoms
1 × 5-cm/2-inch stick of cinnamon
vegetable oil for deep frying

Preparation time: 3 hours
  30 minutes
Cooking time: 45 minutes

Sift the flour into a bowl. Pour in the yogurt, mix well in and put to one side. Put the saffron threads into a cup and pour on enough boiling water to three-quarters fill the cup. When the water has cooled to blood heat, sprinkle in the yeast with 2 teaspoons of the sugar. After 15 minutes or so, pour this water into the flour and yogurt mixture and stir to produce a batter, about the consistency of double cream. If necessary add a little more water. Whip the batter with a fork, put the bowl to one side in a warm place for 3 hours.

Meanwhile, prepare the syrup. Heat the water in a saucepan and add the sugar, cloves, cardamoms and stick of cinnamon. Bring to the boil and boil for 20 minutes so as to make a thick syrup. Put the syrup to one side.

When the batter is ready, heat some clean cooking oil in a deep frying pan. When a small amount of batter flicked into the oil immediately sizzles and rises to the surface, it is ready. Spoon the batter into a forcing bag fitted with the smallest nozzle. Squeeze the batter in swirls into the hot oil, making each swirl about 8 cm/3 inches across. Cook until the Jallebi turns golden brown, remove from the oil with a slotted spoon and transfer to the syrup. Repeat this until all the batter is used up. Jallebis are best served hot, freshly cooked and immersed in the warm syrup. They can also be served cold and they will keep for up to 1 week in a refrigerator.

From left to right: Beveca, Gulab jamun and Jallebi.

Nut fudge
Bombay halwa

Just as the best fruit cakes are in the West, the best halwas are measured by the amount of nuts and other rich ingredients. This recipe is rich in butter and in pistachios and almonds.

300 ml/½ pint water
350 g/12 oz soft brown sugar
1 tablespoon cornflour
50 g/2 oz almonds
50 g/2 oz pistachio nuts
100 g/4 oz butter
6 cardamoms
6 cloves
1 lemon

Preparation time: 15 minutes
Cooking time: 15 minutes plus
    chilling time

Put the water into a saucepan, bring to the boil, add the sugar and dissolve it in the water. Continue to boil to drive off the water. Mix the cornflour with a little of the syrup to form a smooth paste and add this paste to the saucepan.

Roughly chop the almonds and pistachio nuts. In a frying pan heat the butter and fry the almonds and the pistachio nuts. Remove the seeds from the cardamoms and fry those too with the nuts. Crush the cloves and add to the frying pan, fry for a further 2 minutes and then transfer the contents of the frying pan to the saucepan. Continue to stir until the mixture becomes very stiff. Squeeze in the juice from the lemon. Scoop a little of the mixture out and drop it onto a cold plate. If the mixture immediately solidifies, then it is ready to pour out into a shallow tin.

Put the tin in a cool place and then in the refrigerator. When it is solid cut it into traditional diamond shapes with a sharp knife and serve. Halwa will keep for up to a month in an airtight tin set in a cool place.

Carrot pudding
Gajrela

This is a very popular recipe particularly in the north of India. It uses large amounts of cream to make a thick sauce in which are soaked sweetened grated carrots. It is certainly one of the easier Indian sweet dishes to make.

500 g/1 lb carrots
100 g/4 oz ghee or 120 ml/4 fl oz
    cooking oil
6 cardamoms
6 cloves
1 × 5-cm/2-inch stick of cinnamon
900 ml/1½ pints milk
225 g/½ lb soft brown sugar
100 g/4 oz chopped almonds
50 g/2 oz sultanas
300 ml/½ pint double cream

Preparation time: 10 minutes
Cooking time: 1 hour 10 minutes

Scrub the carrots and grate them on the coarsest side of the grater. Heat the ghee or cooking oil in a saucepan. Remove the seeds from the cardamoms and fry them, together with the cloves and cinnamon, broken into small pieces, for 2–3 minutes. Add the grated carrot and stir it so that it is well mixed in with the ghee.

Pour on the milk and add the sugar. Bring to the boil and stir to dissolve the sugar. Continue to boil for 30 minutes until the milk begins to thicken. Reduce the heat and add the almonds and sultanas. Pour in the double cream and continue to cook for a further 15 minutes. Serve hot. Gajrela is sometimes served cold, but to my mind it is not as appetising as the ghee tends to coagulate when the dish is chilled.

Sweet rice
Meeta chawal

Clearly, with so much rice grown in the Indian subcontinent it would be surprising if there were not a number of sweet dishes made with rice. This particular dish is cooked almost like a savoury Pillao but using sweetened water instead of stock.

225 g/½ lb Basmati rice
100 g/4 oz ghee or 120 ml/4 fl oz
    cooking oil
6 cloves
6 cardamoms
1 × 8-cm/3-inch stick of cinnamon
½ teaspoon mace
50 g/2 oz soft brown sugar
½ teaspoon saffron threads
2 tablespoons honey
50 g/2 oz sultanas
50 g/2 oz sliced almonds
50 g/2 oz pistachios

Preparation time: 10 minutes plus
    4 hours soaking
Cooking time: 45 minutes

Wash the rice well and pick it over to remove any impurities. Cover with cold water and leave to soak for 4 hours.

Heat the ghee or cooking oil in a large, heavy saucepan. Fry the cloves, cardamoms, cinnamon and mace for 3 minutes. Drain the water from the rice and add the rice to the saucepan, stirring well to ensure that the rice is well coated with oil. Now pour on enough boiling water to cover the rice. Add the sugar and bring back to the boil. Add the saffron threads. Cover the saucepan and cook for 15–20 minutes until the rice is *al dente*. Fold in the honey, sultanas, almonds and pistachios and cook for a further 5 minutes. Serve piping hot.

Sweet dumplings with cream Chuckolee

This is rather a rich dish, if somewhat rarely eaten these days. Traditionally the dumplings are cut into geometrical shapes, usually diamonds, but sometimes squares, oblongs and rhomboids. The shape, needless to say, makes very little difference to the taste! The version of this dish cooked in the south of India calls for coconut milk, however, I have used cream to add extra richness to it.

170 g/6 oz flour
½ teaspoon salt
50 g/2 oz butter
1 egg
1.2 litres/2 pints milk
1 × 8-cm/3-inch stick of cinnamon
4 cloves
4 cardamoms
3 tablespoons honey
150 ml/¼ pint double cream

Preparation time: 15 minutes
Cooking time: 25 minutes

Sieve the flour and the salt together. Rub in the butter and break in the egg to form a hard paste. Knead for at least 5 minutes until a very smooth and pliable mixture is obtained. Roll the dough out to about 0.5 cm/¼ inch thick and cut into geometrical shapes.

Heat the milk in a heavy saucepan, together with the cinnamon, cloves, cardamoms and honey. Bring to the boil and simmer gently while dropping each individual piece of pastry into the mixture. Cook for 10 minutes. With a slotted spoon scoop out the cinnamon, cloves and cardamoms (or as many as you can). Reduce the heat and gently stir in the cream so as not to break up the dumplings. Serve immediately.

From above: Bombay halwa, Gajrela, Meeta chawal and Chuckolee.

Semolina pudding
Suji halwa

For many people in the West, semolina pudding reminds them of terrible school meals. However, the Indians have developed much better uses of semolina and I am sure if you try Suji Halwa you will not even know that there is semolina in the recipe!

600 ml/1 pint milk
100 g/4 oz semolina
350 g/12 oz soft brown sugar
50 g/2 oz ghee or butter
10 cardamoms
1 tablespoon chopped almonds

Preparation time: 5 minutes
Cooking time: 45 minutes plus
     chilling

Bring the milk to the boil. As it warms, remove a couple of spoonfuls to mix in with the semolina. At first make a thick paste and then thin it down with more milk. Once the semolina is well mixed in, add to the milk in the saucepan. Continue to boil gently and add the sugar, stirring to dissolve it.

Heat the ghee or butter in a frying pan. Remove the seeds from the cardamoms and crush them with a rolling pin. Fry the seeds gently together with the chopped almonds for 1–2 minutes. Pour the ghee, cardamoms and almond mixture into the milk and continue to boil gently. As the mixture thickens, stir constantly to ensure that it does not stick to the bottom or sides of the saucepan. When the mixture is very thick and on the verge of turning solid, transfer it to a buttered dish, level out the surface and allow to cool. Once it is cool, cut it into the traditional diamond shapes and serve. Suji Halwa will keep in an airtight tin in a cool place for up to 3 weeks.

Pistachio sweetmeat
Pista barfi

Not many people in India attempt to make the various sweetmeats or Barfis at home as they are quite often better made in bulk by the specialist sweetmeat shops. However, you can obtain a very fresh-tasting sweetmeat by making it yourself. The essential thing to remember when making this recipe is to watch the mixture in every stage of cooking, to ensure that it does not stick or burn.

1.2 litres/2 pints gold top milk
350 g/12 oz soft brown sugar
170 g/6 oz chopped pistachios
1 tablespoon rice flour
50 g/2 oz ghee
½ teaspoon almond essence

Preparation time: 10 minutes
Cooking time: 1 hour plus 1 hour
     chilling

Put the milk into a large, heavy saucepan and bring to the boil, dissolving the sugar into it. Boil gently for 30 minutes or so, until the milk has reduced and begun to thicken. Stir in the chopped pistachios. Sieve in the tablespoon of rice flour. Continue to cook for another 20 minutes until the mixture is really thick. Stir in all but a teaspoonful of the ghee and cook for a further 5 minutes. Add the almond essence.

At this stage it is important to keep scraping the sides of the saucepan with a spatula and turning the mixture constantly to ensure that it does not stick. Use the remaining ghee to grease a large, flat tin and pour the mixture onto the tin, spreading it out flat. Allow to cool for an hour and then cut into traditional diamond shapes and serve. Barfi may be kept in a cool place, sealed in an airtight tin, for up to a month.

Carrot pudding
Gajjar ka halwa

This is one of the most popular of puddings although it is not strictly a Halwa as it does not keep for as long as the traditional Halwas do. Because of the fresh carrot content it has to be eaten within 3 or 4 days. It is certainly one of the simplest of Halwas to make and probably a good one to make if you are new to cooking Indian puddings.

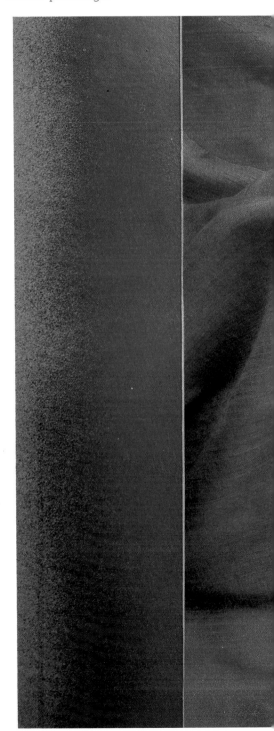

From above centre clockwise: Suji halwa, Gajjar ka halwa and Pista barfi.

900 ml/1½ pints milk
100 g/4 oz soft brown sugar
225 g/½ lb carrots
100 g/4 oz unsalted butter
50 g/2 oz sliced almonds
50 g/2 oz sultanas
10 cardamoms
¼ teaspoon mace
2 tablespoons honey

Preparation time: 10 minutes
Cooking time: 1 hour 30 minutes

Heat the milk in a large, heavy saucepan and bring to the boil. Add the sugar. While this is happening scrub the carrots and grate them coarsely. Add them to the milk. Once it is boiling reduce the heat to just below boiling point and cook, with the pan uncovered, for 45 minutes, stirring from time to time to ensure the carrots do not stick to the bottom of the saucepan.

Heat the butter in a large frying pan, and when it has melted fry the almonds and sultanas gently for 2 minutes. Remove the seeds from the cardamoms and crush them between two pieces of greaseproof paper using a rolling pin. Add the cardamoms, together with the mace, to the frying pan and stir in well. Then add the honey, stirring in well, and cook for a further 1 minute.

Pour the milk and carrot mixture, which by now should be quite thick, into the frying pan. If there is too much liquid at this stage, pour part of it in and continue to boil off the liquid, adding more from the saucepan when there is room. Continue to boil gently, stirring constantly, until the mixture begins to stiffen and goes solid. Once it is beginning to solidify remove from the heat and transfer to a baking dish and allow to cool. When cool cut into the traditional diamond shapes and serve.

Honey snacks
Shehed tukra

ᲗᲔᲗᲔᲗᲔᲗᲔᲗᲔᲗᲔᲗᲔᲗᲔᲗᲔᲗᲔᲗᲔ

This is a very simple recipe to follow. It consists of squares of puff pastry coated with a rather tasty, aromatic syrup. As with most pastries it is best eaten fresh, but it will keep chilled for up to a week.

225 g/½ lb self-raising flour
50 g/2 oz ghee or butter
½ teaspoon nutmeg
pinch of cinnamon
150 ml/¼ pint milk
cooking oil for deep frying
4 tablespoons thin clear honey
1 × 5-cm/2-inch stick of cinnamon
4 cloves
4 cardamoms

Preparation time: 15 minutes
Cooking time: 20 minutes

Sieve the flour into a bowl. Heat the ghee or butter gently in a saucepan and stir into it the nutmeg and cinnamon. Rub the melted ghee or butter into the flour and add the milk to make a good, hard dough. Knead the mixture well for at least 5 minutes, then roll out to between 0.5 and 1 cm/¼ and ½ inch thick. Cut into 2.5-cm/1-inch squares. Heat some clean cooking oil in a deep frying pan and deep fry the squares until they are golden brown.

While this is happening, gently heat the honey in a saucepan together with the stick of cinnamon, cloves and seeds from the cardamoms. Allow to boil gently so that the honey reduces slightly and takes up the flavour of the cinnamon and cardamoms. When golden brown drain the squares of puff pastry on kitchen paper. Arrange them in a dish and pour on the honey, straining the cloves, cardamoms and cinnamon. Serve.

Saffron egg
Safran anday

ᲗᲔᲗᲔᲗᲔᲗᲔᲗᲔᲗᲔᲗᲔᲗᲔᲗᲔᲗᲔᲗᲔ

It is quite unusual to find all-egg puddings in India, mainly because there is still very much an emphasis on puddings that will keep for some time, such as the Halwa and other sweetmeats. Egg puddings of course have to be eaten virtually as soon as they are cooked as they do not keep very long.

4 eggs
150 ml/¼ pint milk
1 tablespoon ground almonds
½ teaspoon saffron threads
75 g/3 oz butter
100 g/4 oz soft brown sugar

Preparation time: 10 minutes
Cooking time: 1 hour 20 minutes

Above left to right: Shehed tukra and Malpura; below left to right: Safran anday and Shahi tukra.

Beat the eggs together with the milk and stir in the ground almonds. Put the saffron threads into a cup and pour over enough boiling water to three-quarters fill the cup.

Heat the egg and milk mixture very gently together with the butter in a heavy saucepan and bring slowly to the boil, adding the sugar, stirring to ensure that it is dissolved. Simmer gently for 5 minutes. Pour in the saffron water, straining the threads. Stir in well and continue to simmer. When the mixture begins to thicken pour it into a greased baking dish. Bake in a preheated medium oven, 180°C/350°F/Gas Mark 4, for 1 hour until it is brown. Serve immediately.

Indian pancakes
Malpura

ৡ৵ৡ৵ৡ৵ৡ৵ৡ৵ৡ৵ৡ৵ৡ৵ৡ৵ৡ৵ৡ৵

These are very popular throughout the whole of India. Traditionally they are cooked not in a frying pan but in earthenware pans or chatties. These chatties are set in hot charcoal and rubbed with a little ghee on the inside. The pancake batter is then poured in and the chatties immediately spun to make the batter swirl to the outside of the chatti to cook very quickly until crisp and biscuit-like. Frying pans serve just as well to make this dish and you will find no problem in following the recipe. Malpuras can be eaten on their own or with other dishes, for example with one of the vermicelli or rice puddings.

170 g/6 oz wholemeal flour
1 teaspoon baking powder
300 ml/½ pint milk
2 tablespoons honey
½ teaspoon aniseed
50 g/2 oz ghee or butter

Preparation time: 20 minutes plus
  2 hours resting
Cooking time: 15 minutes

Sieve the flour and baking powder into a bowl. Warm the milk gently and dissolve the honey into it. When the milk reaches blood heat, mix in the flour to form a fairly thick batter. Gently crush the aniseed to release some of its flavour and beat it into the batter. Whip the batter well and put to one side to rest for 2 hours. Whip it once again just before cooking the pancakes.

In a large, heavy saucepan heat the ghee or butter until it is foaming. Using a jug, pour a little of the batter into the centre of the frying pan, allowing it to spread to the sides of the pan quite quickly. Fry gently over a medium heat, turning the pancake to ensure that it is brown on both sides. Lift out and drain off any excess fat. Put to one side in a warm oven to keep until you have made the rest of the pancakes. Malpuras are best served just warm.

Royal bread pudding
Shahi tukra

ৡ৵ৡ৵ৡ৵ৡ৵ৡ৵ৡ৵ৡ৵ৡ৵ৡ৵ৡ৵ৡ৵

This is regarded as one of the richest dishes ever produced by the Moguls, containing pistachios, almonds, cream and saffron.

170 g/6 oz ghee or 175 ml/6 fl oz
  cooking oil
25 g/1 oz chopped almonds
75 g/3 oz pistachios
1 teaspoon saffron threads
8 slices white bread, at least
  0.5 cm/¼ inch thick
150 g/¼ pint milk
300 ml/½ pint double cream
300 ml/½ pint water
225 g/½ lb soft brown sugar
2 teaspoons kewra water

Preparation time: 10 minutes
Cooking time: 30 minutes plus
  2 hours chilling

Heat the ghee or cooking oil in a large, heavy frying pan and gently fry the almonds and pistachios for 2 minutes. Scoop them out with a slotted spoon and put to one side. Put the saffron threads into a cup and pour on sufficient boiling water to half fill the cup. Put to one side. Take the bread slices and remove the crusts. Cut each slice into half and fry the bread pieces in the ghee until they are light brown on both sides. It is important at this stage not to overdo the frying of the bread. Remove the bread slices and put to one side.

Heat the milk, cream and water together in a heavy saucepan and stir in the sugar as it comes to the boil. Continue to boil until it begins to thicken, then pour in the saffron water, squeezing any colour from the threads. Continue to cook for a further 10 minutes until a thick syrup is obtained.

Arrange a layer of bread slices in a dish, sprinkle on some of the pistachios and almonds and pour on some of the milk and cream mixture. Then add crossways another layer of bread, more almonds and pistachios and pour on the rest of the cream and milk mixture.

Allow to cool to room temperature, sprinkle in the kewra water, put in a refrigerator and chill for 2 hours before serving. Shahi Tukra will keep in the refrigerator for 3–5 days.

Banana puffs
Kayla pustholes

۞۞۞۞۞۞۞۞۞۞۞۞۞۞۞۞

Pustholes are very popular in the south of India. They can be filled with virtually anything but this recipe uses a mixture of bananas and coconut. Feel free to experiment with other fillings.

2 bananas
225 g/½ lb strong white flour
1 teaspoon salt
50 g/2 oz butter
2–3 tablespoons milk
½ fresh coconut
kewra water
cooking oil for frying

Preparation time: 20 minutes
Cooking time: 15 minutes

Sieve the flour and salt together. Rub in the butter and knead into a firm dough with the milk. Knead until the dough is pliable and roll out to about 0.25 cm/$\frac{1}{16}$ inch thick. Cut into 8-cm/3-inch circles. Mash the bananas and grate the fresh coconut into it. Sprinkle in 2 or 3 drops of kewra water. Place small amounts of the mixture in the centre of each circle, wet the edges of the pastry and gather them together to form a parcel.

Heat some clean cooking oil in a deep frying pan and fry the pustholes until they are golden brown. Lift out with a slotted spoon, drain on kitchen paper and serve while still warm.

Mango aroma
Am illaichi

۞۞۞۞۞۞۞۞۞۞۞۞۞۞۞۞

This is a good recipe for using up overripe mangoes, which you may be able to find in shops at knockdown prices. It does not matter if the mangoes are bruised and very soft.

900 g/2 lb fresh mangoes or a
    350-g/12-oz tin of mango pulp
¼ fresh coconut
450 ml/¾ pint milk
¼ teaspoon saffron threads
2 tablespoons honey
50 g/2 oz chopped almonds
5 cardamoms
½ teaspoon cinnamon
½ teaspoon yellow colouring

Spicy fruit salad
Chaat

꠸꠸꠸꠸꠸꠸꠸꠸꠸꠸꠸꠸꠸꠸꠸꠸꠸

Throughout India, Pakistan and Bangladesh there are thousands of small stalls dotted along the roadside serving chilled fruit, cut up into small pieces and spiced with a mixture of chilli powder and black pepper. More often than not, salt is sprinkled onto the fruit as well. The collective name for this type of dish is Chaat and the stalls where it is sold are known as Chaat houses. The fruit is spiced and salted, not only to add flavour but to increase perspiration and in so doing rid the body of all kinds of toxic wastes. The salt serves to replace that lost through perspiration. Chaat can be made with virtually any combination of fruits. The essential thing to remember is not to cut the fruit too thin or into too small pieces otherwise the fruit will go mushy. The ingredients given in the following recipe may, of course, be varied according to the fruit available.

2 bananas
1 apple
1 pear
½ honeydew melon
2 oranges
1 lemon
2 teaspoons black pepper
1 teaspoon chilli powder
1½ teaspoons salt

Preparation time: 30 minutes plus
  2 hours chilling

Remove the seeds from the melon and cut up the flesh into 4-cm/1½-inch cubes. Peel and core the apple and pear and cut into large chunks of similar size. Peel the oranges and chop roughly into pieces about 2.5 cm/1 inch big. Remove the skin from the bananas and chop into slices about 2 cm/¾ inch thick. Mix with the other fruit and squeeze on the juice from the lemon. Gently turn the fruit mixture, sprinkling in the salt, black pepper and chilli powder. Chill in the refrigerator for 2 hours and serve.

Left: Kayla pustholes; centre above: Chaat; centre below: Am illaichi; right: Am.

Mangoes
Am

꠸꠸꠸꠸꠸꠸꠸꠸꠸꠸꠸꠸꠸꠸꠸꠸꠸

The main problem with importing mangoes into Western countries is the fact that they are among the most perishable of fruits and once picked they begin to ripen very quickly. Certainly if they are picked ripe, by the time they arrive here, even if brought by air, they will generally be past their best. So far, there has been no real way of slowing this ripening process. Bananas, when they are shipped from the West Indies, are often cooled and surrounded by Ethylene gas to slow the ripening process. This does not seem to work with mangoes.

The key to buying mangoes is to buy ones that are just at their peak. Colour is not a great help as mangoes come in a number of different types. Colours can range from green or yellow to almost bright red. There are two basic kinds of mangoes. In India these are known as Cartna Wallah, which are for cutting, and Chusne Wallah for sucking. For serving with an Indian dinner you should choose the larger, cutting mangoes, which are firmer to the touch and which make good-size mango pieces. One large mango, about 23 cm/9 inches long, will provide more than enough fruit for a dessert for two people (or use one smaller mango per person). All mangoes have a large, flat stone inside and the trick is to be able to trim away the flesh from the stone as cleanly as possible. This is not as easy as it sounds as the stone is covered in hairs which grow out into the flesh and these have to be cut through as you cut the mango.

Stand the mango on end and with a sharp knife cut down one side of the mango, parallel with one side of the flat stone. Do the same with the other side. You now have two side slices of mango. In the middle will be left the stone surrounded by a relatively small amount of flesh. Trim this away as cleanly as you can and throw the stone away. It is inevitable that you will lose some of the mango, as it sticks to the hairs on the stone. The skin of the mango can be trimmed away from the remaining pieces or the mango can be served with the skin intact and you then scoop the flesh with a spoon.

Preparation time: 10 minutes
Cooking time: 30 minutes plus
  chilling time

Peel the mangoes and remove the flesh from the central stone. Finely grate the coconut and mix it together with the mango pulp in a liquidiser. Heat the milk in a heavy saucepan and add the saffron threads, honey and chopped almonds. Remove the seeds from the cardamoms, crush them with a rolling pin and add to the milk, together with the cinnamon.

Bring the milk to the boil and reduce its volume by about a quarter. Stir in the mango and coconut mixture and yellow colouring and continue to boil gently until it begins to thicken. When you have a very thick sauce, cool the mixture and then whip it with a whisk. Transfer to a serving bowl and chill.

Sugar cane
Gunna

Sugar cane is not generally found in the fruiterers in the West, however, if you do find it on offer, buy it because it makes a very good and interesting dessert. The skill in serving it is to make sure that you have cut it into small chunks, no more than 4 cm/1½ inches long, and if the sugar cane is more than 2.5 cm/1 inch in diameter, split the chunks in half. Also, try to remove as much of the outer bark of the cane as possible. Arrange the chunks in a bowl, chill before serving and preferably serve on a bed of crushed ice. Guests then chew pieces of the sugar cane, sucking away the juice and spitting out the leftover pulp.

Papaya
Papita

The papaya or paw-paw as it is often known, is very highly regarded for its digestive quality. It certainly makes a very good dessert. As with all soft fruits it is important to make sure the papaya is not overripe. Choose a fruit that is of a good, deep colour. The flesh should be firm but yield against pressure. Cut the paw-paw in half lengthways and scoop out the seeds. Be careful when dealing with the paw-paw as it produces an enzyme which causes some people to come out in a rash. If you are prone to allergic responses to fruits, then wear rubber gloves to prepare the fruit. Scoop away the black seeds from the centre of the paw-paw – these are of no use, except that in southern India they are said to have mysterious medicinal qualities, producing all kinds of effects if consumed by people! Cut the halves of paw-paw into half once again, lengthways and serve just as you would a melon. The paw-paw is best served chilled.

Lychee
Leechee

Most people in the Western world are familiar with tinned lychees. But if you are able to get hold of fresh lychees, they are well worth serving as an accompaniment to an Indian meal. Lychees grow on small trees and they are covered with a hard but brittle outer skin. Serve them in their outer skin just as you would grapes, or prepare them by peeling away the skin and removing the glossy stone from the inside of the lychees. As you do this, be careful not to squash the lychee too much, otherwise you will lose some of the juice from the fruit. A bowl of lychees always tastes better if chilled. When buying lychees just gently squeeze them to see that they are still firm in their outer peel and beware of being given any crushed ones as they go off very quickly.

Guavas
Amrood

Guavas are not indigenous to India. They were imported into India from South America, where they were discovered by the Spaniards. They can vary in shape, from being almost spherical to elongated like a large Victoria plum. They bruise very easily so it is important to choose ones that have not been damaged. They should be firm but just slightly yield to gentle pressure. Check to see also that the skin is smooth and yellow. Serve in a fruit bowl or cut up, with the hard, glossy seeds inside scooped away to make a fruit salad. As with apples, you will need to squeeze a little lemon juice onto the guava to prevent it browning if you do cut it up for fruit salad.

Pineapple
Ananas

Pineapples are now grown throughout India on a commercial basis. Whilst they are not exclusively an Indian fruit I have included them here as many people would love to serve fresh pineapple but are not too sure how to prepare it.

The first thing is to choose a good, ripe pineapple, free of any large areas of green. A good pineapple should be bright orange and if pressed with the thumbs around the crown of leaves it should have a little give in it. The leaves too should be bright green and should not be blemished by browning. The best way to serve it for a dessert is, I think, to make Pineapple Boats.

This is done by standing the pineapple upright and cutting down with a sharp knife to form two halves and then cutting each half lengthways into two or three, depending on the girth of the pineapple. If you can manage it, leave the leaves on when you do this. I have found that a serrated knife is best for cutting pineapple, but whatever sort you use it has to be good and sharp. Prepare the wedges for the table by cutting the flesh through with a knife and then crossways in chunks, so that your guests can consume the pineapple with the minimum fuss.

Water melon
Tarbouz

Water melons are eaten extensively in the Indian subcontinent and a large wedge makes a very good starter or dessert for an Indian meal. Usually half a water melon of average size, about 45 cm/18 inches in diameter, is sufficient for four people. Chill the water melon well before serving and remember that a much larger wedge is needed, about twice the size in fact than with the conventional honeydew melon.

Above left to right: anana and tarbouz; centre left to right: am and amrood; below left to right: papita and gunna.

Chapter Ten
Snacks and drinks

In the cities of the Indian subcontinent literally millions of people rely on snacks as a major part of their daily diet. Office workers and the up-and-coming class of clerical workers crowd round the stalls selling any number of savouries during their lunch-breaks and buy such varied delicacies as puff pastry filled with tamarind water, thin pancakes and pasties stuffed with minced meat or vegetable curry. Similarly, when invited to tea at any well-to-do house, it is considered impolite not to offer some kind of savoury refreshment to go with the tea. There are any number of different snacks served in Indian cooking and this chapter contains some of the most popular ones.

Traditionally Indians do not drink alcohol with their food. However, in recent years increasing numbers of people, particularly in the cities, have developed a liking for beer, although wine is still very seldom found. There are, though, many non-alcoholic drinks, which accompany Indian food far better than alcoholic ones. Number one, of course, is tea, universally grown and drunk throughout the Indian subcontinent. The average person in India tends to drink tea very, very sweet, and if he can obtain it, with quite a lot of milk. Tea is also made quite strong and there are a number of various ways of serving it. There are also the drinks based on a combination of sweetened essences, such as sandalwood and mint, and the milk-based drinks. Some of the drinks in this chapter are good taken just on their own on a hot summer's day, particularly the recipe for Nimboo Pani or Lemon Water.

Stuffed pastry cases
Samosa

Samosas are, I suppose, the Indian equivalent of Cornish Pasties. However, the cooking is very different. Instead of being baked in an oven, a Samosa is filled with precooked vegetable or minced meat curry and deep fried until crisp. A couple of Samosas make a very filling snack.

For the fillings I suggest you use either Keema Pimento as described on page 85 or Aloo Bogar, as described on page 131. However, any dry dish, vegetable or meat, can be used for the filling. Feel free to experiment. This recipe makes 15–20 samosas.

100 g/4 oz flour
$\frac{1}{2}$ teaspoon baking powder
$\frac{1}{2}$ teaspoon black pepper
$\frac{1}{2}$ teaspoon salt
$\frac{1}{2}$ teaspoon cumin seeds
50 g/2 oz margarine
2 tablespoons natural yogurt
vegetable oil for deep frying

Preparation time: 30 minutes
Cooking time: 15 minutes

Sieve the flour, baking powder, black pepper and salt together into a bowl. Sprinkle in the cumin seeds and mix in well. Rub in the margarine and then add the yogurt to form a hard dough. Knead well, adding more flour or yogurt to obtain the right consistency. The dough should be fairly moist, but hard. Break off balls, approximately 2.5 cm/1 inch in diameter.

On a well-floured board, roll them out so they are wafer thin, less than 2 mm/$\frac{1}{16}$ inch. This is quite difficult to do and you may find you need several attempts at rolling the dough out thinly. It is not too critical if the dough is not rolled out to form perfect circles. Place each successive disc of dough on top of another, separated by a good dusting of flour.

Cut the pile of dough circles in half, you should now have approximately 15–20 semicircles of dough. Take each semicircle, spoon in a little filling, being careful not to put in too much. Fold the semicircle of pastry into a triangular shape and seal by moistening the edges of the dough with a little water.

When you have filled all the cases, heat some clean vegetable oil in a deep frying pan until a small piece of dough thrown into the oil immediately sizzles and floats to the surface and goes golden brown. Fry the Samosas until they are golden brown and crisp. Lift out with a slotted spoon, drain on kitchen paper and serve either hot or cold.

Fritters
Pakora

Pakoras are to be found on offer in any bazaar of any city in India. They are very simple to make, consisting of deep-fried batter made from chick-pea flour. This recipe is for basic batter. It is possible to use the batter to coat any number of different vegetables cut into slices and in some cases spinach leaves are dipped into the batter and fried. However, Pakoras are just as tasty when the batter itself is fried.

100 g/4 oz chick-pea flour
$1\frac{1}{2}$ teaspoons salt
$\frac{1}{2}$ teaspoon chilli powder
1 teaspoon turmeric
1 teaspoon garam masala
2 tablespoons natural yogurt
cooking oil for frying

Preparation time: 15 minutes plus
 1 hour resting
Cooking time: 20 minutes

Sieve the chick-pea flour into a bowl, using the back of a spoon to force any lumps through the sieve. Sprinkle in the salt, chilli powder, turmeric and garam masala. Mix in well and add the yogurt. Stir well, adding a little water to make a fairly thick batter. Whisk with a fork and leave to stand for 1 hour.

Whisk the batter once more. Heat some cooking oil to a depth of 5–8 cm/2–3 inches in a frying pan. Drop a small piece of batter into the oil and if it immediately sizzles and floats to the surface and starts to brown, the oil is ready. Drop spoonfuls of the batter into the hot fat and cook until golden brown. Lift out with a slotted spoon, drain on kitchen paper and serve.

*Samosa and Pakora;
Shami kebabs.*

Ground meat patties
Shami kebabs

Shami Kebabs are, to my mind, one of the best kebabs in Indian cuisine. They do require a double cooking process, where the meat is first of all cooked together with the lentils. Then it is ground to a fine paste, formed into patties and fried again. The Kebabs are good served either hot or cold. A freshly cooked Shami Kebab always tastes better than one kept for a day or two.

500 g/1 lb minced meat
100 g/4 oz ghee or 120 ml/4 fl oz
   cooking oil
2 medium onions
2 cloves garlic
1 × 2.5-cm/1-inch piece of fresh
   ginger
2 teaspoons coriander seeds
6 cloves
6 cardamoms
1½ teaspoons black pepper
½ teaspoon ground cinnamon
1½ teaspoons chilli powder
2 tablespoons chick peas or channa
   dal
1 teaspoon salt
1 teaspoon onion seeds
2 tablespoons natural yogurt
1 tablespoon chopped coriander
   leaves
1 egg
cooking oil for frying

Preparation time: 15 minutes
Cooking time: 1 hour

Heat the ghee or cooking oil in a heavy saucepan. Peel and finely chop one of the onions and fry until it is soft. Peel and finely chop the cloves of garlic and the ginger. Add those to the saucepan and fry for a further minute and then add the coriander seeds, cloves and the seeds from the cardamoms. Sprinkle in the black pepper, cinnamon and the chilli powder. Mix in well and cook for a further 30 seconds.

Add the minced meat, turning constantly to ensure that the spice mixture is well dispersed in the meat. Reduce the heat so that the meat cooks very slowly. Wash the chick peas, put into a saucepan, cover with water and boil until they are soft.

Drain the water from the chick peas and mix them with the meat. Increase the heat and mix in well. Add the salt and onion seeds and continue to cook until the meat has totally changed colour. Now mix in the yogurt. Remove from the heat and pass through a very fine grinder or use a mortar and pestle or a blender. The idea is to end up with a very fine paste. Knead the paste well, peel and finely chop the remaining onion and add to the paste mix. Form the paste into kebabs about 5 cm/2 inches in diameter and 1 cm/½ inch thick. Press a few chopped coriander leaves into the centre of each kebab. Beat the egg well. Dip each kebab in the egg and shallow fry in as little oil as possible until brown on both sides. Lift out with a slotted spoon, drain on kitchen paper and serve.

Nut puffs
Kachori

❀❀❀❀❀❀❀❀❀❀❀❀❀❀❀❀

Kachoris are a very unusual snack, and apart from the spices it is hard to decide whether they are sweet or savoury. They consist of pastry cases filled with a purée made from cashews, almonds and pistachios and flavoured with peas. The purée must be made very stiff. As with Semolina Fritters, Kachoris do not keep too well and are best served still warm from the frying pan.

225 g/½ lb flour
1 teaspoon salt
½ teaspoon bicarbonate of soda
100 g/4 oz ghee
25 g/1 oz pistachios
25 g/1 oz cashew nuts
25 g/1 oz chopped almonds
2 teaspoons chilli powder
1 teaspoon garam masala
50 g/2 oz desiccated coconut
100 g/4 oz frozen peas
cooking oil for deep frying

Preparation time: 15 minutes plus
  1 hour resting
Cooking time: 45 minutes

Sieve the flour into a bowl with the salt and bicarbonate of soda. Rub in 50 g/2 oz of the ghee and then add sufficient water to make a hard dough. Put the dough to one side to rest for 1 hour. Heat the remaining ghee or 60 ml/2 oz cooking oil in a frying pan and gently fry the pistachios, cashews and almonds. Sprinkle in the chilli powder and garam masala and add the desiccated coconut.

Now add the peas and continue to cook until the peas are heated through. By this stage most of the ghee should have been absorbed by the nuts. If it has not, then strain the ghee from the frying pan. Put the mixture into a liquidiser and blend to form a fine purée. This should be quite stiff. If it is not sufficiently stiff add a little more coconut.

Break off pieces of the dough and form into balls about 4 cm/1½ inches in diameter. Roll out into circles about 10 cm/4 inches across. Spoon the purée into the circles, gather up the corners and pinch to seal the circles into patties. Heat some clean cooking oil in a deep frying pan and when a little of the dough added sizzles and rises to the surface, the oil is ready. Deep fry the patties until they are golden brown. Lift out with a slotted spoon, drain on kitchen paper and serve.

Fried rice balls
Tali chawal

❀❀❀❀❀❀❀❀❀❀❀❀❀❀❀❀

This recipe is simple. It consists of cooked rice, mixed with a few spices and coriander and deep fried. It is a good way of using up leftover boiled rice.

170 g/6 oz rice
1 teaspoon salt
2 teaspoons chilli powder
½ teaspoon garam masala
1 tablespoon chopped coriander
  leaves

Preparation time: 30 minutes
Cooking time: 15 minutes

Wash the rice well and remove any impurities. Put into a saucepan and cover with water. Bring to the boil and cook until the rice is *al dente*. Drain the water off and grind the rice to a fine paste, using a liquidiser. Mix in the salt, chilli powder and garam masala and form into small balls, 2.5 cm/1 inch in diameter. Press a few of the coriander leaves into each ball.

Heat some clean cooking oil in a deep frying pan and drop in a small piece of rice dough. If it immediately sizzles and floats to the surface the oil is ready. Fry the balls until they are crisp and serve immediately.

Above: Tali chawal; below left to right: Kachori and Suji pakora.

Semolina fritters
Suji pakora

ᘓᘒᘓᘒᘓᘒᘓᘒᘓᘒᘓᘒᘓᘒᘓᘒᘓᘒᘓᘒᘓ

This is one of the many semolina recipes to be found in Indian cooking. These fritters are easy to make, combining semolina with natural yogurt and a little spice. They tend not to keep very well, so they are best served within an hour or so of cooking.

100 g/4 oz semolina
1 teaspoon garam masala
1 teaspoon salt
2 teaspoons chilli powder
2 tablespoons natural yogurt
150 ml/¼ pint water
1 medium onion
1 clove garlic
1 tablespoon chopped coriander
    leaves
cooking oil for frying

Preparation time: 20 minutes plus
    30 minutes resting
Cooking time: 15 minutes

Sieve the semolina into a bowl, together with the garam masala, salt and chilli powder. Mix in well. Add the yogurt. Mix the yogurt into the semolina to form a stiff paste, then add sufficient water to make a thick batter. Transfer the batter to the goblet of a liquidiser. Peel and finely chop the onion and garlic. Add to the liquidiser and liquidise together for 2 minutes, so the onion and garlic are fully mixed in with the batter. Leave to stand for 30 minutes. Then liquidise again for 30 seconds and mix in the chopped coriander leaves.

Heat some oil in a deep frying pan and when a small drop of batter immediately sizzles and floats to the surface, the oil is ready. Pour in spoonfuls of the batter and fry until crisp. Lift out with a slotted spoon, drain on kitchen paper and serve.

Stuffed coconut pancake Alebele

This is a very typical dish on the west and south coast of India and although it is generally eaten as a snack, it is certainly very filling. To obtain the true flavour one should use fresh coconut although it can be made successfully with desiccated.

100 g/4 oz flour
½ teaspoon salt
pinch of bicarbonate of soda
2 eggs
½ fresh coconut or 100 g/4 oz desiccated coconut
450 ml/¾ pint milk
50 g/2 oz ghee or 60 ml/2 fl oz cooking oil
1 teaspoon fresh aniseed
1 × 2.5-cm/1-inch piece of fresh ginger
100 g/4 oz soft brown sugar
ghee or cooking oil for frying

Preparation time: 20 minutes plus 1 hour resting
Cooking time: 30 minutes

Sieve the flour, salt and bicarbonate of soda into a bowl. Beat in the eggs and milk to form a batter. Whip well and leave to stand for 1 hour. Grate the meat of the coconut, using the coarse side of the grater.

Heat the ghee or cooking oil in a frying pan. Sprinkle in the aniseed and fry gently for 1 minute. Peel and finely chop the ginger, add to the frying pan and fry for a further minute. Then sprinkle in the grated coconut, or desiccated coconut if using, turning well to ensure it is well mixed in with the aniseed and ginger. Reduce the heat and add the sugar. By now the filling should be quite thick. Mix the sugar in well with the coconut and put to one side.

Clean the frying pan and heat enough ghee or cooking oil to cover the bottom of the pan. Whisk the batter once again. Pour a tablespoon of batter in to the centre, allowing it to spread to the sides of the frying pan. Gradually increase the heat and when the pancake is virtually cooked spoon in a little of the filling, fold over and fry for a further 30 seconds. Lift out with a fish slice and put to one side. Repeat with the rest of the batter and filling.

Rice pancakes Dosa

These pancakes are quite delicately made and traditionally served with a selection of chutneys. They are well worth the preparation time and very simple in themselves to make. Try them with Tomato Chutney (see page 28) or just on their own.

50 g/2 oz Basmati rice
50 g/2 oz red split lentils
2 tablespoons natural yogurt
½ teaspoon chilli powder
1 teaspoon salt
½ teaspoon baking powder
75 g/3 oz ghee or 90 ml/3 fl oz cooking oil for frying

Preparation time: 15 minutes plus soaking overnight
Cooking time: 15 minutes

Wash the rice and lentils well and soak overnight. The next day, grind the rice and lentils in a liquidiser, adding a little water if necessary. Mix in the yogurt, chilli powder, salt and baking powder. Mix well together in the liquidiser and leave for a further 4 hours. Whisk again in the liquidiser.

Heat the ghee or cooking oil in a small frying pan. Pour a tablespoon of the batter into the centre, tilting the pan to allow it to spread out. Fry gently on both sides until the pancake just begins to brown. Eat while still warm from the pan. Repeat with the rest of the batter. Dosas are best eaten warm. Keep them warm if necessary in a tea towel. They can be served chilled also.

Above: Numkeen roti; below left to right: Alebele and Dosa.

Savoury toast
Numkeen roti

❖❖❖❖❖❖❖❖❖❖❖❖❖❖❖❖❖❖❖❖

This recipe is very similar to the recipe for French toast found in the West. It has virtually the same ingredients based on an egg batter; however, as you might expect it is a little more aromatic and spicy, with the addition of ginger and chilli powder.

4 thick slices bread
3 eggs
150 ml/¼ pint milk
½ teaspoon black pepper
½ teaspoon salt
1 teaspoon chilli powder
1 clove garlic
1 × 2.5-cm/1-inch piece of fresh ginger
cooking oil for frying

Preparation time: 10 minutes
Cooking time: 10 minutes

Cut the bread into strips about 5 cm/2 inches wide. Beat the eggs together with the milk, black pepper, salt and chilli powder. Peel and finely chop the garlic and ginger. Beat into the egg, pour the egg mixture over the bread and fry each piece until it is golden brown. Serve piping hot.

Savoury biscuits
Sev gatia

Sev Gatia is the Indian equivalent of Cheese Straws. It is easy to make and will keep in an airtight tin for several weeks. It is a very good accompaniment and a good alternative to peanuts to be served with alcoholic drinks.

170 g/6 oz chick-pea flour
1 teaspoon turmeric
1 teaspoon chilli powder
1 teaspoon salt
50 g/2 oz ghee
$\frac{1}{2}$ teaspoon aniseed
1 teaspoon black pepper
150 ml/$\frac{1}{4}$ pint water
cooking oil for frying

Preparation time: 20 minutes plus
   1 hour resting
Cooking time: 15 minutes

Sieve the chick-pea flour into a bowl, using the back of a spoon to force any lumps through the sieve. Sieve in the turmeric, chilli powder and salt. Mix together well and rub the ghee into the flour. Sprinkle in the aniseed and black pepper. Add the water gradually to form a dough. Knead this dough well for at least 5 minutes and put to one side to rest for 1 hour.

Put the dough into a forcing bag with a nozzle about 3–5 mm/$\frac{1}{8}$–$\frac{1}{4}$ inch in diameter. Heat some clean oil in a frying pan. Drop a small lump of dough in and if it immediately sizzles and comes to the surface, the oil is ready. Squeeze long strips of dough into the fat and fry until golden brown and crisp. These strips may be broken up into smaller pieces to allow them to be stored although they are very good served hot straight from the fat.

From above: Podina ka sharbat, Sharbat, Lussi, Lussi numkeen and Sev gatia.

Yogurt drink
Lussi

In the past, Lussi was the name given to buttermilk or whey left from the butter-making process. More recently though it has tended to be a drink made from a combination of milk and yogurt and this recipe is just that. It is very sharp and designed to quench the thirst in hot climates. This version is called Lussi Meeta.

300 ml/$\frac{1}{2}$ pint natural yogurt
450 ml/$\frac{3}{4}$ pint chilled milk
a few ice cubes
1 lemon
3 teaspoons sugar
1 teaspoon kewra water

Preparation time: 10 minutes

Put the yogurt and the milk into the goblet of a liquidiser together with a few ice cubes. Squeeze over the juice of the lemon and add the sugar and kewra water. Liquidise for a minute or so until the ice is crushed and the yogurt/milk mixture well mixed. Pour immediately into chilled glasses and serve.

Salted yogurt drink
Lussi numkeen

This is an acquired taste. The addition of salt to normally sweet dishes is found in hot countries throughout the world. The idea is quite simple – to replace the salt lost through sweating. To that end there are several Indian drinks containing what to the average Western palate is rather too much salt. However, once you have acquired the taste for Lussi Numkeen you may well find that you are hooked on it!

300 ml/$\frac{1}{2}$ pint natural yogurt
450 ml/$\frac{3}{4}$ pint chilled milk
1 lemon
a few ice cubes
3 teaspoons salt
$\frac{1}{2}$ teaspoon kewra water

Preparation time: 10 minutes

Put the yogurt, milk and juice from the lemon into a liquidiser, together with some ice cubes. Add the salt and kewra water and liquidise for a minute, until the ice cubes are crushed and the yogurt and milk is well mixed. Pour into chilled glasses and serve.

Sherbets
Sharbats

A Sharbat is a name given to any sweet, aromatic drink. In the Indian subcontinent sharbats are generally served by street vendors, who have endless bottles of brightly coloured sweet liquids, to which they add ice and water and sometimes sugar to make up the sharbat. You can make a sharbat from virtually any basic ingredient with the addition of large amounts of sugar and some aromatics. The following is a general sharbat recipe.

600 ml/1 pint water
500 g/1 lb sugar
1 × 2.5-cm/1-inch stick of cinnamon
10 cloves
10 cardamoms
$\frac{1}{2}$ teaspoon kewra water
food colouring of your choice

Preparation time: 15 minutes plus chilling

Bring the water to the boil and stir in the sugar. When it has dissolved add the cinnamon, cloves and cardamoms. Continue to boil gently to reduce the liquid to a thick syrup, then sprinkle in the kewra water and the food colouring. (To follow the Indian tradition – the brighter, the better!) Allow the syrup to cool. Bottle in a screw-top bottle and serve suitably diluted with ice-cold water.

Mint drink
Podina ka sharbat

This is Sharbat made with mint and is one of the more refreshing of the summertime drinks. It must be made with fresh mint leaves as something in the preservatives used commercially for bottling mint seems to impart a bitter flavour to the drinks.

300 ml/$\frac{1}{2}$ pint mint leaves
1 teaspoon aniseed
900 ml/1$\frac{1}{2}$ pints water
225 g/$\frac{1}{2}$ lb sugar
1 × 2.5-cm/1-inch stick of cinnamon
green food colouring

Preparation time: 2 hours
30 minutes plus chilling

Wash the mint leaves and coarsely chop them. Mix together with the aniseed. Heat the water and the sugar together, bring to the boil and stir well to dissolve the sugar. Add the cinnamon. Put the mint and aniseed mixture into another saucepan. Pour the sugar and water mixture over the mint. Cover and leave to infuse for 2 hours.

Then strain the mixture into another saucepan and add 2–3 drops of green food colouring. Bring to the boil to reduce the liquid by half, allow to cool and mix with water and ice cubes to make a refreshing drink. If necessary add a little more sugar to taste.

Milk drink
Doodh ka sharbat

କ୍ଷକ୍ଷକ୍ଷକ୍ଷକ୍ଷକ୍ଷକ୍ଷକ୍ଷକ୍ଷକ୍ଷକ୍ଷକ୍ଷ

This is an unusual drink using only goats' milk, but it is popular in certain parts of India. It tends to be served more as a pudding rather than a straight cooler as it is very rich, containing almonds and pistachios. It is a very useful drink to serve after a heavy Indian meal where a pudding would probably be too much to take!

600 ml/1 pint goats' milk
½ teaspoon saffron threads
2 tablespoons honey
25 g/1 oz chopped almonds
25 g/1 oz chopped pistachios
5 cloves
5 cardamoms
1 teaspoon kewra water

Preparation time: 1 hour plus
    chilling

Heat the milk in a saucepan together with the saffron threads, until just below boiling point. Stir in the honey and dissolve it. Boil gently for 30 minutes. Add the almonds and pistachios. Remove the seeds from the cardamoms and crush them and the cloves with a rolling pin. Add to the milk, return to the boil and boil for a further 5 minutes, allowing everything to mix in well. Remove from the heat and when cool transfer to the goblet of a liquidiser. Sprinkle in the kewra water and liquidise together to form a smooth drink. Serve well chilled. This drink is so rich that it is served in rather small glasses.

Sandalwood drink
Sharbat sandal

କ୍ଷକ୍ଷକ୍ଷକ୍ଷକ୍ଷକ୍ଷକ୍ଷକ୍ଷକ୍ଷକ୍ଷକ୍ଷକ୍ଷ

Sandalwood is the bark of a tree and is very similar to cinnamon. The main difference in the flavouring is that sandalwood is far subtler, more aromatic and less sweet. It is interesting to note that the Indian name for cinnamon is Dal Cheeny, which actually means 'sweet lentils'. Sandalwood has a much more heavily perfumed flavour. It can be bought in small packs at some Indian grocers and it is well worth having on hand to make fresh Sandal Sharbat.

25 g/1 oz sandalwood
900 ml/1½ pints water
4 cloves
4 cardamoms
350 g/12 oz sugar
2–3 drops of yellow food colouring
1 lemon

Preparation time: 30 minutes plus
    chilling

Boil the sandalwood together with the water, cloves and cardamoms. Add the sugar and stir to ensure it is well dissolved. Continue to boil until a thick syrup is obtained, allow to cool and add the drops of yellow colouring, to produce a bright yellow syrup. Squeeze in the juice from the lemon, put into a screw-top bottle and store until needed. To make the Sharbat simply dilute the Sharbat mixture with chilled water, adding more sugar if needed.

Lemonade
Nimboo pani

କ୍ଷକ୍ଷକ୍ଷକ୍ଷକ୍ଷକ୍ଷକ୍ଷକ୍ଷକ୍ଷକ୍ଷକ୍ଷକ୍ଷ

This is one of the best cooling drinks in India. It is very similar to what the French call *Citron pressé* and the effect is very much the same. One difference is that Nimboo Pani contains salt as well as sugar.

1 tablespoon sugar
600 ml/1 pint water
2 lemons
1½ teaspoons salt

Preparation time: 15 minutes

Dissolve the sugar into the water. Squeeze in the juice from the lemons and include as much of the pulp as possible, taking care to strain out the pips. Stir in the salt just before serving. Moisten the rim of each glass with a little juice from the squeezed lemon skin and dip the glasses in coarse salt so the rims become encrusted. Carefully pour in the Nimboo Pani and serve.

Tamarind water
Imli ka pani

କ୍ଷକ୍ଷକ୍ଷକ୍ଷକ୍ଷକ୍ଷକ୍ଷକ୍ଷକ୍ଷକ୍ଷକ୍ଷକ୍ଷ

This drink is only for the brave! It is a particularly difficult drink to acquire a taste for. However, it is popular in India, particularly in cities such as Bombay, where tamarind water is often used to dip pieces of pastry into before eating. It does make a refreshing drink if you can take the bitterness of the tamarind and it certainly cuts through and quenches the thirst. You need to start the preparations the day before.

50 g/2 oz tamarind
900 ml/1½ pints water
½ teaspoon chilli powder
1 teaspoon salt
1 tablespoon sugar
1 teaspoon ground ginger
1 lemon
1 tablespoon chopped mint

Preparation time: 15 minutes plus
    overnight soaking

Put the tamarind into a bowl. Bring to the boil 300 ml/½ pint of the 900 ml/1½ pints of water and pour over the tamarind. Leave to soak overnight.

Next day squeeze the tamarind over its water and discard the pulp. Put the tamarind water into a liquidiser and add the chilli powder, salt and sugar, ginger powder and the juice from the lemon. Liquidise well together and add the rest of the water. Mix in the chopped mint, chill and serve.

Traditionally very small cups of Tamarind Water are served as an accompaniment to Indian food, the smaller the cups the better as I am sure you won't find too many people who can take a second cup!

Tea
Chai

There is so much information about tea that a whole book could be written. Here, it might be useful just to state one or two of the Indian methods of making tea. Most tea in India is served very sweet and quite often with a great deal of milk. However, when tea is used to accompany a meal it tends to be served without milk and rather weaker than the stronger blends served in the tea houses. To this end choose some of the more delicate teas, such as Darjeeling, and perhaps mix in a little Earl Grey tea on a ratio of one teaspoon of Earl Grey to four teaspoons of Darjeeling. The oil of bergamot, which is used to give the Earl Grey its distinctive flavour, serves to add an aromatic, smoky taste to the tea, which when taken with the Darjeeling is not too overpowering. Have on hand, apart from a large teapot, a pot of hot water so that guests can dilute their tea so it may be taken easily without the tea tasting too strong. Nowadays, jasmine flowers may be bought, either dried or in some cases fresh, at some Asian stores and it is nice to add 1 heaped tablespoon of these to the teapot too, occasionally even using the odd flower as decoration, floating on the surface.

From above: Sharbat sandal (in bottle), Chai with jasmine flowers, Imli ka pani, Nimboo pani, Doodh ka sharbat and Sharbat sandal.

Index

Illustration acknowledgments

The British Library: pages 142 and 143.
The Fotomas Index: pages 16, 17, 18 and 19.
Michael Holford: pages 10, 11, 36, 37, 110 and 111.
The Rainbird Publishing Group: pages 68, 69, 124, 125, 142 and 143.
The Victoria and Albert Museum (Crown Copyright): pages 4, 5, 6, 7, 8, 9, 52, 53, 90, 91, 158, 159, 176 and 177.

If you have difficulty in obtaining any spices you can contact The Curry Company, PO Box 1, Sutton Scotney, Winchester, Hampshire SO21 3NW.